The uses of poetry

The uses of poetry

DENYS THOMPSON

CAMBRIDGE UNIVERSITY PRESS

CAMBRIDGE

LONDON · NEW YORK · MELBOURNE

Published by the Syndics of the Cambridge University Press
The Pitt Building, Trumpington Street, Cambridge CB2 1RP
Bentley House, 200 Euston Road, London NW1 2DB
32 East 57th Street, New York, NY 10022, USA
296 Beaconsfield Parade, Middle Park, Melbourne 3206, Australia

© Cambridge University Press 1978

First published 1978

Printed in Great Britain at the
University Press, Cambridge

Library of Congress Cataloguing in Publication Data

Thompson, Denys, 1907–
Uses of poetry.

Includes bibliographical references and index.
1. Poetry. I. Title.
PN1111.T5   809.1   77-82517
ISBN 0 521 21804 7 hard covers
ISBN 0 521 29287 5 paperback

Contents

Preface

This book aims to make a general map of a large territory: the needs met by poetry and the purposes proposed for it from the earliest times. Ideally music would be considered too, as it used to be much more than an accompaniment to words, but lack of knowledge precludes this. Ideally too there should be related anthologies as illustrations.

Speech and probably poetry have been in existence for many thousands of years, but the effective life of printing is only about five hundred years. During this time the part played by poetry, once very large, in the life of man has steadily diminished; though there are still countries where poets are punished and imprisoned for writing poems, an activity necessarily dissident under any form of tyranny. As the utility of poetry has decreased, there is less to be said about it; so that poetry before print gets a good deal of attention. But it must be stressed that there is no intention of idealising any past era; an age remarkable for beautiful poetry can be unpleasant and dangerous to live in. The period that produced Shakespeare and other poets was remarkable for vicious religious intolerance, capricious injustice, hideous punishments and a system of police spies.

In a sense the volume is propaganda for poetry. It stems from a belief that the restrictions on thought and language that have been imposed with the devotion of great resources to science have thwarted human beings and stifled their development; and that emotional education such as that given by the arts is needed for the growth of whole men.

Grateful thanks are due to Michael Black of the Cambridge University Press for suggestion and advice; to Christopher Parry for reading some drafts; to Kenneth and Sara Priestley for typing; to the staffs of the University and City Libraries in Cambridge; and to the Arts Council for a grant in 1974.

Acknowledgements

Permission to quote the following translations is gratefully acknowledged to the authors (or their representatives) and publishers: Dr J. Mascaro, Rig-Veda x 129 from *Lamps of Fire*, C. M. Bowra and Weidenfeld and Nicolson Ltd for 'Elephant Hunter Take Your Bow' from *Primitive Song*, and Sir Arthur Grimble and John Murray for 'The Lifting of the Head' from *Return to the Islands*.

1

The nature of poetry

The deep roots of speech

There is little point in trying to site a dividing line between the territories of poetry and prose, for some of the corralled inmates will leap over any barrier. Dickens in his novels broke into verse in more than one place, the best-known example being the comment on the death of Little Nell in chapter 72 of *The Old Curiosity Shop*:

> Oh! it is hard to take to heart the lesson that such deaths will teach, but let no man reject it, for it is one that all must learn, and is a mighty, universal Truth. When Death strikes down the innocent and young, for every fragile form from which he lets the panting spirit free a hundred virtues rise – in shapes of mercy, charity and love – to walk the world, and bless it. Of every tear that sorrowing mortals shed on such green graves, some good is born, some gentler nature comes.

One might also cite the description of the steeple at the beginning of *The Chimes* and of the tower in the third quarter of the same story. George Eliot too wrote a kind of verse in *Adam Bede*, in the account of Hetty's troubles after she met Arthur Donnithorne, and in Dinah Morris's interview with Hetty in prison. Moreover *poèmes trouvées* can be found in scientific prose:

> There is no force, however great,
> Can stretch a cord, however fine,
> Into a horizontal line
> That shall be absolutely straight.

And from a prose translation of Linnaeus (quoted by Elizabeth Sewell) an arrangement in verse form:

> *Mollusca*
>
> Are naked,
> furnished with tentacula
> or arms; for the most part
> inhabitants of the sea;
> and, by their phosphorous quality,
> illuminate
> the dark abyss of waters, reflecting
> their lights to the firmament. Thus

what is beneath the water
corresponds
with that which is above.
(*Systema Naturae*, vol. 4.)

Evidently powerful feeling or intense interest can cause a writer to move into verse when he needs a form of expression marked by a pronounced rhythm and a concentration achieved with the aid of imagery. Hardy wrote some good sense about this:

> The shortest way to good prose is by the route of good verse. The apparent paradox – I cannot remember who first expressed it – that the best poetry is the best prose ceases on examination to be a paradox and becomes a truism. Anybody may test it for himself by taking any five lines in verse and, casting off the fetters of metre and rhyme that seem to bind the poet, trying to express the same ideas more freely and accurately in prose. He will find that it cannot be done: the words of the verse – fettered as he thought them – are the only words that will convey the ideas that were intended to be conveyed.
> (Hardy 1967, p. 14)

The content of poetry is usually denser and more memorable, the style is more incisive and makes a more immediate impact. But, once more, the borderline is vague, and we must be satisfied with the obvious point that the effective rhythms of speech in all their variety underlie every piece of good writing, whether poetry or prose. We therefore start by considering the part played by speech in human life.

Human beings are not just passive automata. They do not merely suffer the effects of influences from outside, but react positively to every disturbance. It rains, and men put on waterproof clothes; it freezes, and the birds puff out their feathers to get some insulation. All creatures exhibit a consciousness, a general awareness, a disposition to try out their environment, and a drive to 'achieve intellectual control over the situations confronting them' (Polanyi, p. 132). Most people except convinced reductionists will recognise on their own experience and observation the truth of the statement that

> Directiveness and creativeness are fundamental characteristics of life, shared by no inorganic system; that they are not to be explained in terms of mechanism or purpose; that human directiveness and purposiveness in thought and action are a specialised development of the directiveness and creativeness inherent in life...Psychological activity issuing in purposive behaviour is to be regarded as a specialisation of vital activity...Organic and psychological activities are closely akin.
> (Russell, p. 178)

This vital activity is seen at its most developed in man, whose special concerns are to rid himself of fear and to attain a mastery over his material environment. This directiveness towards biological ends (Russell adds) is the very essence of life.

Again it was towards biological ends that our impulses were profitably directed when consciousness evolved as a result of its value in the struggle for survival. Self-consciousness followed as social life developed; man became more aware of his fellows and acquired the power of speech, which was physically a part of the central machinery for the control and co-ordination of behaviour (Firth, pp. 145, 152). Speech also was another aid to survival; it enabled groups to keep in touch, and it may be that the families in which the young responded quickly to speech had the best chance of continuing. At some stage came true human communion and communication, for the alarm noises and the sounds that early man made just to keep in contact in the forest are shared with the animals, and are not real speech. Thus human speech reaches very deeply into 'the formative layers of experience' (Masserman, p. 174).

The infant's early cries of discomfort and his noises of comfort express his response to bodily conditions, and his awareness of these utterances is inseparable from his experience of his bodily condition (M. M. Lewis, p. 15). This integration is never dissolved; the body cannot be regarded as a purely material system; the mind's activity is only a function of a complete living organism, so that in any human action the whole being is involved. Here is a small example: 'To help yourself determine how closely you approach a purely auditory image of a word without an actual twittering of vocal organs, try the classic test of attempting to hear yourself think the word "bubble" while holding the lips rigidly apart by the insertion of a couple of fingers between the teeth' (Downey, p. 43). The unity of thought and feeling precludes any compartmentalising of language into language-as-poetry and language-as-science:

> The human organism, that body which has the gift of thought, does not have the choice of two kinds of thinking. It has only one, in which the organism as a whole is engaged all along the line. There has been no progression in history from one type of thought to another. We are merely learning to use what we have been given, which is all of a piece. This means too that we have to admit and reaffirm our solidarity with the thinking of the child and the savage.
> (Sewell, p. 19)

The wholeness of the organism is exemplified from another angle

3

by the way in which habitual emotions have cumulative physiological effects, and leave their mark on face, posture and movements (M. B. Arnold, p. 267). The unity of the human being appears very clearly in the study by Wolf and Wolff of a man who, as the result of an accident had for many years to insert food directly into his stomach by hand – after chewing it – introducing it straight into the stomach, failed to satisfy his appetite. Thus they were able to observe the stomach, not as an isolated organ, but as a working unit in a whole integrated organism. When the subject was sad and discouraged and self-reproachful, his stomach too suffered prolonged pallor; when he blushed, his gut blushed too (Wolf and Wolff). (The authors commented that therapy should care for the man rather than his stomach, p. 177.) Another example is the fact that pitch discrimination is not a purely aural matter but involves the central nervous system and the brain; it is a functional activity of the mind and not an organic reaction of the body (Howes, p. 114). Elizabethan English reflected the unity we are discussing when it referred to 'bowels of compassion' (1 John 3: 17); and in *King Lear* Regan excuses herself from replying to an insult on the ground of her illness: 'else I should answer From a full-flowing stomach'. Even today there are survivals in our application of 'liverish' and 'hearty' to moods, and our inability at times to 'digest' information or 'stomach' an experience. It is worth mentioning too that a study of the finger responses of deaf mutes during thinking indicated that their hands and arms were the seat of both their spoken and written speech.

To the physically energetic William Morris the writing of poetry sometimes seems to have been almost another form of manual exercise (P. Henderson 1967, p. 23); and in the poetry he enjoyed A. E. Housman felt a bristling of the skin and other physical manifestations. These trifles are worth noting only as small examples of the combined expressiveness of poetry and the body, now vestigial but once so close that even now, in R. G. Collingwood's view, every kind of language is but a specialised form of total bodily gesture. Viewed thus it is the offshoot of an original bodily expression of emotion, dominated by thought in its primitive form as consciousness, so that each one of us, whenever he expresses himself, is doing so with his whole body, and is thus actually talking in this 'original' language of total bodily gesture (Collingwood, pp. 243 ff). 'It is the enactment by the body, through changes of rhythm and stress and intonation, of the dramatic content of poetry, that links spoken verse with the dance' (Bodkin, p. 321).

4

A man's voice is just one element in a situation in which he speaks with his whole body, with his body muscles as well as with his breathing apparatus. On this fact complete theories of the origin of language have been based, notably that of Sir Richard Paget, which are illuminating so far as they go. Before we cite some poems that illustrate the impossibility of separating the voice from the whole man, here is a single example from Greek. The word *kataptustos* means 'contemptible', and it may be that some readers will agree that its meaning is felt before it is translated. If so, they may care to know that it is derived from *ptuo* (I spit), a gesture word if ever there was one, and that it simply means 'spittable-upon'. There are many instances of this muscular English in Anglo-Saxon, but none is quoted here because the necessary translation would lose the impact of the original. However there are numerous examples in the alliterative poetry of the fourteenth century, which at its best 'conveys sensations of bodily action and movement through effects of rhythm and types of imagery not confined to the purely visual or auditory' (Speirs, p. 30). Here a knight is enduring a rough journey in winter:

> Sumwhile with wormes he werres,   and with wolves als,
> Sumwhile with wodwos,   that woned in the knarres,
> Bothe with bulles and beres,   and bores otherwhile,
> And etaines, that him anelede   of the heghe felle;
> Nade he ben dughty and drighe,   and Drighten had served,
> Douteless he hade ben ded   and dreped ful ofte.
> For werre wrathed him not so much,   that winter was wors,
> When the colde cler water   fro the cloudes shadde,
> And fres er hit falle might   to the fale erthe;
> Ner slain with the slete   he sleped in his yrnes
> Mo nightes then innoghe   in naked rokkes,
> There as claterande fro the crest   the cold borne rennes,
> And henged heghe over his hede   is hard iise-ikkles.
> (*Sir Gawayne and the Grene Knight*, 720–32, Penguin edition)

(Sometimes he warred with dragons, and with wolves also, sometimes with wild men of the woods that dwelt among the rocks, with bulls and bears and boars at other times, and giants that pursued him on the high fells. Had he not been doughty and strong, and served his God, he would doubtless have been slain and slaughtered many times. Yet the warring worried him not so much, the winter was worse, when the cold clear water fell from the clouds, and froze before it could fall to the pale earth. Near dead with the sleet, he slept in his armour more nights than enough among the naked rocks, where the cold stream ran clattering from the crests above, and hung high over his head in hard icicles.)

If read aloud with vigour a good deal of its forcefulness comes across even to those who are not familiar with all of the vocabulary. Another passage worth reading aloud is the description of Avarice in *Piers Plowman* v, 188–99 (quoted in chapter 6). Much later, it is impossible to read the well-known lines on the difficulty of reaching the truth, in Donne's third Satire, without feeling a sense of muscular effort:

> On a huge hill,
> Cragged and steep, Truth stands, and hee that will
> Reach her, about must, and about must goe;
> And what the hill's suddenness resists, winne so
>
> (*suddenness*, steepness)

And the sense of weary uphill plodding is marked in Blake's

> Ah, Sun-flower! weary of time,
> Who countest the steps of the Sun,
> Seeking after that sweet golden clime
> Where the traveller's journey is done

In Shakespeare too there are many lines where the words enact the meaning, so that it is felt before being apprehended.

Rhythm

Other effects of the movement of poetry may rest on a physiological basis – the contraction and expansion of the lungs for example, the pulse of the blood and the beat of the heart. The ear too can enjoy the recognition in poetry of the sound of wind and sea and the drumming of rain. The poet who writes for reading aloud or singing can utilise the upbeat or intake of breath before a singer begins; thus the beginning of a line is sometimes more stressed than the end. It is worth noting that speech can alter not only the respiratory cycle of the speaker, but also that of his listener. It is a familiar fact that something in listeners causes them to impose a non-existent rhythmic structure on a random time pattern of stimuli (Minifie, p. 230), and that the mind will tend to group evenly intense sounds by accenting them, using stress (more sound), duration, or most commonly physical movement. 'A motor theory of rhythm has been very widely accepted as the fundamental explanation, according to which the experience of rhythm is the result of finely ordered bodily movement, its pleasures those of response to disciplined muscular controls' (Howes, p. 119). The poet is thus able to exploit his listeners' innate sense of rhythm for his own purposes.

6

In the brain there is a continuously oscillating electric current, known as the alpha-rhythm, which can be recorded on an electro-encephalograph. This rhythmicity is the motor for a great variety of rhythmic movements, including speech and perhaps even syntax (Lenneberg 1967, p. 119). There seems to be a basic speech rhythm that plays a part in general psychological and neuro-physiological processes; it serves as an organising principle and possibly as a timing device for articulation; it enables speakers to phrase their utterances, and listeners to impose a rhythmic structure on any speech they may hear (Minifie, p. 230). But in spite of the universal appeal of rhythm in language, not much is known of its exact nature. It may be that the study of kinesthesis will help – the group of senses involved in the perception of movement and position, whose receptors are found in the muscles, tendons and joints; senses basic to the feeling that your body belongs to you and without which it is impossible to imagine yourself. The consciousness of one's own body and what it is doing operates all the time we are awake, and makes us aware of rhythm in what we are doing. There certainly seems to be firm physiological ground for the emotional effects of poetry, controlled and shaped and made communicable with the aid of rhythm in words and music. Words go far back into the subconscious, to the obscure primary zone where human language emerges from a 'pre-vocabulary' of biological and somatic stimulus and recognition:

> The emotional life engendered by an articulate culture is, of course, primordially rooted in the emotions of inarticulate creatures. We have seen that the exhilaration shown by apes and babies when solving a problem prefigures the intellectual joys of science... Laments for the dead and songs of love are likewise formulations of earlier shapeless emotions, which are refashioned and amplified into something new by words and music. The originally experienced sentiments are not expressed but alluded to, just as objects are alluded to rather than represented in a painting.
> (Polanyi, p. 194)

The deep-rootedness of rhythmic speech may explain why certain rhythms and metres, with the aid of a few key words and tones and changes in the voice, can induce feelings of dissociation, exaltation or relaxed calm, before any intellectual meaning is taken in by the hearer.

Our knowledge of young children and their development affords more evidence for the existence of this innate sense of rhythm. They begin early to engage in rhythmic movement, near to dancing, and to enjoy and make rhymes and jingles almost as soon as they can use language. When their speech is rhythmic, it is not necessarily because they have learned it; it is not certain that the adults round a child can determine the onset or development of his language – there is no direct mirroring of the input. The child constructs language by himself, and the ability to learn and use language is so deeply rooted that children learn it even in the face of dramatic handicaps, such as congenital blindness, congenital deafness and gross parental neglect (Lenneberg 1964, p. 67). Normally however the child is open to a variety of stimuli from adults, and then he is likely to follow Arnold Gesell's time-table. In his first five years of life the child at eighteen months listens to short rhymes with interesting sounds – he has been responding to music, pictures and rhymes for many months. At twenty-four months the interest in rhymes is developed; his own language is often rhythmical and repetitive; and at forty-eight months he delights in nonsense rhymes. Commenting on the satisfaction that children used to derive from their singing games, Willa Muir wrote:

> The satisfaction cannot arise, the tradition cannot survive for long, unless the unformulated energies of the underworld [of feeling] have found a shape to flow into which is accepted directly, without question, by all the participants. It looks as if the shape to be achieved takes a rhythmic form naturally and spontaneously. Human beings are symmetrically fashioned and each day is rounded for them by the sun; when they run or skip or hop they cannot help doing so rhythmically any more than waves on the sea can help following a rhythm. Children combining in play shape a rhythm for their games without thinking about it. (p. 31)

These are findings about 'normal' children, but there is interesting evidence from an autistic case. An autistic boy was fond of music from a very early age; he could reproduce tunes and was soothed by them. Then one day his parents read to him Beatrix Potter's *Apply Dapply's Nursery Rhymes*. Soon he started repeating and joining in, and eventually could say the whole set of poems through with his parents. Stories meant nothing to him, but a rhyme or rhythm would seize his attention. After a couple of readings of Lear or Lewis Carroll he would know whole poems, and by the time he was three he was still not talking except in poems. He was offering his parents something, and the contact grew closer to the normal contact between parent and child (Rowlands, *passim*). The majority of adults seem always to have been able to respond to the crude reiteration of sounds. There are survivals from primitive religions to exemplify this, and if the hideous noises of Nazi rallies are by now forgotten we still have the political rally and football matches. After mere noise came the repetition of slogans and phrases at revivalist meetings:

> Throw out the lifeline, throw out the lifeline,
>   Someone is drifting away;
> Throw out the lifeline, throw out the lifeline,
>   Someone is sinking today.

But the mere repetition of loud noises, such as those which batter pop fans into insensibility, hardly comes under the heading of rhythm. Some writers on rhythm make a distinction:

> Rhythm is important in two quite different areas, in efficiency of movements and in esthetics. Natural rhythms for bodily movements can be utilized to advantage in performing work with least expenditure of effort – walking in the preferred rhythm is less tiring... Rhythm is probably the most basic esthetic expression in the entire animal world.
> (Wenger, p. 120)

But there probably never was a clear-cut distinction; the singer of a spinning song may have got through the work more easily, but she also unburdened herself of her joys and sorrows. Many 'work' songs became 'art' songs. Karl Bücher's observation that fatigue was diminished in many occupations by rhythmic effort led him to trace the origin of poetry to the making of concerted effort accompanied by the songs and chants of workers; he traced the main source of rhythm to the habit of fitting vocal sounds to bodily movements. The sounds produced by work, like the noise of the feet in treading, came to be accompanied by words. Then came the sound of tools in use, with a periodicity imposed by breath, muscle and the nature of the task. The hammering of stone and metal, the flail-strokes of threshing, the fanning of husks, are examples of tasks with their own rhythms; other patterned sounds developed when co-operative jobs, like the hauling of a log or the moving and rowing of a heavy boat, were undertaken. As it was found that rhythmical action marked by shouting made work easier, the reflex action of the voice incidental to muscular action was followed by primitive labour songs.

The sense of rhythm in man is thought by some writers to have developed from his necessarily living by the rising and setting of the sun and the changes of the seasons, but it is not easy to see how this happened. It seems more likely that the natural tendency of human beings to impose a pattern of rhythm on the noises around them came into action when they heard the sounds of wind, waves and rain and the cries of birds and animals, and needed (in the

9

interests of magic, for instance) to imitate them. Here for example is an almost wordless rain chant, with the last line imitating the call of the plover as it is heard before the rain, made up by Australian aborigines:

Rain Chant

Dad a da da
Dad a da da
Dad a da da
Da kata kai

Ded o ded o
Ded o ded o
Ded o ded o
Da kata kai
(Bouquet, p. 28)

And here is a fertility song of the Navajo Indians:

Corn Song

The corn grows up.
The waters of the dark clouds drop, drop.
The rain descends.
The waters from the corn leaves drop, drop.
The rain descends.
The waters from the plants drop, drop.
The corn grows up.
The waters of the dark mists drop, drop.
(*Journal of American Folklore*, 7, p. 191)

Rhythm in poetry sets up a pattern of expectation in the hearer, and to a less extent in the reader of the printed page; the written poem cannot rely on being as effective as the spoken, because the reader can always be interrupted or stand aside and be critical. A monotonous pattern may first be used, to secure some control over the hearer; the most primitive form is the physical stimulus of repetition which may induce unusual states of mind and lull the superficial parts of consciousness. Further:

> As the wild rhythms of the ancient dance tended to annul the participant's consciousness of separate personality, exalting him to union with his group and with its God, so, in fainter degree, the rhythms of poetry still serve to hold the reader apart from this everyday self and cares, caught up into the thought and feeling communicated.
>
> (Bodkin, p. 321)

The instinctive inclination to group recurrent sense impressions in such a way as to derive pleasure from the arrangement may be part of the human being's desire for order, for controlling his

environment in the interests of survival and adjustment. The satis-
faction derived from making patterns, evident in early art long
before any poetry we can know, must be the expression of a psychic
need. Masserman regards rhythm as one of the magic *ur* defences
of man, the miraculous transformation of chaos into pleasurable
order, with a sense of familiarity as the first stage (Leedy, p. 59).
Especially when speaking aloud the poet groups his words into
phrases, and by the inflectional pattern of his voice puts his material,
from the simplest jingle upwards, into a form as positive as that of
a piece of music. The attention of his audience once gained, he
can introduce variety of intensity, pitch quality, and movement;
fulfilling or disappointing expectations according to his need. If he
is skilful he can involve the whole personality of his hearers to the
point of readiness for muscular and motor response. Another view
is that rhythmical poetry produces quite different effects in listeners;
the degree of hypnosis exerted enables them to resolve the discords
of reality in fantasy, entering a less individualised world where they
have more in common with other people (G. Thomson 1945, p. 19).

That is a Marxist view, and makes no appeal if one believes that
good poetry is life-enhancing. It would not have appealed to St
Augustine. According to his *De Musica* 'numbers' (i.e. rhythms)
contained 'manifestations of reality in the intimate core of being
from which poetry or music drew its power. To Augustine numbers
were the structure of being, and it was through numbers, whether
as rhythm or mathematics, that intuition could reach the nature of
being' (Blackmur, p. 326). He almost gave the impression that if you
kept your verse in good order, your soul and the soul of your poetry
would also be in good health. And though we can know little of
Greek music, we believe that the Greeks followed a musical melody
with an intensity unknown to us, and that they set a high value on
it. At a time when music and poetry were not divorced, the Spartan
Lycurgus made music a part of education. The songs to be sung
must not offend the spirit of the commonwealth; they should extol
the fatherland and lead to a sense of order, lawfulness and a
capacity for quick decision. In Athens Solon was the champion of
music as the promoter of morals and citizenship (Lang, p. 13).

Symbolising

The use of symbols in poetry is an extension of a specifically human
capacity: the ability to understand signs and shapes, from traffic
signals upwards, that stand for things or states or activities. The

essence of using such graphic symbols successfully is the making of connections, and the same is true of verbal symbolising. The latter is not a consciously applied device, but rather an effect of the central nervous system in a way not yet understood, though no doubt the neurologists will be able one day to tell us why (in T. S. Eliot's words) 'the human soul in intense emotion strives to express itself in verse'. No one logically and rationally searches out the symbols he uses, for 'the human organism thinks as a whole, and our division of it into mind and body is the result of our over-emphasis on logic and intellect in mere isolation' (Sewell, p. 35). Donne noted an example of this thinking-as-a-whole when he wrote, in his 'Second Anniversary':

> her pure and eloquent blood
> Spoke in her cheeks, and so distinctly wrought,
> That one might almost say, her body thought.

The language of such unified thinking is poetic, and symbolism is one of the devices it employs to apprehend the unity of experience. From the earliest times of which we have knowledge, symbols have helped men to master themselves and to feel that they were exercising a degree of control over their environment. Symbols for instance were utilised for their potentiality as magic; and a surviving pre-industrial people, the Australian aborigines, still make use of rain-magic and other songs that are heavy with symbolism (Berndt, p. 311).

People derive their symbols from their experience and their environment. As we use cars and aircraft, so African pastoral people make up their metaphors from animal life, especially cattle, and introduce them into their panegyrics (Finnegan, p. 248). For most of mankind, agriculture, guided by the seasons and the heavenly bodies, has been the richest source of symbols.

> Most likely it was (at least through the horticultural stage) an inven-
> tion of women, who perceived in the fecundity of seed and soil an
> image of their own sexuality. From that initial poetic insight the
> technics of cultivation burgeoned into a splendid variety of sexual-
> spiritual symbols. The new agrarian culture saw the earth as a
> mothering womb, the seed and rain as sperm, the crops as a bearing
> of offspring.
> (Roszak, p. 373)

It is easy to see how the great vegetation myths originated in the cycle of birth, maturity, death and re-birth, and that the related symbolism became part of a knowledge of the agricultural round. On these pagan foundations Christian symbolism established itself;

the whole visible universe was charged with hidden meaning, and nature was one vast allegory. But Christianity did not destroy the older pagan symbols; they lived on, almost undisguised in some religious poetry and most evidently in folk song, which expressed the various kinds of love by means of flowers. Folk songs lasted long, because they were true and contained a wealth of meaning and of knowledge worth having, which penetrated the different layers of the reality of love.

Among the Santal people of north-east India, for instance

> Symbolism, which is second nature, comes into its own and 'the right true end of love' is described in terms of natural phenomena – birds, animals, trees, flowers, fruit, rivers, clouds, storm and rain. There can be little doubt that by this instinctive recourse to parallels drawn from nature and to symbolic imagery of this kind, Santals are able to communicate intimacies of feeling that might otherwise defy sensitive expression.
> (Archer, p. 233)

The symbolism that comes to people dependent on the agricultural round is found in many countries. The ancient love songs of China originally possessed a ritual value and contained a moral: men, like nature must do things at the right time. They seem originally to have been improvised on certain set themes in the course of ritual dances at agricultural festivals, and they included practical information about plants and animals. Confucius is said to have compiled an anthology of these poems in order that the practice of virtue might be learned from them; it became a book of instruction in schools, and like the *Song of Solomon* the subject of symbolic interpretation (Granet, p. 11).

Since symbolising starts with the perception of similarities by human beings who are basically the same, against a common background of earth and sky and sea and the seasons, one finds the same metaphor independently generated in different languages; nearly everywhere light stands for life, and darkness for death. The working of some of these universal images is explained by I. A. Richards in reminding us not to attach too much importance to their sensory qualities:

> What gives an image efficacy is less its vividness as an image than its character as a mental event peculiarly connected with sensation. It is a relict...of sensation and our intellectual and emotional response to it depends far more upon its being...a representative of a sensation, than upon its sensory resemblance to one.
> (Richards 1924, p. 119)

The transfer of a sense impression enables one experience to be described in terms of another. R. L. Stevenson, for example, wrote, 'Bright is the ring of words'; Aeschylus said, 'The trumpet sets the shore ablaze'; and in an Old English poem the air was darkened with the voices of the dying. And every day we talk about loud colours, abrasive manners and brilliant speeches. Just as a child discovers how to substitute speech for physical acts, begins to prise his words out of the context in which they have been locked and supplements activity by the use of symbols, so the adult goes a stage further and with the aid of such metaphors as those just cited frees his brain from 'the tyranny of sense perception'. There seems to be a natural human proclivity to produce symbolic versions of experience and to extend meaning by making the connection between one level of experience and another. This is managed by the kind of metaphor we have mentioned, by a kind of personification ('April is the cruellest month, breeding lilacs') and by treating abstractions as animate ('A terrible beauty is born'). Such verbal means help the individual to come to terms with his experiences, 'The tide of sensations of internal bodily origin [which] comes into consciousness', and assist the interpretation of such changes. Something of the kind seems to have taken place in Greek thinking:

> The men who created the first European rationalism were never – until the Hellenistic Age – 'mere' rationalists: that is to say, they were deeply and imaginatively aware of the power, the wonder, and the peril of the Irrational. But they could describe what went on below the threshold of consciousness only in mythological or symbolic language; they had no instrument for understanding it, still less for controlling it.
> (Dodds, p. 254)

However symbolism, the short-circuiting of thought to produce light, is not to be regarded as a *pis aller*, for it enlarges the consciousness in a unique way, and offers a means of acquiring and exploring knowledge, and of handing on the results. Even simple elemental words like air, water, earth and fire, despite a load of information about their chemistry and physics, still prompt an emotional response, and convey a sense of their lasting value as the essences of the material creation.

One value of symbolising to men lies in its harmonising power; it enables them to identify and resolve inner conflicts, and to establish an equilibrium. An aspect of this power is illustrated by Kathleen Raine:

It is from myths, fairy-lore, and imaginative poetry that we normally learn of those supernatural persons, actions, and events which inform our own interior worlds; and through these symbolic embodiments learn to know ourselves. The hunger of children for that world is natural; for it is before we set out that it is most necessary to learn in advance the map of interior country through which we are about to travel; of the situations we shall encounter in our own re-enactment of the human experience of birth, love and death.
(Raine, p. 128)

The need for symbolising is as great as ever it was, at all stages of our lives. An eleven-year-old boy comes to terms with experience in his poem called 'Temper':

> Temper is a red hot hate which glows inside you
> It takes over all love and boils it
> And flows through your body like bolting lightning
> It sticks in you like knives of thunder
> And feels as if you want to destroy
> And to make a revenge which you cannot make
> To fight when you cannot fight
> And to rise against your enemies
> But this is the abominable that is not visible to us
> But all we can see is a stubborn way of revenge
> That leads us astray to wander for ever.
> (Thompson, p. 158)

Again, from a secondary school, a teacher reports that when she read myths and fairy-stories to leather-jacketed adolescents of fifteen they listened with rapt attention – all they wanted in addition were stories of animals and babies. They had been starved of the symbols that help young people to grow up.

Symbolising (in Melanie Klein's words) 'is the basis of all talents, that is, the basis of those skills by which we related ourselves to the world around us'. The old myths enabled man to take his bearings in relation to conflicts, frustration, the chief events of life, and death; they helped man to understand experience. 'The great step from fairytale to myth is taken, when not only social forces – persons, customs, laws, traditions – but also cosmic forces surrounding mankind, are expressed in the story; when not only relationships of an individual to society, but of mankind to nature, are conceived through the spontaneous metaphor of poetic fantasy' (Langer 1948, p. 155). The transition to interpretive myth was aided by taking from nature the great permanent symbols: the heavenly bodies, the seasons, the tides, which seemed to obey a divine rule, and so laid down for human beings the limits of their activity. 'They are the most obvious metaphors to convey the dawning concepts of life-functions – birth, growth, decadence, and death.' The archetypal imagery that gave man his identity and his place in the universe was absorbed by Christianity, and there are many medieval religious poems with tough pagan fibres in them. Greece supplies another example of continuity. In ancient ritual laments the descent of a god or a hero to the underworld symbolised not only the burial of the crops but also a journey deliberately undertaken to combat Hades and save mankind from death. The later Christian laments dwell on light as the symbol of the wisdom and knowledge of God; and in the popular tradition Christ's descent to the underworld is the descent of Herakles, Orpheus or Apollo in antiquity. To the Greek peasant the Resurrection signals the liberation of both dead and living from their miseries, and the return of spring; it was sometimes believed to ensure the safety of the year's crops. In medieval Europe symbolism combined nature, history and religion in a vigorous unity that is inconceivable in a scientific age, and offered men a conception of the world that satisfied their needs. By contrast we suffer nowadays from the making of artificial distinctions between various modes of experience; and the valuable poets are those who bring out the wholeness of our being.

Below the cosmic level symbolism can supply the small change of daily living and make for harmony between people; it has been called the glue which holds together societies and cultures. The rhymed rituals of children are an insurance against possible conflict; their gnomic verses symbolise the principles of their conduct:

> Mind your own business,
>   Fry your own fish;
> Don't poke your nose
>   Into my clean dish.

Sayings of this kind 'become a main instrument in the development of "mutuality" in children's conduct [and give] each child the experience of the force of common assent' (M. M. Lewis, p. 224). Among still existing non-literate people the symbolic statement is one of the most highly appreciated stylistic features, and can be used to express an idea which the speaker does not wish to put bluntly. In the East symbolism is a part of life, and when it appears in poetry it is only an extension into verse of an everyday habit, since people converse all day long in symbols. Discussing the folk songs of the Maikal Hills in India, Verrier Elwin wrote: 'The symbolism of the songs . . . is simply the symbolism of everyday set to music. The Gond and Pardhan actually do think and talk in symbols all their lives. A symbol is the readiest cure for embarrassment, and can smooth over a business transaction or a hitch in one's love-making' (Elwin 1944, p. 113).

Symbols discover the relationships and meaning of diverse things and throw new light on what is familiar; they are practically useful. However in an age of scientific knowledge the old symbols derived from the natural world are losing their power, and are not being replaced – in fact they probably cannot be replaced in most modern minds, with so little in the way of shared beliefs and feelings. Even Christianity has lost its capacity for thinking in symbols such as 'light and darkness, the tree of life, the bird of the soul, voyage and road and river... terms of symbolic discourse, the only language we have in which to express not merely the appearances but the content, the quality of experience'. (Raine, p. 111).

Without recourse to a range of well-charged positive symbols, life is deprived:

> The peculiar degeneration of consciousness from which we suffer – the diminishing awareness of symbolic resonance – is especially a crisis of language. In our culture, almost uniquely, we have invented the hierarchical relationship between rhapsodic declaration and literal prose, between matters of myth and matters of fact. Rhapsody and myth – the prime linguistic carriers of symbolic resonance – have long since ceased to be regarded as sources of knowledge...the one-dimensional language of the logician, scholar and critic – and eventually of the technician and scientist – has been promoted to a position of omnipotence among us.
> (Roszak, p. 382)

In both our formal and informal education the spirit of Gradgrind, with its neglect of anything that is not factual and 'useful', is still too much with us. The way we think and the way we learn limit our knowledge and the range of our thought, so that scientists of a kind can react with shock and indignation even to another kind of science, such as parapsychology, that threatens to widen their limited vision. Perhaps it is arguable that deliberately to ignore and play down symbolic discourse results in a deprivation of an essential human characteristic.

Symbols that were originally flashes of perception, illuminating what had not been apprehended before, pass into a language as metaphors. There they serve a variety of purposes, providing useful definitions, the means of stressing a particular aspect of a subject, of focusing attention, of catching a fleeting experience, of introducing a synonym that tells us something of the user's feeling and intention. In time the original symbolic meaning weakens, but nearly always a resonance remains; in a particular context a well-worn expression like 'the dying year' may still convey a precise shade of meaning. And clichés though they are, such phrases as 'a flood of complaints', 'a torrent of abuse' and 'a shower of congratulations' are charged with more meaning than can be carried by the equivalent quantitative epithets. At a humble level metaphors are valuable labour-saving devices; on a larger scale they enable language to handle effectively a vast number of things and experiences. They are additions to knowledge; they make for lasting understanding and help us to be at home in our surroundings – for they are a device 'by which we claim power over our existence and protection from the menacing darkness that presses upon our most determined enlightenment' (Nash, pp. 170, 171). Symbolic values evolved slowly, and came to incorporate various survival and adjustment mechanisms; 'this symbol-making and symbol-sustaining ability is believed to be the primary reason for man's survival as a species' (Key, p. 196).

2

In the beginning

Dance

'The foundations of language are ultimately to be found in the physical nature of man – anatomy and physiology – and that language is best regarded as a peculiar adaptation of a very universal physiological process to a species-specific ethological function: communication among members of our own species' (Lenneberg 1967, p. 106). Language, as we have noted, had a survival value in enabling members of a group to keep in touch and avoid danger; it is certainly so deeply rooted that children construct language for themselves out of the raw material available to them. No one has ever taught a child to speak his own language.

It seems unlikely that speech developed to name objects or convey concepts; rather its beginning lay in the sounds produced by emotions, sounds from which a vocalised speech was evolved. In its original state 'language is imaginative and expressive...it is an imaginative activity whose function is to express emotion' (Collingwood, p. 225). From these original emotive utterances developed the referential, practical use of language, but it has never achieved independence. R. J. Pumphrey describes intelligence as coming in an envelope of emotion; 'the intelligence conveyed by the message is only part of the whole information carried by speech' (cf. Grene, p. 181). Thus the first language was poetic rather than prosaic in character, and when all qualifications have been admitted this is borne out by what we know of so-called primitive languages; preliterate peoples do not recognise any difference between prose and poetry. It is worth recalling that Milman Parry believed that the similes in Homer retained their force because his language was so firmly grounded in daily and communal speech. And Michael Oakeshott accounts for our vestigial respect for poetry: 'Our disposition to seek in poetry a guide to conduct; our confusion of poetry with wisdom or with entertainment...may be understood as a survival from bygone times before poetry had emerged and been recognised' (Oakeshott, p. 238).

Music and dancing are almost as old as humanity; pieces of

ancient bone flute are evidence of the first, and for the second there is the witness of cave paintings. This dancing, it may be surmised, was in a ring round a fire or tree or standing stone, with the shouts of the dancers matching their bodily movement and with primitive chanting to mark the rhythm. Thus the earliest language may have been a verbal supplement to dancing, developed from the rhythmic beating and vocal noises that accompanied the communal ecstasies. 'The emotional speech in which exact rhythm began was the loud and repeated crying of a throng, regulated and brought into consent by movements of the body, and getting significance from [that] of the festive occasion' (Gummere, p. 94). The whole expressive side of man was engaged in an activity that combined music and movement and poetry; 'in this sense it may be said that the dance is the mother of all languages'. The meaningless vocables that we find ourselves making up to fit any insistent rhythm, like the sound made by the wheels of a train passing over joints in the rails, were converted into words or replaced by them. By the late palaeolithic age dances had probably developed into magical rites connected with man's desire to exert his will over animals, and eventually, perhaps over thousands of years, words separated out from what was at first a single function of dance, music and poetry. Here we may trace the beginning of lyric poetry and the choral odes that were related to the myths which interpreted the seasons and the life of the crops (Donovan, p. 138). These odes in turn grew into the Attic drama, when in the sixth century B.C. a choir leader, Thespis, inserted a spoken character part into the sung narratives performed in honour of Dionysius at Athens. Songs were also evolved in very early times to co-ordinate the movements of a labouring group and mark the rhythm of various manual tasks – a development which some Marxist critics regard as the origin not only of poetry but of all speech. At some point music and song came to be performed with little or no movement, and within historical time words became independent of music.

It is reasonably clear that poetry came before prose and was linked with ritual dancing; this is fully consistent with our knowledge that in many countries poetry used to accompany dancing and that traces of the connection are well marked in old poems, and in some of the terms, such as rondeau and rondel (reminding us of round dances), used to describe verse forms. We can feel this when we hear poetry in common metre of fourteen or sixteen syllables – the iambic tetrameter of Greek prosody; the common metre 'agrees with certain common tendencies in the human mind.... This type of verse is natural because it runs in periods of 4, 8, 16, which one may call the natural rhythm for the human race, the rhythm of all popular tunes and dances' (Ker 1966, p. 205). An example can be heard in the opening sentence of Wordsworth's 'Lines Written in Early Spring':

> I heard a thousand blended notes
> While in a grove I sat reclined

The rhythms of country tunes account for the broken line metres that Herrick favoured, lines which correspond with the 'set and turn single' of country dance steps, as in his 'Up Tailes All' (Gibbon, p. 64). And for the closeness of the three modes, dancing, music and poetry, surviving till recently in folk song and dancing, we may cite Cecil Sharp:

> Fiddlers...associate the tune with the dance in precisely the same way as singers connect the air of a song with its words. I have often heard them say that if only they could recall the dance they would remember the tune also. They seem quite incapable of playing a tune if they have forgotten the form and figures of the dance to which it belongs. On one occasion, a concertina player, from whom I had just noted down a Morris tune, innocently remarked, 'Now, sir, you know all about the dance.' On cross-examination, I discovered that he really believed that a knowledge of the tune carried with it the knowledge of the figures of the dance also.
> (Sharp, p. 21)

And Willa Muir wrote of the singing games of her childhood: 'they were strongly rhythmical; the dance-steps, the tune corresponded to the beat of the word-stresses, and much repetition fixed the shapes indelibly in our memories. It is worth noting that the dancing never hampered the singing or the actions; the governing rhythm was never broken' (Willa Muir, p. 32).

Dance with song was the magical art of agricultural peoples, found wherever men settled down to farming, and practised to encourage the crops to grow, the beasts to breed, and themselves to do the work. It is in the background of most of the world's poetry; in Greece, for example, where dance was the foundation of the oldest folk songs; and remained important for many years. The Greek lament for the dead, with its history of two thousand and five hundred years, expressed in its early form an old idea rooted in fertility magic: that by the burial of the dead and by making offerings of fruit and grain and flowers the earth would be repaid for the gift of life, and so fertility would be promoted. It involved movement as well as wailing and singing – 'the scene must have resembled a dance, sometimes slow and solemn, sometimes wild and ecstatic' (Alexiou, p. 6). Another example is that of ancient Chinese poetry, which developed from the ritual dances that were performed at agricultural festivals. Nearer home, E. K. Chambers describes the connection between poetry and dance: 'At critical seasons of the agricultural year...our primitive ancestors went in procession about the fields of their village, to secure fertility to their crops, gathering finally in a ring of ecstatic dancing round some notable copse or tree...originally the song which accompanied it may have been no more than an inarticulate outcry' (E. K. Chambers, p. 69). The origin of the dances-with-song was always with the 'uneducated' people. The medieval carole, for instance – the ring dance to be mentioned below – was not an aristocratic genre, and the conventions of courtly love hardly touched it at all; 'the carole of ladies and knights probably had little to distinguish it from the ring-dances of the folk, who originated the pastime' (Greene, p. xxxv). Even the *Song of Roland,* the epic about the defeat of Charlemagne at Roncevaux in A.D. 778, performed at courts and not a popular product, incorporated the shouted refrain that was first heard in dances, and 'on the visual level there is an element of ritual dance which, however frenzied, has its own aesthetically satisfying patterns' (Owen, p. 23).

Christianity seems to have missed an opportunity in not utilising the dance for its own purposes, as it succeeded in doing with other pagan customs. The apocryphal Acts of John, which date from before A.D. 170, impute to Christ and his disciples the accompanying of a hymn with a round dance on the eve of the Passion. He made his disciples stand in a ring, and sang a hymn after each line of which they were to say 'Amen'. After the hymn Christ is said to have delivered a discourse in which he remarked, 'I would keep time with holy souls'. Then 'thus having danced with us the Lord went forth'. The Franciscans in their efforts to re-Christianise the revelry of Christmas seem to have used a number of popular refrain poems that were once danced, but leaving out the dancing part; and the Franciscan poet, Jacopone of Todi, used dance forms for his poems. Dance-with-song seems to have been genuinely popular in the early Middle Ages, not restricted to any one rank but understood and enjoyed by all: 'Particularly, it was a favourite custom to dance and sing in this way on the vigils or eves of saints' days, when people assembled from some distance at the church where the day was to be observed. Dancing parties were often held at these "Wakes"; they were often held in the churchyard' (Ker 1969, p. 61). Preachers in

the vernacular quoted popular poems; one of these, from about
1350, retains in its refrain an echo of the linkage between song and
dance (the second 'make' means *mate*):

> Hound by hound we schulle ous take,
> And joye and blisse schulle we make,
> For the devel of elle man haght forsake,
> And Godes Sone is maked our make.
> (E. K. Chambers, p. 80)

The vitality of pagan spring and winter customs especially was
a problem to the church for centuries, as we gather from Bede. In
most cases the pagan observances were successfully assimilated, but
the attempt does not seem to have been made with the dance. A
number of decrees specifically exclude dancing from the neigh-
bourhood of churches (Davies, p. 30), and it became secularised.
Giraldus Cambrensis records an anecdote about a parish priest who
heard dancers singing all night round his church a song with the
refrain 'Swete lemman, thin are' (Sweetheart, have mercy), and
then next morning repeated the words in saying mass in church.
The church however did not prevent one of its most popular forms
of words to music, the carole, evolving from the Old French carole.
This was a ring dance in which the dancers themselves sang the
governing music; this was what Chaucer understood by 'carol'; and
when in *Sir Gawayne and the Grene Knight* the author describes the
knights of the Round Table as going to the court 'caroles to make',
they were going to dance. The song accompanying the dance was
divided between a leader and the rest of the chorus; the leader sang
successive new lines, while the rest of the dancers holding hands
in a ring joined in the refrain. Thus the proper meaning of 'carol'
is a lyric in which regularly repeated burdens show the poem's
descent from the dancing circle of the 'carole', which had an
enormous vogue as a social pastime. It has been suggested that carols
were written to divert interest from 'those pagan songs, with their
wild dances, which, even as late as the fifteenth century, made
Christmas a trying and dangerous period for the church' (Ward and
Waller, pp. 376 ff). Then the dance movements went out, leaving
the rhythms of dancing in traditional carol tunes, as in 'Gabriel to
Mary Came' (No. 1 in the *Penguin Carol Book*). But not many carols
have preserved their dance tunes; most of the music that has
survived with carols is not simple dance song.

Another form that was originally danced is the ballad. Anglo-
Scandinavian ballads, for example, were designed to be danced
while a precentor chanted the narrative verses. They are charac-

terised by a refrain or double refrain, which is sung by the dancers as they pause between two movements. Many ballads were once used to regulate the steps of a dance, and S. Baring Gould may well have been right in saying that 'it was the fiddle that banished the ballad as a song accompaniment to a dance' (Gummere, p. 326). There is an interesting little piece of evidence at the end of this account of Cecil Sharp's:

> As time went on, dance and song became divorced, each taking on a separate and independent existence...With this separation the words 'ballet' and 'ballad' became differentiated, the former being applied to the dance only, and the latter to the song. Curiously, the synonymous use of these two words still survives. The English peasant will often say that he has learned a particular song 'off a *ballet*', meaning thereby a 'ballad-sheet', or, 'Never had no ballet to it' – as a singer once said to me.
> (Sharp, p. 93)

The opening lines of 'The Cruel Mother' are an example of a singing dance:

> She sat down below a thorn,
> *Fine flowers in the valley,*
> And there she has her sweet babe born,
> *And the green leaves they grow rarely.*
> (Hodgart, p. 13)

Many English dance poems must have been lost; there was no one to write them down, as there was with religious poems. John Speirs suggests that the (possibly thirteenth-century) 'Lenten is come with love to toune' and 'Between Mersh and Averil' originate from songs and dances celebrating the return of spring; one that speaks for itself as a dance song is:

> Ich am of Irlaunde
> And of the holy londe
> Of Irlande.
>
> Gode sire, pray ich thee,
> For of sainte charite,
> Come and daunce wit me
> In Irlaunde

Another possible vestige of the ring dance was the custom of folk singers, observed in Ireland and other countries, to hold the hand of a neighbour and sway it slowly, or more energetically at a deeply affecting passage. The ring dance survived in north Somerset until late in the last century in the form of the Apple Tree Wassail, danced in an orchard in the evening. And behind much medieval music and poetry one can sense the impulse of the dance, notably in the goliardic Carmina Burana.

Other examples of the unity of dance and song may be found in mimetic dances, encouraging crops to grow and rain to fall, that are reported from all over the world; in African dance songs, often joined by members of the audience; in the hey-day of Polish folk songs, for all events from the cradle to the grave, all danced as well as sung; and in Eskimo song-fests. In the latter the music is provided by a team of two, one drumming and the other dancing and singing. The singer forgets everything about him and falls into a trance, and the audience joins in with a refrain. 'Nothing in such a performance would be haphazard. The song had a tune; the words had to follow the drumbeats and also the dance that was bound by a certain rhythm' (Freuchen, p. 273).

The earliest poetry

Many of the explorers, missionaries and anthropologists who have made contact with peoples labelled 'primitive' recorded examples of their poetry and noted the part it played in their lives. There is no reason to suppose that these peoples resemble the earliest human beings more than us, products of western civilisation; they are only primitive in a limited sense. Like our ancestors they may have no agriculture or little; they may be nomads and have few possessions – but over millennia they have developed codes of behaviour, forms of social organisation, and languages of complexity and rich expressiveness, none of which can be styled 'primitive'. Their economy may sometimes resemble that of the men who first gathered food or hunted their prey, and their poetry in each case arises from their conditions of living; but that is about as far as we can go in trying to assimilate early man and more recent groups.

But for the purposes of this book the primitive, pre-literate peoples are producers of unwritten poetry, and as theirs is the only work, of its kind we have to go on we shall use it to make guesses about the earliest poetry; there is a clear division between the products of industrial civilisation on the one hand and the first men and pre-literates on the other. We are to imagine the earliest men as developing noises (that eventually became words) to accompany the rhythm of dance movements; and that from using poetry to accompany communal dances they began to apply it to other occasions, such as the co-operative moving of a log, or the paddling of a canoe, where organised effort was needed. Once language had developed, it may not have been long before poetry came to accompany all seasonal festivities: the tasks that went to making a living, the attempts to come to terms with real or imagined influences, and the major events of human existence, from birth to death. Certainly in the oldest culture of which we have knowledge poetry was at the same time 'ritual, entertainment, artistry, riddle-making, doctrine, persuasion, sorcery, soothsaying, prophecy and competition' (Huizinga 1970, p. 142). This multi-functional verse is reported from many parts of the world. In China, for example, the words inspired by the seasonal festivities took on the character of love poetry and provided source material for moral instruction, history and education. From Greece the oldest surviving verse shows that the life of the people from beginning to end was attended by poetry for every circumstance and every emotion that involved them (Smyth, p. 489). And in ancient Israel, poetry

> was indispensable to the sports of peace, it was a necessity for the rest from the battle, it cheered the feast and the marriage (Is. 5: 12; Amos 6: 5; Judg. 14); it lamented in hopeless dirge for the dead (2 Sam. 3: 33); it united the masses, it blessed the individual, and was everywhere the lever of culture. Young men and maidens vied with one another in learning beautiful songs, and cheered with them the festival gatherings of the villages, and the still higher assemblies at the sanctuary of the tribes. The maidens at Shilo went yearly with songs and dances into the vineyards (Judg. 21: 19); and those of Gilead repeated the sad story of Jephtha's daughter (Judg. 11: 40); the boys learned David's lament over Jonathan (2 Sam. 1: 18); shepherds and hunters at their evening rests by the springs of the wilderness sang songs to the accompaniment of the flute (Judg. 6: 11). The discovery of a fountain was the occasion of joy and song (Num. 21: 17). The smith boasted defiantly of the products of his labour (Gen. 4: 23). Riddles and witty sayings enlivened the social meal (Judg. 14: 12; 1 Kings 10).
>
> (Reuss, 'Hebrew Poesie' in *Herzog. Encykl.*)

Among surviving 'primitive' peoples poetry is woven into the fabric of life. The Todas, a pastoral tribe of Southern India, compose poems for all sorts of subjects and all their major interests – marriages, funerals, dairy operations, husbands, children, a woman's beauty (Emeneau, p. 543). It is (or was) the same with the aboriginals of another part of India, Chattisgarh, one of whose folk songs runs

> How am I to cross the hills?
> Without you the level plain
> Is like a mountain
> Without you the flooded river
> Is a parched plain in time of drought
> Without you the sarai tree in bud
> Is dry and blackened in a forest fire.

26

In Australia the aborigines 'have songs for almost all occasions, and the range of subject matter is as varied as life itself' (Berndt, p. 307). Once again, poetry came before prose and persisted for a long time since it was the main and only adequate means of expressing the important concerns of a society.

> For the utterance of solemn or holy things poetry is the only adequate vessel. Not only hymns and incantations are put into verse but lengthy treatises such as the ancient Hindu sutras and sastras or the earliest products of Greek philosophy. Empedocles pours his knowledge into a poem and Lucretius still follows him in this. The preference for verse form may have been due in part to utilitarian considerations; a bookless society finds it easier to memorise texts in this way. But there is a deeper reason, namely, that life in archaic society is itself metrical and strophical, as it were. Poetry is still the natural mode of expression for the 'higher' things.
> (Chapman, p. 81)

Early poetry did not voice individual emotions and convictions, for the people were audience and performer too. Both led the same kind of life, without class or wealth distinctions; and they shared a slighter consciousness of themselves as individuals than is normal with us today. The poet spoke for his audience as they wanted to speak, of themes and occasions of common interest, and expressed their joy or grief or their desire to communicate with supernatural powers. The words of the poet were characteristic of the society he belonged to; its members 'learned from the flora and fauna of their surroundings, conversed with them, worshipped them and sacrificed to them. They were convinced that their fate was bound up intimately with these non-human friends and foes, and in their culture they made a place for them, honouring their ways' (Roszak, p. 7).

In so far as it survives translation, the style of pre-literate poetry often reminds one of English writing, popular in origin and style, up to about the time of Shakespeare. It is concrete, it is good at conveying sensation, emotion, and impressions; it often expresses an immediate reaction to sights or experiences; the response is full and uninhibited. Both the pre-literate and the English poets were in close touch with the environment from which they wrested a living; they saw the seasons pass and felt the weather directly; they knew by personal experience what they were talking about. Thus there is an immediacy in the language of both. The comparison can only go so far; it stops at the point at which we note how English poetry relies on the associations of words, built up by previous use, in religious contexts especially. The pre-literate has none of this capital to draw on; instead he relies on the experience he shares with his audience of the basic facts and events of human life. What the Berndts write about aboriginal poetry in Australia has a wide application:

> In sacred songs especially, the style, the way of saying things, is not a prosaic literal affair: there is a heavy use of symbolism; a single word may convey a whole range of images – most notably in short compressed songs where each word has a number of mythical and other implications apart from its literal meanings. This is not always clear in translation...The construction of songs often shows considerable technical skill, in the choice and arrangement of words, the use of metre and stress in total patterning, the matching of sounds – and the relation of the whole to a particular tune, or to its musical accompaniment. (p. 311)

To read the translations of pre-literate poetry collected during the past two hundred years is to be moved by the humanity of the work. The poems record the thoughts and feelings of complete human beings, struggling to exist and cope with the changes and chances of life, in a way that brings them near to us. To readers living in an age subject to strong dehumanising influences they reaffirm what is important to mankind; they evoke not condescension but the respect due to people who are certainly not less than our equals and have much to offer. It is not difficult to see in them the growing point of humanity; they seem to show us that the emotions and responses they offer did not exist before they were given shape in words. The thought of the poems is concrete and direct, their use of symbols spontaneous, their rhythm and syntax – as far as one can tell – closely connected. Here art is not something laid on from outside, but the means that men and women developed in finding their humanity and maintaining it.

Work songs

Songs to accompany every activity of the working day are among the oldest of all poetry. They must have flourished before the epic; in Book 18 of the *Iliad* Homer describes the shield of Achilles, on which was depicted the scene in a vineyard. A boy sang 'the lovely song of Linus in a treble voice to the sweet music of his tuneful lyre. They all kept time with him and followed the music and the words with dancing feet'. The Greeks evolved songs for most occupations – weaving, stamping barley, treading grapes, making ropes, carrying water and baking bread; watchmen and shepherds also had their songs. One of the oldest survivors – if we can allow it to pass as a work song – is a spring begging-song of the seventh century B.C. for the children of Rhodes:

> The swallow has come, has come,
> Bringing fine days and fine weather.
> She is white in the belly, and black in her back.
>
> Roll out the pudding from your rich house,
> And a beaker of wine, and a basket of cheese.
> Buns too and pulse-cake the swallow will not reject.
> Are we to get it or to go away?
> If you will give us something, well and good.
>
> But if not, we will not put up with it.
> Let us take the door or the lintel,
> Or the lady who is sitting inside.
> She is small and we will easily carry her.
>
> But if you will give us something,
> You may get something big in return!
> Open, open the door to the swallow.
> For we are not elders – we are children.
> (Chadwick 1932, I, p. 428)

There are countless examples from other times and other parts of Europe – a spinning song from Russian peasants, from Iceland a grinding song of about A.D. 1230, found in some manuscripts of the Prose Edda, and from France a Gascon ballad sung by women as they washed clothes and beat the linen in cadence.

Outside Europe there are thousands of poems, from a variety of occupations. Polynesia produced a large range of work songs – for marching, canoe-building, paddling, boat-launching, and hauling heavy timber, to give only a few instances. In India the people of the Maikal Hills had songs for weaving, fishing, weeding, and for cowherds, potters and road menders; and while husking rice with a long-handed pestle the women would sing poems celebrating the virtues of the winnowing fan, the broom and rice-pounder. In the Chattisgarh district, in addition to those for weeding and threshing and weaving, there were songs for reaping, grinding, churning and fishing. From Africa an enormous number of work songs have been reported; here is a characteristic account:

> It was their invariable habit to sing when paddling. They seldom put in more than a few strokes, before someone started a song, to keep time for the paddlers; all the men joined in the chorus... The king often sent for the canoe-men to come and sing their songs; when they came, they marched round and round in one of the courtyards, working their arms as though paddling, and singing at the same time.
> (J. Roscoe, *The Baganda*, 1911)

And also in Africa there are numerous co-operative songs accompanying work that can go to a rhythm, such as

> hoeing, weeding, mowing, launching a boat, sawing, hauling in fishnets, pounding, floor-beating, throwing up water from deep wells in a human chain, carrying a chief in his hammock, hanging up beehives, or rubbing animal skins to make them soft; there are domestic and solitary songs for women grinding corn or pounding rice; there are gang songs for pulling trucks, for road work, for factory hands, and for miners.
> (Finnegan, p. 231)

In short, work songs have sprung up wherever monotonous work has had to be done by human muscle; they imposed or brought out rhythms that made labour both easier and more efficient. Very striking testimony to the power of work songs has been collected by Bruce Jackson in the prisons of Texas, where the convicts he talked to were vocal and articulate. One told him that

> I can do a whole lot more work workin' by time than I can workin' loose. Why? Well it looks like it's more fun. Even picking cotton, I likes to sing. When I sing, picking cotton, before I know anything I be three blocks ahead of the squad.

In wretched conditions the men took pride in working faster and better; another man declared:

> When a man gets to singing he doesn't get time to think about his problems or the work. I believe it's easier being a leader because the group is pushing you and you're pushing the group. And it urges you to go just a little bit stronger with the group pushing you. You got to go.

The best-known and the most numerous of British work songs are the sea shanties of the merchant ships. One of the collectors, Richard Runciman Terry, derived their name from Antigua. There the shanties of West Indians were movable wooden huts, and when a move was desired they hauled away on wheels pulled by two long ropes; the shantyman mounted the roof, and sung a song with a chorus, which is the exact musical parallel to the sailors' pull-and-haul shanty. However, the general view is that the word represents the French imperative, '*Chantez!*' 'Sing!' One of the earliest references to this type of song is in the work of a Dominican, *The Book of the Wanderings of the Brother Felix Fabri*, who made a note of 'Mariners who sing when work is going on...a concert between one who sings out orders and the labourers who sing in response' (Hugill, p. 3). Few shanties can be dated before 1800, though the *Complaynt of Scotland* (1549) records a simple one:

Haill all and ane.
Haill all and ane.
Haill him up til us.
Haill him up til us.
 Hou hou.
 Pulpela pulpela.
 Boulena boulena.
 Darta darta.
 Hard out strif...
(Lloyd, p. 290)

Shanties took the form of verses enounced by the shantyman, with choruses from the crew working on a particular task, and their aim was to produce rhythmical and thus effective application of manpower. In the Navy, where shantying seems to have been forbidden, this was achieved by a fiddler. There were two main types: first, halyard shanties, most of them fairly short, for spasmodic hauling jobs, such as heaving up the yards; examples are 'Reuben Ranzo' and 'Boney':

Boney was a warrior,
 Away-i-oh;
Boney was a warrior,
 John François.

Boney fought the Proosh-i-ans,
 Away-i-oh;
Boney fought the Proosh-i-ans,
 John François... etc.

The second kind consisted of capstan shanties, where the men walked round the capstan, pushing a spoke-like bar in front of them; the work (of heaving up the anchor chain, for example) went to slower-moving songs such as 'Rio Grande', 'Shenandoah' and 'Sally Brown'. The best of them have beautiful and memorable tunes, but the words are less interesting, for to hold the interest of the men there was a great deal of improvising. Thus a good shantyman was worth his weight in gold, especially if he was quick-witted and inventive. He was privileged and might be excused hard work, because (according to a saying of the sea) 'when the men sing right, the ship goes right'. As with folk song, no two singers ever sang the same shanty in the same manner, and the 'adlibbing' was probably often bawdy.

Apart from the shanties few work songs have survived in the British Isles. A good spinning song comes from the Isle of Man, and a number of songs in Gaelic for different occasions and kinds of work were recorded at the end of the last century. In Scotland too this early twentieth-century record takes us back to a distant period:

On a day in harvest, more than a hundred years ago, when every
sort of outdoor work was accompanied by songs of suitable rhythms,
a party of reapers assembled at Ebost, in Bracadale, divided them-
selves into two rival bands representing the poetesses who had orig-
inally sung the words of strife, and while working with all their might
to be first at the other end of the field where they were reaping, sang
the song with so much fervour that they unconsciously cut themselves
with their sickles.

(Frances Tolmie, 1911)

Also in nineteenth-century Scotland several cases are recorded of
a farmer engaging a piper to lighten the work of the harvesting;
in Banffshire 'a proper ploughman of the eighteenth century would
not drive his team afield without a piper to play in addition to the
ordinary gaudsman' (Buchan, p. 180). It was the gaudsman's
business to encourage the team of oxen by whistling, often psalm
tunes. In Gaelic there were songs for milking, reaping, spinning,
weaving and grinding with the quern; and old rowing songs came
to be used for rope-waulking (D. Thomson, p. 75). In the Hebrides
there were songs for fulling wool to make tweed.

Examples of English song directly linked with work are not
common. The 'Bird Starver's Cry' from Somerset runs:

Hi! Shoo all o' the birds
    Shoo aller birds
    Shoo aller birds

Out of master's ground
Into Tom Tucker's ground

Out of Tom Tucker's ground
Into Luke Collis's ground

Out of Luke Collis's ground
Into Bill Vater's ground

Hi! Shoo aller birds
    Kraw! Hoop!
(James Reeves, *The Idiom of the People*)

The songs mentioned so far, most of them quite utilitarian, were
all fairly closely integrated with an occupation, to make the work
smoother and more effective. Cecil Sharp several times remarked
on this integration: 'I have many times sat by the side of a stone-
breaker on the way-side and taken down songs – at the risk, too,
of my eyesight, for the occupation and the song are very often
inseparable' (Fox-Strangways, p. 35). Another Somerset singer he
collected from could only sing a song when she was ironing, and
yet another woman in the same village sang best on washing day.

'There now', said a woman who had forgotten a song Sharp wished to note, 'if only I were driving the cows home I should remember it at once'; and a man managed to recall a Robin Hood song when he remembered that he sang it while milking. R. R. Terry has a relevant anecdote:

> A friend of mine who lives in Kerry wished a collector to hear some of the traditional keening, and an old woman with the reputation of being the best keener in the district, when brought to the house to sing the funeral chants, made several attempts and then replied in a distressed manner, 'I can't do it, there's no body.' This did not mean that she was unwilling to keen in the absence of a corpse, but that she was unable to do so. Just before giving up in despair my friend...asked her if it would suffice for him to lie down on the floor and personate the corpse. When he had done this the old woman found herself able to go on with the keening.   (p. ix)

It seems likely that rhythmical beating and varying tones formed part of primitive man's communal dances at festive meetings, and that these first noises came to be used for marking the rhythms and so making concerted human action more effective. The rhythms are inherent in certain elementary tasks, such as heaving logs and striking wood or stone with some sort of tool. Then one of two developments took place. According to Karl Bücher language was invented at this early stage, emerging as part of the technique of production: 'speech evolved from the reflex actions of the vocal organs incidental to the muscular efforts involved in the use of tools' (G. Thomson 1945, p. 16). Alternatively, already existent words were fitted to the rhythms of work, onomatopoeic or nonsensical at first, with meaning eventually imposed – much as thousands of years later the medieval sequence (a piece of verse or rhythmical prose inserted between the Gradual and the Gospel in the Mass) developed from the felt need to supply words for the lengthy modulations on the final 'a' of 'alleluia'. The first to link the origin of poetry to work, specifically agriculture, was the Roman poet Tibullus:

> agricola adsiduo primum satiatus aratro
>   cantavit certo rustica verba pede,
> et satur arenti primum est modulatus avena
>   carmen, ut ornatos diceret ante deos.
> (II, i, 51–54)

> (The farmer, fed up with endless ploughing, was the first to sing of country matters in a definite rhythm; and, full of food, was the first to make a poem on the dry oat pipes to sing before the gods he had decorated.)

33

Later the idea that the rhythms of poetry stemmed from the singing of workers on the job found favour with Marxist writers.

It is certainly true that many songs made up to lighten labour and increase the efficacy of work came to be performed as 'art' songs; this happened with the singing of the Baganda canoeists, as we noted earlier in this chapter. Another development was the augmenting of the Polynesian chants used as work songs by mention of the great occasions in the past when similar actions had been successfully performed. St Augustine is said in his later sermons to have borrowed with good effect the rhythmic chants of labourers in the fields; (Brown, p. 258) and it was from chants like these that arose the tradition of accentual Latin which produced the great medieval hymns. In English poetry the sea shanties are only one example of the way in which words and music developed for utilitarian purposes have come to satisfy quite other demands. Negro spirituals too, some of which evolved to meet conditions of slavery, have survived and spread over the world as songs in their own right.

Most of the songs already mentioned have been enmeshed in common tasks, though their life has continued in meeting new and different needs. In addition, many other songs were sung at work, some on the subject with which the task or enterprise was concerned, others much more personal, the vehicle for the thoughts and feelings of a person working on his or her own with time and opportunity for individual expression. African hunters, for example, on their way to the forest sing in praise of the animals they are going to hunt; in particular there is a remarkable Pygmy song for elephant hunting, with a beautifully expressed sense of the forest darkness and the business they are engaged on:

> On the weeping forest, under the wing of the evening,
> The night, all black, has gone to rest happy;
> In the sky the stars have fled trembling,
> Fireflies which shine vaguely and put out their lights;
> On high the moon is dark, its white light is put out.
> The spirits are wandering.
> Elephant-hunter, take your bow!
> *Elephant-hunter, take your bow!*

> In the frightened forest the tree sleeps, the leaves are dead,
> The monkeys have closed their eyes, hanging from branches on high.
> The antelopes slip past with silent steps,
> Eat the fresh grass, prick their ears attentively,
> Lift their heads and listen frightened.
> The cicada is silent and stops his grinding song.

Elephant-hunter, take your bow!
Elephant-hunter, take your bow!

In the forest lashed by the great rain,
Father elephant walks heavily, *baou, baou,*
Careless, without fear, sure of his strength,
Father elephant, whom no one can vanquish;
Among the trees which he breaks he stops and starts again.
He eats, roars, overturns trees and seeks his mate.
Father elephant, you have been heard from afar.
Elephant-hunter, take your bow!
Elephant-hunter, take your bow!

In the forest where no one passes but you,
Hunter, lift up your heart, leap, and walk.
Meat is in front of you, the huge piece of meat,
The meat which walks like a hill,
The meat which makes glad the heart,
The meat that will roast on the hearth,
The meat into which the teeth sink,
The fine red meat and the blood which is drunk smoking.
Elephant-hunter, take your bow!
Elephant-hunter, take your bow!
(Bowra 1962, p. 44)

Some of these hunting songs have become general entertainment
– and so have other songs from all over the world, made for a
variety of enterprises, such as an expedition to obtain salt, to gather
medicinal herbs, herding cattle, trading, gambling and a hundred
other occasions. And then there are numbers of unspecialised songs,
not related to any particular task, but providing an outlet when the
work was solitary or tedious.

Waggoners used to sing to their teams and thus ease the hardships
of the road; the lumberjacks of Maine, who had to make their own
entertainment, enjoyed a large repertoire of songs of only moderate
quality, though an employer would pay more to a lumberjack who
could sing than to the others. Scottish housewives, according to their
descendants, used to sing a great deal at their cooking and cleaning;
and African girls still sing of their lovers as they pound the yams.
The liveliest evidence of what singing can do for men working under
conditions of near-slavery comes from the Texan convict camps
(already mentioned), where all the prisoners are black. The rhythm
imparted by singing not only made the work go faster; it also was
useful for survival in cutting down trees, just as the 'roustabouts'
on the Mississippi River and Chesapeake Bay used songs to time
their steps on swaying gang planks, to avoid being swung into the
water. With all work going at the same pace there could be no

singling out of the slower men for punishment. Most important, the songs supplied an outlet for the convicts' tensions and frustrations and angers (Jackson, p. 29). A prisoner spoke of 1938:

> You get worked to death or beat to death. That's why we sang so many of these songs. We would work together and help ourselves as well as help out our fellow man.

And another:

> They really be singing about the way they feel inside. Since they can't say it to nobody they sing a song about it. I mean, you know, long time ago when the penitentiary was kind of rough they used to sing songs about the bosses.

And noting that the most poetic of the prison work songs are those which are used for untimed activity, Bruce Jackson comments, 'The songs change the nature of the work by putting the work into the workers' framework rather than the guards'. By incorporating the work with their song...they make it theirs.'

Mnemonics

The earliest forms of poetry, associated with communal dances, became the vehicle for religious thoughts and feelings. Quite early it must have been found that verse was the right shape for moulding charms and spells, and from that stage it would have been easy to develop mnemonic forms of weather lore and agricultural knowledge. The bookless societies that have been normal for most of human history needed verse for purely utilitarian needs, as well as for the expression of more exalted matter; good memories were important.

There are many instances of the power of memory in non-literate peoples. The sacred books of India, the Rig (or Royal) Veda, were composed between 1500 and 1000 B.C. and though writing existed in India in the third century B.C. they were not written down till the eighth or ninth century A.D., having lost nothing in transmission. This was so accurate that admirers of oral transmission, which is characteristically flexible and selective, regard it almost as belonging to the history of print, because in none of the transmitting periods were any alterations made to suit the needs of the time. English ecclesiastics also used to have retentive memories. Wilfrid, abbot of Ripon, who flourished in the first half of the seventh century A.D., knew a hundred-and-fifty Psalms off by heart – not an outstanding performance for monks at that time – and when imprisoned by

King Egfrith he passed his time singing the Psalms (Decarreaux, p. 264). A thousand years later Dr Robert Sanderson of Oxford could repeat all the *Odes* of Horace, Cicero's 'Offices' and much of Juvenal and Persius without books (Walton, p. 398). In the eighteenth century children in England were taught to recite verses from the Gospels or Psalms, a reward of fivepence a hundred verses being offered in Cornwall; one child recited four hundred verses and got his one-and-eightpence (Mathews, p. 59). Cecil Sharp often remarked on the excellent memories of the people from whom he collected folk songs. Of one man he records: 'He told me that he was a coalminer; that he had heard the song when he was a boy, fifty or sixty years ago; that it was sung by a tramp who was passing through his village; that it had pleased his fancy, and that he had never forgotten it.'

Sometimes the memory was supported by visual aids. Carved sticks in Polynesia, knotted cords in Peru, Benin bronze plaques, cult objects and even the landscape were among the aids; and it is possible that some forms of art may have supplied a learning technique to the bards and story-tellers of these islands. Frances Yates observes most relevantly:

> In the ancient world, devoid of printing, without paper for note-taking or on which to type lectures, the trained memory was of vital importance. And the ancient memories were trained by an art which reflected the art and architecture of the ancient world, which could depend on faculties of intense visual memorisation which we have lost... The artificial memory is established from places and images ... The art of memory is an inner writing.

The way in which Langland presents such qualities as gluttony by means of almost three-dimensional visual imagery comes to mind. He was only following the practice of the preachers. Here for example is John Ridewell, an English Franciscan of the fourteenth century visualising idolatry as a blind and deaf harlot, diseased and with a disfigured face:

> Mulier notata, oculis orbata,
> aure mutilata, cornu ventilata,
> vultu deformata et morbo vexata.
> (Smalley 1960, p. 112)

His rhymes were written down to help him memorise points for a sermon. Habits of attention and retention must also have worked very powerfully when it came to listening to anything in the form of verse. In fact before print there existed what Havelock has termed 'a total technology of the preserved word'. In this memory was made easier by a psychological mechanism – 'a state of total personal involvement and therefore of emotional identification with the substance of the poeticised statement that you are required to retain'.

Mnemonic verse has served a variety of purposes. In St Matthew 7 and St Luke 6 there is a parable in a verbal form that is common to both; and it has been maintained that these and similar parables in the Gospels were in their original Aramaic actually spoken in a simple and familiar metrical form that could be easily and surely memorised. The Frisian legal codes, the first to be written down in any Germanic language, contain metrical and semi-metrical passages the form of which made them easy to memorise; and alliterative formulas had the practical purpose of emphasising and defining legal ideas. (This is one of the points at which one catches a glimpse of the power and prestige that used to attach to the poet.) There are many instances, especially from Africa, of verse being adopted for genealogies, catalogues and other historical material. In Indo-China the game of question and answer in verse form has served to store up a whole mass of useful knowledge:

> A girl has just accepted her swain, and together they intend to open up a shop. The young man asks her to tell him the names of the medicaments and the whole treasury of the pharmacopeia follows for answer. The art of arithmetic, the knowledge of various commodities in business, and the use of the calendar in agriculture are most succinctly passed on in this way.
> (Huizinga 1970, p. 149)

Material on the art of navigation and information about weather and coast-lines have often been versified, and an Arab manual collecting resources of this kind has been discovered, written in iambic verse, for the use of ships in the Indian Ocean (Gibb, p. 143). Round the coasts of Newfoundland and Canada skippers made up rhymes, known as 'pilot verses', which were a serious aid to survival on those coasts. A coasting guide for Newfoundland, called 'Wadham's Song' was put on record in the Admiralty Court, London, soon after it was composed in 1756, as it was considered the best coasting guide for the area up to that date. For fishing vessels sailing to the Tyne from the Lincolnshire coast there were these lines:

> First the Dudgeon, then the Spurn,
> Flamborough Head comes next to turn,
> Scarborough Castle standing high,
> Whitby Rocks lay northerly.
> Sunderland lay in a bight, etc.

The old fisherman who recorded these verses in 1965 added, 'They used to tell these aboard the boat. All these different rhymes, well, you being a boy, you used to pick 'em up and you'd learn 'em, you see.' Some weather lore from the same source ran:

> When the sun sets in a bank
> Westerly wind you shall not want.

> Sun go down as clear as a bell,
> Easterly winds as sure as hell.

> Mackerel's back and mare's tails
> Makes lofty ship carry low sails.
> (*Over to You*)

Landsmen also had many traditional weather forecasts, such as:

> When Bredon Hill puts on his hat
> Ye man of the vale, beware of that;
> When Cheviot you see put on his cap
> Of rain ye'll have a wee bit drap.

Sayings about the weather and the seasons were only part of a corpus of verse connected with agriculture; it may have been one of the main methods of handing down farm experience (Evans, p. 177). The fact that it was written in verse had something to do with the immediate acceptability and long life of Thomas Tusser's *A Hundred Good Pointes of Husbandrie*. The author (?1524–1580) came of good Essex stock, was educated at Eton and Trinity College, Cambridge, and after a spell at Court took to farming in Essex. His book was published in 1557, and gave farming advice, arranged by months. Several editions were called for in his lifetime; he enlarged his hundred to five hundred and later thought up another five hundred; altering his advice as he changed his farm, and adding material on gardening and housekeeping, together with precepts on conduct in general. It was reprinted steadily till 1710, but was then lost sight of till a new annotated edition appeared in 1812, after which it became a curiosity. A sample of his unpretentious verse:

> In harvest-time, harvest-folk, servants and all,
> Should make, all together, good cheer in the hall;
> And fill out the black bowl of blythe to their song,
> And let them be merry all harvest-time long.

> Once ended thy harvest, let none be beguiled,
> Please such as did help thee, man, woman, and child;
> Thus doing, with alway such help as they can,
> Thou winnest the praise of the labouring man.

There was scope for a social conscience in a handbook of technology.

In England no laws ever found a versified form, but a great deal of advice has been made memorable by rhyme and metre. Charms and spells and recipes in verse go back to before the Conquest; and when, at the end of the fourteenth century, English replaced French and Latin medical treatises appeared in some quantity, many of them in verse for ease of memorising (Talbot, p. 186).

> The lyric, to us traditionally the most intimate form of poetic composition, was often, at the end of the Middle Ages, of an eminently practical nature; verses were copied, as they were composed, to preserve in memorable form useful information or wise sayings. Poems about alchemy are found stained with chemicals, devotional verses were certainly used in private prayer.
> (Stevens 1961, p. 117)

Of the proverbs and maxims about health that survive today, the 'Early to bed, early to rise' one is at least as old as 1554. The habit of using verse for anything that needed to be remembered appeared in a parish register at the end of the eighteenth century at Cottenham near Cambridge; the close seasons for marriages were set forth in rhyming couplets:

> Advent marriage doth thee deny,
> But Hilary gives thee liberty,
> Septuagesima says thee nay,
> Eight days from Easter says you may.
> Rogation bids thee to contain,
> But Trinity sets thee free again.

In this century Walter De la Mare found these lines in a laboratory:

> An alkali swallowed! – to make the patient placid
> For alkali corrosives give an acid.
> An acid swallowed! – then reverse the matter
> And give an alkali to kill the latter.
> The acid antidotes in household use
> Are table vinegar and lemon juice.
> What alkalis there are needs no revealing –
> Take whitewash, chalk, or plaster from the ceiling.

For most of the thousands of years during which education has been going on it has been mainly an oral process, with extensive recourse to mnemonics. In the fourth century of Christianity Commodian made up eighty acrostic or alphabetical poems, intended to be learned by heart by converts. Paul the Deacon in the eighth century composed 'grammatical hymns' to be used in school in the teaching of Latin grammar; and in the nineteenth century (circulating well on into this one) Kennedy's *Latin Primer* contained very full rhyming lists of nouns, designed to fix the gender of the words in the learner's mind for life. They succeeded:

Third nouns masculine prefer
Endings o, or, os and er...
Third nouns feminine we class
Endings is, aus, x and as,
S to consonant appended,
Es in flexion unextended...

In the second half of the ninth century Sedulius Scotus at Liège compiled a work on the duties and responsibilities of kings, interspersed with mnemonic verses to recapitulate the preceding prose. A similar purpose caused medieval preachers to pepper their sermons and homilies with verses, both to help the speaker recall the chief divisions of his theme and to do the same for his congregation. There were also popular rhyming summaries of the sacraments and the ten commandments (Owst 1926, pp. 271, 3), as well as rhyming handbooks of instructions for priests.

The use of verse for emphasis and summary in the body of a prose work is not limited to English sermons. In the Sanskrit *Panchatantra*, a collection of moral tales of about 200 B.C., the exposition of a philosophical and moral theme is put into verse; wise sayings are also versified, to sum up the narrative or introduce the next tale. The prose sagas of Wales, Ireland and Scandinavia all resort to poetry at moments of great emotional intensity, and the verse additions to the Icelandic *Story of Burnt Njal* look as if they have been inserted for the same reason. Augustine employed a rhetorical, near-poetic prose, with rhymes to strengthen passages of feeling or pathos. Bunyan is our last example; he introduced both parts of *The Pilgrim's Progress* with substantial explanations in verse, put hymns into the mouths of his characters (including the well-known 'Who would true valour see'), and used brief poems for comment or emphasis:

What danger is the pilgrim in,
How many are his foes!
How many ways there are to sin,
No living mortal knows.
Some of the ditch shy are, yet can
Lie tumbling in the mire;
Some, though they shun the frying-pan,
Do leap into the fire.

The examples above illustrate the application from outside, as it were, of poetic devices to commonplace purposes. More might have been said here about spells and charms, were it not that in their case metrical and other devices are essential – there from the start for their incantatory and hypnotic power – not just for their efficacy as aids to memory. On the other hand jingles about the weather or forbidden days for weddings contain no poetic value but merely make use of the mnemonic quality of rhyme and metre. However it seems likely that a society which knew the utilitarian worth of poetic devices would take poetry for granted and regard learning by heart as normal. Perhaps this acceptance assured a welcome for the huge class of didactic poetry, the form of which was determined by the convention that serious and lofty matter required, not so much memorability as the serious and lofty treatment afforded by poetry. As for the present, mnemonics are less necessary in an age of tapes and printing, and learning by heart is educationally unfashionable, though given the right help and technique children enjoy learning by heart. It would have been better in the schools to improve the methods of memorising and make its usefulness understood by learners instead of jettisoning it. There is much to be said for learning good poetry by heart if it leads to understanding and possession, perhaps for life. As it is, it looks as if the only users of mnemonics today are the advertiser and propagandist, who exploit the methods of poetry to pick the locks of our minds and implant their devices within.

3

Rites, bards, ballads

Praise, propitiation, magic

The earliest poetry must have been religious, the means whereby
man came to terms with supernatural powers, found himself, and
gave meaning to life. As often, we turn to 'primitive' peoples for
pointers. The Papago Indians for example believe that animals have
been ordained as man's food. This privilege has been granted by
the animals themselves and it must not be abused, for the slightest
waste or cruelty will cause them not only to withdraw the supply
of food but also to punish men by disease. The way to cure disease
is to please the animals by virtuous living and thus acquire the power
to overcome evil. 'The cycle is complete. The connection of practical
economy with religious belief has been worked out by this frugal
people as far as by anyone.' And Ruth Underhill continues:

> Not only the animals are living powers. Every part of the natural
> environment is also personified and must be treated with circum-
> spection and respect. The individual, when going about his duties,
> should never attack nature roughly, but explain his need and ask for
> help. 'I have come to get clay,' says the woman who is digging
> material for her pots, 'be favourable to me.' The hunter, bending
> over a dead deer, apologizes: 'I have killed you because I need food.
> Do not be angry.' The planter, taking a handful of corn kernels from
> his pouch, adjures them: 'I am dropping you into the earth. Now
> ripen well.' It is a religion whose every act is focused upon the forces
> of nature, constraining them to help man or, at least, not to hinder
> him in his arduous tasks.
> (Underhill, p. 15)

The sense of at-oneness with their environment is evident in this
religious chant of the Yokuts of central California:

> ...My words are tied in one
> With the great mountains
> With the great rocks,
> With the great trees,
> In one with my body
> And my heart...
> And you, day,
> And you night!

All of you see me
One with this world.
(Kroeber, p. 511)

Gratitude for the beauty of light and life is felt in this song of the
Mudbara tribe in the Northern Territory of Australia:

> The day breaks – the first rays of the rising Sun, stretching her arms,
> Daylight breaking, as the Sun rises to her feet,
> Sun rising, scattering the darkness, lighting up the land...
> With disk shining, bringing daylight, lighting up the land...
> People are moving about, talking, feeling the warmth,
> Burning through the gorge she rises, walking westwards,
> Wearing her waistband of human hair.
> She shines on the blossoming coolibah tree, with its sprawling roots,
> Its shady branches spreading.
> (Berndt, p. 319)

Comparable expressions of praise of the sun as giver of life come
from all over the world. There is not space to print Psalm 104 from
the Authorised Version, but because it is less generally available the
opening of Akhenaton's 'Hymn to the Sun' must be quoted. As
the product of a civilisation that had existed already for about two
thousand years it has nothing 'primitive' about it, but it is clearly
a late version of previous hymns to the sun. The opening lines below
praise the universal splendour and power of the sun; the remaining
sections deal with night, day and the good it does to man, animals,
plants and rivers, the creation of man and animals, and finally the
whole of the creation:

> The dawning is beautiful in the horizon of the sky,
> O living Aton, Beginning of life!
> When thou risest in the eastern horizon,
> Thou fillest every land with thy beauty.
> Thou art beautiful, great, glittering, high above every land,
> Thy rays, they encompass the lands, even all that thou hast made.
> Thou art Re, and thou carriest them all away captive;
> Thou bindest them by thy love.
> Though thou art far away, thy rays are upon earth:
> Though thou art on high, thy footprints are the day.
> (Bouquet, p. 68)

Religion grew out of man's relationship with his whole environment,
and it came to be the means whereby he assured himself of his place
in it, so that (in Martin Buber's words) to primitive man 'Everything
is...full of sacramental substance, everything. Each thing and each
function is ever ready to light up into a sacrament for him' (Buber,
p. 133). Everyday repeated actions – washing, eating, drinking –
came to be performed in settled ways, accepted first as correct and

then regarded as having a secondary meaning, a symbolic as well as a practical function.

> Washing away dirt is a simple, practical act; but its symbolic value is so striking that one might say the act has a 'natural meaning.' Eating, likewise, is a daily practice, but is so easily significant of the kinship among those who eat together, and the even closer connection – identification – of the eaters with the eaten, that it has a certain sacramental character...habitual patterns are exalted into sacred procedure.
>
> (Langer 1948, p. 140)

These repeated acts of daily life came to have poems of their own. The hunter had little songs or spells of his own to help him, like this Eskimo spell – an aid to catching game, and the secret property of a West Greenlander:

> Why am I no longer able?
> Why cannot I now make a kill?
> What prevents me – what prevents me?
> Hither, thou my quarry!
> Hither, thou my quarry!
> (Birket-Smith, p. 170)

In northern California and parts of Oregon the salmon-catching season did not open till a leading medicine-man had conducted a ceremony with prayers which propitiated the salmon and caused them to run abundantly. Many other common and seasonal activities have been promoted with the aid of spells, reported from all over the world. As numerous as spells of the chase are the medical charms, in Book 19 of the *Odyssey* for example we are told that 'the dark flow of blood' inflicted on the hero by a wild boar 'was stanched with a rune'. Also in Greece, about 665 B.C., Thaletas the Cretan is said to have composed purification spells by which he stopped an outbreak of plague in Sparta. The early literature of India includes spells in abundance – against diseases, for the recovery of straying cattle, to encourage love affairs. Till late in the nineteenth century Norfolk girls would try to get a sight of their future husbands by pinning their garters to the wall with nine pins in the shape of a cross, saying this charm:

> I pin my garters to the wall,
> Hoping to hear my true love call;
> Whether I wake or whether I sleep,
> I hope to hear my true love speak.
> (Dew, p. 82)

The Norsemen had spells, as did the French of the ninth century who used many ancient ones (to make barren land fertile, to encourage the swarming of bees), and in England the *Exeter Book* of the tenth century records some pleasant Anglo-Saxon poems which once again served a particular purpose such as bringing about the swarming of bees and the recovery of cattle. Another was the 'Charm against Wens':

> Wen, wen, little wen,
> Here thou shalt not build, nor stay.
> But thou must go north to the hill hard by,
> Where thou hast a brother in misery.
> He will lay a leaf at your head.
>
> Under the foot of the wolf, under the wing of the eagle,
> Under the claw of the eagle, ever mayest thou fade.
> Shrivel like coal on the hearth!
> Shrivel like muck in the wall!
> Waste away like water in a bucket!
> Become as small as a grain of linseed,
> And far smaller too than a hand-worm's hip-bone,
> And become even so small that at last thou art nothing.

And Bede in his *History of the English Church and People* (IV, 22) records the case of a young man whose bonds were miraculously freed when anyone tried to fetter him; he was asked whether he possessed any written charms. Before they died out spells were generally Christianised; this one from Cornwall was for the wound caused by the prick of a thorn:

> Christ was of a virgin born,
>   And he was pricked by a thorn,
> And it did never bell nor swell,
>   As I trust in Jesus this never will.
> (Wright, p. 247)

In the Finnish national epic *Kalevala* the hero wants to build a boat. He starts by going to fell an aspen, but the tree asks what he wants, and tells him that this kind of timber is not suitable. A pine tree says its wood is too knotty, and finally an oak agrees that its timber is suitable and that the omens are good. The hero then 'built with magic songs the vessel', but

> When the boat's ribs were constructed,
> And the sides were fixed together,
> Still he found three words were wanting,
> Which the sides should fix securely,
> Fix the prow in right position,
> And the stern should likewise finish
> (Rune XVI)

So he went in search of them. The Navajo Indians of America had songs (for example) to maintain and prolong life, to heal the sick and to encourage the power of germination; here the words were even more important than elsewhere. Words for them preceded the creation, and were the ultimate source of material success; a Navajo said, 'I have always been a poor man. I do not know a single song' (Astrov, p. 21). In Africa the number of spells was reduced by Christianity, but the Yoruba of Nigeria still use magic formulas to accompany the application of healing herbs; 'this kind of "functional" poetry is never recited in public for obvious reasons, and such potent words are not readily revealed by those who know them' (Beier 1970, p. 22).

Absolute accuracy – and often secrecy – in the use of spells is normal. Eskimo spells had to be expressed in exactly the right words and be performed with the right actions, because survival might depend on these observances. Among the Chippewa Indians long and healthy life was sought by initiation at which songs were acquired, some self-composed, others bought expensively. The Navajo also insisted on accuracy in their long song sequences for healing ceremonials; they contained the inward experience of generations, so 'no word may be altered or omitted, no gesture, dance or ceremony changed'. If such a cure proved ineffective it was taken to mean that some mistake must have been made in the performance. The magic power of the karakia, the mantic chant of Polynesia, depended on the form and manner of recitation; it must always be poetry and it always had to be sung – 'The power lay, not in the words alone, but in the combination of words with vocal music' (Chadwick 1940, III, p. 336). Poetry became magical because it was sung. In general the style of spells is simple. Composed for practical needs, there had to be no uncertainty about them, so they tend to be explicit and reduced to the indispensable requirements. They used all the devices possible, of accent, alliteration, repetition, rhythm, exclamation and so on, and thus came to need a practised orator for their proper interpretation. In the Irish bardic schools for example, which flourished with scarcely a break from A.D. 590 to the seventeenth century, magical incantations were part of the course for poets – one of the spells was yet another for the recovery of lost cattle. In Scotland too the bards up to about 1700 were known to be clever magicians (Hyde, p. 241). Thus in Europe and perhaps in Asia spells played an important part in the early history of both poetry and music. The best words for a purpose were arrived at, and they were arranged in the most memorable form. Poetry was developed because it was needed, as an art in which words do more than just make statements; and the

way in which we still metaphorically speak of enchantment is a
survival from a time when poetry was practical and purposeful.

Those who used magic were not trying to get something for
nothing; they did not think for example that the course of nature
could be altered for their benefit.

> No magician believes that he can get what he wants by merely
> wanting it, or that things come about because he thinks of them as
> happening. On the contrary, it is because he knows that there is no
> immediate connexion of this kind between wish and fulfilment...that
> he invents and adopts this technique as a middle term to connect the
> two things.
>
> (Collingwood, p. 19)

What the 'primitive' wanted was to commune with the forces of
nature, to make contact with them as if they were mindful. In an
agricultural society magic expressed the peasants' attitude towards
their flocks and crops and farming gear, and at the various seasons
canalised and strengthened their feelings – the emotions that would
further the tasks at the right time. There was no feeling that reality
could be controlled, but magical rites put men into the right frame
of mind for getting on with the job. 'The huntsmen whose energies
have been stimulated and organised by the mimetic rite are actually
better huntsmen than they were before' (G. Thomson 1938, p. 14).
And magic against earthquakes induced a readiness to endure what
was to come with courage and hope.

Of course the users of magic hoped for the co-operation of their
environment, which they regarded as alive as much as they them-
selves were. They encouraged the elements to be kind, the crops
to grow and the seasonal events to come round; as a Greek said on
Good Friday, 'If Christ does not rise tomorrow we shall have no
corn this year' (Harrison, p. 73). The encouragement was conveyed
through representation of a kind; in Somerset and the Maikal Hills
of India villagers danced round a tree to stimulate it to be equally
energetic; a dance with leaping reminded the crops to grow up;
leaping dances also helped the rain to descend; and at seed-time
in Brandenburg women used to unbind their hair to encourage the
flax plants to grow as long (Gummere, p. 52). In Susanne Langer's
words the primitive

> dances *with* the rain, he invites the elements to do their part, as they
> are thought to be somewhere about and merely irresponsive. This
> accounts for the fact that no evidence of past failures discourages his
> practices; for if heaven and earth do not answer him, the rite is simply
> *unconsummated*; it was not therefore a 'mistake'.
>
> (1948, p. 139)

48

As with spells, so with more extended rites of magic: it has often been noted that the success or failure of an act is attributed to the use of the right or the wrong word, so that ceremonial phrases are handed down from generation to generation (Diamond, p. 13). This was in part conservatism; but along with it in many cultures went the belief that words were more than conventional signs; the same term stood for the notion of a word and the notion of a thing. In Africa for instance:

> The word and verbal thought in general are conceived in non-literate... societies as having existence in their own right, with powers and vulnerabilities of the same order as the events or acts for which they stand. They are seen, in other words, as being 'behavioural' in the same sense as any other form of action. Much magic incorporates this principle.
> (Carothers, p. 25)

Among many American Indian tribes, such as the Hopi, thought is believed to influence reality; the invading Danes feared writing so much that they threw into rivers all the manuscripts they came across; and even as late as the sixteenth century in England a strong belief in the truth of names – given by God, and found out by Adam – led to a reliance on the power of words through sympathetic magic:

> Where there was a name there was a thing; therefore names could conjure up things. There was, moreover, religious sanction for the traditional belief in the efficacy of words. The verbal authority given to the apostles by the Incarnate Word lived on in the Church's power to bind or loose...Magic relied on the direct efficacy of words for spells, curses and incantations.
> (Mahood, p. 170)

In East Anglia in the last century it was believed that a child never thrived till it was named; and an old woman declared that she 'had been bishopped (confirmed) seven times and intended to be again; it was so good for her rheumatism' (Dew, p. 78).

The aim of all this early religious poetry was to make contact with supernatural powers and to gain their attention and sympathy; it helped men to be more at home in their surroundings and to establish a working relationship with nature, rather than a domineering and exploitative one. They enlisted superhuman aid by means of words, words in the most effective form they knew of, that is, poetry. An early belief in the power of the spoken word is found all over the world; 'the gods are often represented as ruling the world by the oral rites of magic and the origin of the universe ascribed to the creative activity of the holy word. The idea that the gods govern the world through magic formulas is found in the Rig-Veda' (Izutzu, p. 40). Something of the kind may lie behind the opening words of the Gospel according to St John. The putting of man's feelings into words and music and dancing clarified them, and must at some stage have helped him to understand himself. Obviously the earliest poetry was not consciously conceived as such, and it was not deliberately applied; it was not an art but a mode of living, a form of consciousness. It was religious, and included praise, intercession, supplication and celebrations; so that we can trace the emergence of kinds of poetry with which we have become more familiar. The technical skills needed for potent spells or for imitative, sympathetic magic have been employed in poetry ever since – the choice and arrangement of words, the development of incantatory and imitative rhythms, the use of refrains, and 'the matching of sounds – and the relation of the whole to a particular tune, or to its musical accompaniment'. The Berndts add: 'Some of the ordinary rain-magic singing of the deserts is permeated by simple imagery. A Walmadjeri cycle, for example, from Ganingara well, is largely made up of words of this sort: clouds building up, wind blowing from the right direction, the patter of rain drops, little streams starting to run, brimming waterholes, wet ground, and storms.'

This spell from the Gilbert Islands shows that what is formally a spell is for us a beautiful elegy. It was spoken by a young man over the body of the girl, dead from starvation, whom he was to marry; it was intended to make her way straight into the land of her ancestors:

The Lifting of the Head

I lift your head, I straighten your way, for you are going home,
    Marawa, Marawa,
Home to Innang and Mwaiku, Roro and Boaru,
You will pass over the sea of Manra in your canoe with pandanus
    fruit for food;
You will find harbour under the lee of Matang and Atila and Abaiti
    in the West,
Even the homes of your ancestors.
Return not to your body; leave it never to return, for you are going
    home, Marawa, Marawa.
And so, Farewell for a moon or two, a season or two.
Farewell! your way is straight; you shall not be led astray.
Blessings and peace go with you. Blessings and peace.
(Grimble, p. 42)

Rites, myths and epics

Music and ritual dances were performed by the ancient Chinese to keep the world in order; to the Polynesians their religious traditions were important because they upheld their beliefs about the creation of the world, and neglect might lead to natural cataclysms; and other 'primitive' peoples thought that without the proper rituals breath might cease, the sun die and the tides cease to flow. The Papago Indians for example sang seasonal sacred songs to keep the world in order and prevent a flood. In Europe there were rituals to demonstrate the act of regeneration and renewal to the sun, the earth, and the people who observed them. All over the world ceremonies were conducted to allay fears that the universe might collapse and the vital natural forces which enabled men to live might wear out, unless revived. The compilers of the Rig-Veda believed that the origin of the universe was to be found in the creative activity of holy words and that the gods ruled the world through ritual language. A number of the hymns in the Rig-Veda were composed to obtain from the gods the water and warmth needed to produce food; they were inspired by the actual bodily needs of an agricultural people who realised that their lives depended on the ordered sequence of natural processes. Similar beliefs were embedded in the Grail stories and the old Teutonic ritual drama.

Such rituals helped men to understand the mysteries of their existence. The need to master nature prompted them to understand the forces in the world about them; and the spring and autumn ceremonies took shape, stilling anxieties and imparting a reassuring sense of order. With the advent of Christianity the allegorical trend followed by the early believers enabled the pagan rites to be retained and a hidden message extracted from them; the midwinter feasts of fire and light that cheered up the sun were Christianised by the choice of 25 December for the birthday of Jesus; and the ritual drama to which non-Christians were accustomed continued in the shape of the medieval mystery plays.

After ritual came myth, based on the same awareness of the spiritual forces that sustained the life of all nature. To take Greek mythology as an example, because we know so much of its multiplicity and the part it played in Greek life:

> There was a myth behind every rite and every cult-centre, behind new city-foundations, and for more or less everything in nature, the movement of the sun, the stars, rivers and springs, earthquakes and plagues. Myth performed a number of functions: it was explanatory,

didactic and prescriptive. It gave the archaic Greeks their sense of, and knowledge of, their past, their history in other words; it sanctioned cults, festivals, beliefs, the authority of individual noble families...and so on through a range of practices and ideas.
(Finley 1970, p. 130)

It was the specific didacticism of Greek myths, as much as their embodiment of archetypal patterns, that accounted for the prestige and appeal of classical mythology in the Christian era.

When myth flourished and was so much a part of human consciousness, language was suffused with it; there was only one kind of thinking, and only one kind of language, which was poetical. As Owen Barfield has shown in *Poetic Diction*, a word like 'heart' used to have but a single meaning, that is now divided into two separate references, the physical ('heart-disease') and the psychic ('heart-warming'). Consciousness split; and a second kind of language was developed, with a restricted analytical and logical function that has now ousted for all practical purposes (as we characteristically say) the other mode. The poetry produced by the 'primitive' consciousness is in no way remote from us, but intelligible and sympathetic; and if we need an example *King Lear* comes promptly to mind.

In the early stages of civilisation myths supplied cosmology, theology, history and science – or if they did not actually offer scientific explanations they at least rendered the frightening forces of nature less formidable by placing them in reasonably coherent stories. Practical purposes were secured by weather lore, a knowledge of the seasons and a sense of the cycle of procreation, birth, growth and decay – combined with the feeling, so splendidly created by *The Winter's Tale*, that all is not lost when an individual dies. What Malinowski wrote of the indispensable part played by myth in primitive culture has a wide application:

> It expresses, enhances and codifies belief; it safeguards and enforces morality; it vouches for the efficiency of ritual and contains practical rules for the guidance of man. Myth is thus a vital ingredient of human civilization; it is not an idle tale, but a hardworked active force; it is not an intellectual explanation or an artistic imagery, but a pragmatic charter of primitive faith and moral wisdom.
> (Malinowski, p. 19)

The myths of various countries have so much in common in the types of character they describe, their response to recurrent situations, the patterns of behaviour and the attitudes presented, that Jung and others developed the notion of the collective unconscious. Jung went further, and believed that this shared store of archetypal symbols might be the starting point for a renewal of the human capacity for religious experience; and that a true understanding of our collective heritage would reconcile many of the conflicts between science, society and religion. Without accepting Jung's conviction, we cannot however fail to see that the story of Demeter and Persephone tells, upon the natural level, of the sowing and harvesting of corn; on the psychological level, of the death and resurrection of the individual soul...and on the theological, of an aspect of the relation of the divine to the human world (Raine, p. 124). For the insights of myth are by no means all invalidated by the channelling of thought and feeling into well-marked traffic lanes. Myths oblige us to face and accept the conflicts and frustrations of life, and the inevitability of death. The ultimate end of myth 'is not wishful distortion of the world, but serious envisagement of its fundamental truths; moral orientation, not escape' (Langer 1948, p. 153).

Epics developed from myths as the heroes became recognisable human beings and the tales were performed for their entertainment value. But the religious element persisted long, for the traditional oral epic singer

> is not an artist; he is a seer. The patterns of thought that he has inherited came into being to serve not art but religion in its most basic sense. His balances, his antitheses, his similes and metaphors, his repetitions, and his sometimes seemingly wilful playing with words, with morphology, and with phonology, were not intended to be devices and conventions of Parnassus but were techniques for emphasis of the potent symbol.
> (Lord, p. 220)

Traditional epic poems have been enjoyed by most peoples of the world. The hero is strong and courageous; the greatest stress is laid upon friendship and loyalty. The milieu is that of a warrior upper class delighting in hunting, feasting and often cattle-raiding; and behind the heroic expeditions there is occasionally to be detected the shaman's journey to the underworld to achieve something for humanity. Two examples of epic-in-transition-from-myth are thousands of years apart. The Sumerian epic poems included not only some very primitive myths, the origin of the gods and their squabbles over the mastery of heaven, but also the story of man's advance in culture and the deeds of the semi-divine heroes who took part in that advance, and the great deeds of human kings. And then over three thousand and five hundred years later we have the Finnish *Kalevala*, which also contains savage myths, accounts of the creation, and the conflicts of gods, as well as the human story of Aino, the Rainbow Maid, who throws herself into a lake rather than yield to her lover, the magician who was born old. Both the Asian and the European epics show us 'the beginning of that higher mythology wherein the world is essentially the stage for human life, the setting of the true epic, which is human and social' (Langer 1948, p. 153).

Epics generally were recited by professional or semi-professional bards, and towards their end they were performed for entertainment, as in Yugoslavia, but an entertainment that achieved more than the killing of time. There was normally a poetic language for the epic; in England for example the more 'primitive' the language, the wider the gap between the language of prose and that of poetry. This applied as well to the 'peasant' epics of Russia and Yugoslavia, which were performed in an elaborate and highly artificial diction, as well as to epics which maintained their courtly connections. And however exclusively epics came to be the property of the humble, their heroes were always aristocratic – in India, Greece, Russia, England, Yugoslavia and elsewhere it was the same: the poor never got a look in, and the heroic code was admired without question. This may have been because people liked a natural aristocrat to represent the human race when he went on a great quest, or because epics were formed originally at a stage when a tribe or group depended for its survival and success upon a good leader, and the interests of leader and led were identical. Similarly, epics were conformist; they voiced and supported the local ideal, and helped to form and sustain and local way of life. From them, as A. L. Lloyd reminds us, 'the listeners learned how to comport themselves in the face of adversity and dilemma; that is [their] social and artistic purpose...and to achieve it the old epics went far beyond current reality and presented heroic values and actions in high relief' (Lloyd, p. 145). An oral epic of lasting values is close to the society which produced it, and interprets to us the code and attitudes and feelings of that society.

Homer may be an exception to the rule that an oral epic cannot transcend the limitations of the society that produced it. On the one hand the *Iliad* is the story of a particularly unnecessary war, undertaken after a clear hint that the gods disapproved, and embarked on only after one of the heroes had murdered his own daughter to get things going. There is butchery rejoiced in and cruelty unreprimanded. The heroic code, with prowess and honour as its main values, is fully accepted; there is never any rational discussion. 'We should consider what the vision of the heroic created by the *Iliad* has done and might still do to man...The actual influences from the *Iliad* favouring aristocratic self-centred re-gardlessness right through – wherever Homer has had a real part in educating ruling classes – are incontestable' (Richards 1974b, p. 167). Violence, it has been argued, is the real hero of the epic, which pictures 'the wantonness of the conqueror who knows no respect for any creature or thing that is at its mercy or is imagined to be, the despair of the soldier that drives him on to destruction, the obliteration of the slave or the conquered man, the wholesale slaughter...' (Simone Weil in Braybrooke, p. 130).

On the other hand it may be that the *Iliad* brings home the senseless horror of this world of violence, the endless sequence of murder and revenge. The survival of the Homeric epics has been attributed to

> the humanizing of the old heroic saga; it is this which wins Homer a place in our hearts. The scene in which Priam and Achilles, after all the pangs of battle, all the grief and cruelty of unmeasured vengeance, learn to understand and respect each other as men, is at once the culmination of the Iliad and the starting-point of the western conception of humanity.
> (A. Lesky, *A History of Greek Literature*)

M. I. Finley sees in the humanising of the gods 'a step of astonishing boldness', and adds that in Homer there is no distinction between peoples: 'This universality of Homer's humanity was as bold and remarkable as the humanity of his gods.' It is certainly noticeable that Homer presents both hero and commoner, Greek and Trojan, as all beings subject to the common fate of men.

Whichever view one holds, one thing is certain: Homer's poetry embodied much of the knowledge and all of the wisdom of his day, and so far from being mere entertainment it was magisterial and encyclopaedic. In the Homeric formulas 'were framed both law and history and religion and technology as these were known in his society. His art therefore was central and functional as never since. It enjoyed a command over education and government, which was lost as soon as alphabetic literacy was placed at the disposal of political power' (Havelock, p. 94).

Living books

Through such verbal means as praise, ritual and spells men came to terms with the unknown. Words in themselves were thought to be powerful, the formula for a charm would be followed carefully so that there was no deviation from the route to a cure of an illness, the removal of a wart, or whatever the purpose was. Men and women who were skilled in using words came to be relied on for pronouncing spells and anything that needed effective incantation; and the office of medicine-man or shaman came into being. The Eskimos, for example had angakoks, or seers, who 'were usually the best poets, not because they were familiar with the state of trance and the "inspiration" coming out of the trance, but because they, more than anyone else, were experienced in the composition of words' (Freuchen, p. 173). They had in readiness a stock of magic formulas and a special seance language, in which everything was called by a different name or by circumlocution.

Shamans claimed that they were inspired. A case in point is that of the prophet Amos. When (at about 750 B.C.) he was told to go away from Bethel because his prophecies of doom were unwelcome, he defended himself: 'I was no prophet, neither was I a prophet's son, but I was an herdsman, and a gatherer of sycomore fruit. And the Lord took me as I followed the flock, and the Lord said unto me, "Go, prophesy unto my people Israel."' Amos 7: 14–15. Once established, the shaman's function was to approach deities on behalf of men and to announce the messages of the deities to men, in much the same way as Buddhist monks by means of the proper rituals acted as mediators to transmute Buddha's conquest of the dangers that beset human existence into prosperity and untroubled mental states for men (Goody, p. 99). Shamans in different parts of the world used various dramatic means, including poetry, music, ventriloquism and dances, to get into the right state for their explorations, all calculated; the dancing of Russian shamans was wild, but controlled, for even in a confined space they never hit a member of the audience. Their verbal skill must at times have been considerable. The poetic diction which was a large part of a Yakut shaman's equipment amounted to a vocabulary of twelve thousand words, compared with one of four thousand words in ordinary use (Chadwick 1940, III, p. 199). This poetic material was used for the songs which the shaman himself sang first, in order to gain strength.

In his ecstasy the spirit of the shaman visited the sky and the underworld. The purpose of the journey might be (like that of Christ) to combat the powers of evil and save mankind from death. Or it might have a particular immediate aim. There was an Eskimo woman who went through life without even being able to sing a song. On her death a shaman went to spirit land, and there met the woman singing; he told the woman's husband, who then rejoiced that death could not be so bad if it could transform a most unfortunate person into a perfectly happy one. Shamans also applied a form of psychotherapy in the magic songs they chanted to hysterical people, and even in its modern forms 'shamanism may well contribute to mental health by stabilizing the incidence of nervous disorders, since it affords a means of ostensibly controlling the powers which are believed to activate these destructive forces' (I. M. Lewis, p. 204). Among the Navajo it was specifically the spirit of creation that healed, as we shall learn in chapter 8.

As well as by extra-territorial expeditions the shaman gathered knowledge otherwise concealed from man when he took – as he was believed to take – the shape of an animal. In the mythical early days of man, he lived at peace with the animals and understood their speech in a state of harmony that he lost after the Fall. By transformation into an animal, by a knowledge of their language, and by friendship with them the shaman showed that he had recovered the lost state of paradise. Mircea Eliade, after observing that the 'nostalgia for paradise' of the shamanic experience prefigures an early type of Christian mysticism, continues:

> But shamanism is important not only for the place that it holds in the world of mysticism. The shamans have played an essential role in the defence of the psychic integrity of the community. They are pre-eminently the antidemonic champions; they combat not only the demons of disease, but also the black magicians... In a general way, it can be said that shamanism defends life, health, fertility, the world of 'light', against death, diseases, sterility, disaster and the world of 'darkness'... The shaman's essential role depends above all on this; men are sure that *one of them* is able to help them in the critical circumstances produced by the inhabitants of the invisible world. It is consoling and comforting to know that a member of the community is able to *see* what is hidden and invisible to the rest and to bring back reliable information from the supernatural worlds.
> (Eliade, p. 508)

There have never been shamans in England, but in parts of the country the seventh child has been credited with powers like those of shaman. The attributes of such a 'chime child' were

1 To see the dead and the fairies, and to speak with them and come to no harm

2 To have immunity from all ill-wishing, as many of the clergy have

3 To love and control all animals – so chime children often become herdsmen or veterinary surgeons

4 To have a knowledge of herbs and a way of healing others.

This rhyme about them comes from Somerset:

> They that be born of a Friday's chime
> Be masters of music and finders of rhyme,
> And every beast will do what they say,
> And every herb that do grow in the clay,
> They do see what they see and they hear what they hear,
> But they never do tell in a hundred year.
> (Tongue, pp. 2, 3)

From divine inspiration – or hysteric possession – came prophecy, in which the seer was the mouthpiece of the gods, speaking always in poetry; and for a long time there was no clear distinction between poetry and prophecy. The Latin *vates* for example means both seer and poet; in old Arabic the word for 'poet' meant 'knower' – one who had a knowledge of occult things; the Irish 'fili' (bard) is connected with the Welsh 'gweled' (to see) and originally meant a seer; and the Delphic oracles were always delivered in poetic form. Seers uttering inspired verses accompanied by music were highly respected in most European societies; they were revered as messengers between the spiritual and material worlds. Their prophecies included, as well as dips into the future, a knowledge of the past – history and genealogy – and an insight into the hidden present, or what we should call scientific information. In Ireland, for example, bards were organised for more than a thousand years; they were numerous and powerful, for they provided one of the two educated bodies in the country, the other being the priesthood. They were feared for the magic power of their satires, which could bring dishonour and inflict physical injury. Their prophecies are said to have been enormously important; great faith was placed in their verses, and 'every major event was liable to be presented as the fulfilment of a preordained destiny'. The place and influence of bards in Scottish society seems to have been much the same as in Ireland, up to about 1700. These professional bards underwent training in the specialised schools that were established in many European countries. The Welsh had a close guild of poets that maintained their traditions, also for a thousand years; and Irish poets were required to undergo a long apprenticeship and initiation, which led in the later Middle Ages to some uninspired praise poetry. They were taught a memorising system, and grammar, prosody, history and geography; all this instruction was conveyed by word of mouth, most of it in poetry. In Arabia too some, but not all, poets of the Heroic Age (sixth century A.D.) underwent an apprenticeship in schools, which seems as in Ireland to have led to the production of some inferior verse; and in Polynesia professional poets were organised in *areoi*, artistic corporations which were important for their religious associations and intellectual preoccupations.

Among the Arabs and Hebrews the poet was a soothsayer, a magician, and a prophet; and his utterances had a positively utilitarian purpose. To the Arab, as well as being useful in war and a form of propaganda, poetry in its prophetic form preserved 'the collective memory of the past and so gave an element of continuity to the otherwise fleeting and insubstantial realities of the present' (Gibb, p. 29). Ibn Khaldun in the fourteenth century wrote in his *Prolegomena* of the significance that their poetry had for his race:

> Poetry is, of all the forms of discourses, that which the Arabs regarded as the noblest; they also made it the depository of their knowledge and their history, the testimony which would attest their virtues and faults, the storehouse in which were found the greater part of their scientific views and their maxims of wisdom.

But the largest volume of ancient prophetic poetry has reached us from the early Hebrew prophets. These were numerous; Elijah ordered the round-up of four hundred and fifty of them – four hundred were maintained in Jezebel's household – and had the whole lot massacred (1 Kings 18). Their habits are described in the opening chapter of Proverbs:

> Wisdom cries aloud in the open air,
> she raises her voice in public places;
> she calls at the top of the busy street
> and proclaims at the open gates of the city:
> 'Simple fools, how long will you be content with your simplicity?'

They played an influential part in the history of Israel from a very early time. In one of the accounts of the conquest of Canaan Joshua required the sun and moon to stand still until the Israelites had finished slaughtering their enemies, as it was 'written in the book of Jasher' (Joshua 10: 12–14). The female prophetess Deborah directed another battle in which none of the enemy survived, and celebrated the victory in a paean of savage exultation. Another story which illustrates the primitive conception of the poet-seer-magician is that of Balaam, told in Numbers 22 and 23.

The great Jewish prophets of the eighth century B.C. have more to offer than a stone-age morality. They thundered against the loose morals of the pagan peoples around them, with their polytheist beliefs; they preached a god of righteousness, not one that demanded ceremonies and sacrifices; and like so many of the medieval

preachers in England they took the side of the poor and oppressed
against the injustice of the ruling classes. Examples are Amos, his
milder follower Hosea, and Micah, one of the first of all poets to
foresee an era of universal peace, and the source of the famous lines:

> They shall beat their swords into plowshares,
> And their spears into pruninghooks:
> Nation shall not lift up sword against nation,
> Neither shall they learn war any more.
> (Micah 4:3)

The finest poetry of all is found in the work of Isaiah and the other
poet who contributed the later chapters of the prophecies that form
one book. The first Isaiah, who flourished in Jerusalem from 740
to 701 B.C., was a statesman who believed in a saving minority that
would keep the prophetic flame alive till the appearance of a leader,
a Messiah, who would establish justice:

> The wilderness and the solitary place shall be glad for them;
> And the desert shall rejoice, and blossom as the rose.
> It shall blossom abundantly, and rejoice even with joy and singing
> ...Then the eyes of the blind shall be opened,
> And the ears of the deaf shall be unstopped,
> Then shall the lame man leap as a hart,
> And the tongue of the dumb sing:
> For in the wilderness shall waters break out,
> And streams in the desert...
> (1 Isaiah 35)

In the second Isaiah we are given a new interpretation of Jewish
history in the concept of vicarious righteousness:

> It was precisely the function of the innocent to suffer for the
> guilty...the good are those who give their lives for others and
> through their sacrifice the basest are benefited in spite of their own
> unworthiness; and what is true of the individual is true of the race;
> so Israel bore the sins of others and her redemption would mean the
> redemption of mankind...[the] conception of vicarious atonement
> was taken over by many forms of orthodox Christianity, in which,
> however, it was usually narrowed rather than broadened.
> (Bates, p. 559)

Something of the driving rhythm of the original, conveying the
onward rush of the seasons, comes through in these lines:

> For as the rain cometh down, and the snow from heaven,
> And returneth not thither, but watereth the earth,
> And maketh it bring forth and bud,
> That it may give seed to the sower, and bread to the eater:
> So shall my word be that goeth forth out of my mouth:
> It shall not return unto me void,

But it shall accomplish that which I please,
And it shall prosper in the thing whereto I sent it.
(2 Isaiah 55: 10, 11)

One of the utilitarian purposes of Arab and Hebrew prophecy was to rouse and maintain national feeling. Of the Hebrew prophets in particular we know a great deal; they were political and religious leaders, and were regarded as the mouthpiece of their jealous national god. In Wales much of the prophetic material was of a political nature; in the struggle against the Saxons the early bards foretold the return of Arthur, a prophecy that remained a weapon of Welsh nationalism into the fifteenth century (Griffiths, pp. 215 ff). In Scotland the power of the bards was partly a temporal affair, built on their possessions and maintained by their closeness to the chieftain. They held lands in virtue of their office, and seem to have wielded a strong influence in social and political life. In Ireland too bardic families became wealthy and powerful, and in the year A.D. 575 the rapacity of some caused measures to be taken against them. These could not have been effective for long, for in the next century the working classes felt that these idle bardic groups (numbering up to a third perhaps of the free clans and patricians) were an intolerable drain on the country's resources (Hyde, p. 488).

In archaic cultures poetry was at one and the same time ritual, entertainment, artistry, riddle-making, persuasion, sorcery, soothsaying, prophecy and competition. There was only one type of poet for all this, the primordial composite *vates*, of whom Empedocles was a late example, a 'shaman who combined the still undifferentiated functions of magician and naturalist, poet and philosopher, preacher, healer and public counsellor' (Dodds, p. 146). Eventually the poet split into several figures, in roughly two classes: the teacher, including prophet, priest, and philosopher, on the one hand, and on the other the entertainer. In the first capacity the bards were the centre of the intellectual life of their country. They provided education; took part in affairs of state; and shaped laws. The ancient laws of Ireland, for example, which ran from pre-Christian times till about 1500, were handed down orally in poetry; and in Scotland the bards are said to have produced 'an unusually high level of literary awareness and appreciation in the populace at large' (D. Thomson, p. 13). Genealogies were included in praise poems, epics, religious poems and spells; the fourteenth-century *Sir Gawayne and the Grene Knight* opens with a genealogy to place the poem in time. Thus poets were the first historians. Science originated in the poets' accounts of the origin of the universe and its early history; it was sometimes believed that such descriptions helped to keep the world going. The ancient speculations have been displaced, but they had the same purpose and offered similar satisfactions to those of science. As Miss N. K. Sandars commented, in writing of the Babylonian Creation,

> The physical universe – radiation, gravitation, electrical fields, explosions and collisions – is a man-made metaphor, not reality itself...and if for us the general theory of relativity and quantum physics works, then the death and resurrection of Tammuz or Baal and the great Settling of Destinies once a year by Marduk and the assembled gods in Babylon did truly work.

The division of the multifunctional poet into prophet-philosopher and entertainer was not rapid or complete. Religious elements persisted after the original functions of poems had been forgotten; art appropriated the forms of poetry and produced epic and ballad and drama. 'But it is from the dynamic life-principle in myth, the wonderworking tale, that art derived its force. Yet it turned its back on the traditional significance to contemplate the forms as if they were pure form, and from that contemplation to create new meanings' (Lord, p. 220). Entertainment may have been provided by the bards, but it had uses very different from those we associate with the word nowadays. They provided for instance a psychological escape from social and other repressions; in courts their poems were not a mere pastime, but served as a link between ruler and ruled. There were itinerant bards, whose arrival was important and welcome, and there were bards attached to royal and noble houses. In Ireland, for example, before the Anglo-Saxon period,

> Poems, tales, legends and music provided the entertainment at their banquets, based on patriotic or religious themes or inspired by natural sources such as streams and trees, as well as sacred stones or idols standing in the open fields. The bards chanted these old legends in verse, to a harp accompaniment. Together with the *filid* (poets or masters) they were greatly honoured, nor did the missionaries of the future, a certain number of whom came from bardic families, regard them as enemies.
> (Decarreaux, p. 175)

The Greeks had rhapsodes (professional reciters), the Anglo-Saxons scops or gleemen, the Scandinavians skalds, and so on. In the Middle Ages these bards were popular among all classes; they beguiled the leisure and journeys of the nobility and were invariably present at feasts; they performed in the street for ordinary people and were even allowed in church when they sang the lives of the saints and the miracles of the Virgin.

The shamans with their narratives and panegyrics and laments
contributed to the rise of heroic poetry. Epic poetry can perhaps
be traced back through myth to ritual; it was certainly the product
of highly skilled and sometimes professional bards. Shamanist rites
again may be counted among the sources 'of Greek tragedy, as well
as comedy; and survived through the centuries in the plough cycles,
sword dances and epic laments of European peasant societies'
(Mellers 1973, p. 24). The shaman's pre-ecstatic euphoria constituted
one of the universal sources of lyric poetry, for the second state of
his trance 'provides the impetus for linguistic creation and the
rhythms of lyric poetry' (Eliade, p. 510). Out of the early un-
differentiated poetic stuff these particular kinds have developed,
eventually into forms bearing little resemblance to their origin. The
aims and material of the early poetry have faded, but the elements
of its technique have survived. The bardic achievement is summed
up by one of the contributors to *The Outline of History*:

> They mark a new step forward in the power and range of the human
> mind. They sustained and developed in men's minds a sense of a
> greater something than themselves, the tribe, and of a life that
> extended back into the past. They not only recalled old hatreds and
> battles, they recalled old alliances and a common inheritance. The
> feats of dead heroes lived again. The Aryans began to live in thought
> before they were born and after they were dead . . . By the time bronze
> was coming into Europe there was not an Aryan people that had not
> a profession and training of bards . . . These bards were living books,
> man-histories, guardians and makers of a new and more powerful
> tradition in human life.
> (Wells, pp. 233, 234)

Ballad and folk song

A ballad is a fairly short verse narrative, centring on a single
episode, dramatically related. To Wordsworth they were tales

> – of old, unhappy, far-off things
> And battles long ago . . .

– that is to say their themes were simple and world-wide – feuds,
cattle raids, duels, bride-stealing, love and murder. They flourished
in Europe from the twelfth century onwards to about the sixteenth
century, and much later in remote parts. Some of them clearly
embody very ancient material, such as the bits of disintegrating epic
found in Danish ballads; their commonly tragic feeling and tragic
endings seem to connect them with the epic. Originally dramatic
and mimetic, with solo and chorus, they were at first danced. They

were the product of small, close, homogeneous and unlettered communities; and once established they served many purposes, providing a channel for satire, politics, news, protest and stories of robbers and outlaws.

To start with at least, the characters were noble and the setting aristocratic. The singers enjoyed telling their hearers of the luxury and magnificence of aristocratic life; this also distanced the events described. In the typical ballad society the nobles were important, their lives were interesting, they had all the chances of something notable happening to them. In some ways the knight or chieftain represented his people and in a less conscious age lived for them. Moreover 'the same roof often covered the knight and his humblest retainer, the same food fed them, and both were marked by the same standards of action, the same lack of letters, of introspection, of diversified mental employment'. They lived – as Willa Muir said – in the old collective world which did not differentiate much between one human being and another, and in which so much was decided by the people of higher status.

Normally the ballads reinforced the local ethos, not by sermonising but by description and example. Code and customs were those of people living a hard existence, extorting a meagre livelihood from a grudging soil, with disaster always ready to strike. The Border ballads, for example,

> were a unique record of life, in all its joy, superstition, savagery and grief, of a remote and precarious frontier community...unique in their representation, however distorted by time and chance, of the way of life of a medieval-Elizabethan...community tenuously surviving in a world of poverty, violence and superstition, yet singing down the centuries their strange and melancholy tales of love and hate and longing, of thieving and killing, of jealousy, incest, witchcraft and revenge.
> (Reed, p. 7)

Of one such ballad Sir Philip Sidney (in *The Defence of Poesy*) wrote, 'Certainly I must confess mine own barbarousness, I never heard the old song of Percy and Douglas, that I found not my heart moved more than with a trumpet.' Whatever it was – the appeal to local patriotism or the values of the two contestants – that appealed to Sidney, *Chevy Chase* to readers today can hardly be more than a vigorous account of senseless butchery. It is much to the credit of the ballad singers that they let this poem die out years ago; A. L. Lloyd says that despite many reprints there is no trace of it from oral sources. But others, like *Clerk Saunders* and *Sir Patrick Spens*, are more genuinely tragic, representing the world as the peasants saw it and felt about it for hundreds of years, and providing (at least in the Orkneys of Edwin Muir's childhood) their chief imaginative sustenance. Despite their background of lawlessness, hatred, violence and poverty, the story of the ballads is (in R. O'Malley's summing up): 'one of inward dignity, of grief and love felt deeply upon the pulses, of delight and vitality in the teeth of every kind of suffering, and of resignation to the nature of things. They not only depict all this; they enact it. It is there, line by line, in the words that constitute the ballads'.

The decay of the ballad set in with the revival of learning and the spread of the humanist spirit, which divided people into lettered and unlettered classes. Before printing and education finally superseded the ballads the decline could be seen in the broadside versions, for 'only with the advent of general literacy do the moral tags and interjections begin to spread through the ballad texts' (Buchan, p. 81). Even the printed versions, circulating along with hack-writers' verses on murders, executions and monsters, exerted a pull that was felt and envied by Wordsworth:

> I find, among the people I am speaking of, half-penny Ballads, and penny and twopenny histories, in great abundance...I have so much felt the influence of these straggling papers, that I have many a time wished that I had talents to produce songs, poems, and little histories, that I might circulate among other good things in this way, supplanting partly the bad; flowers and useful herbs to take [the] place of weeds.
> (Selincourt 1937, p. 223)

And he did write a number of poems with this aim precisely in mind.

The ballad is a European phenomenon, but folk song is universal, for it is rooted in most human activities: 'among all races there appear certain recurrent, simple idioms that are really nothing but ultimate symbols of their vital consciousness: calls, chimes, cradle-rhythms, work-rhythms; dance-forms, often intimately related to certain bodily movements and steps...in short, all sorts of motifs, in which an undercurrent of popular imagination reveals itself' (quoted in Langer 1948, p. 209). Folk songs filled many practical needs, e.g. as vehicles of the wish for fertility in men and crops and animals. They were originally characterised everywhere by repetitions and refrains and an accommodation of the verse to dancing. The habit of singing means that there must have been a vast quantity of songs, because they accompanied or were actually a part of every event of the day, but of course most of them have been lost. For the great bulk of the material there was no occasion and no means to record it; when writing could have been employed to preserve it, the means was in the hands of people who saw no need to use precious materials for such stuff; and in the Christian era the ecclesiastical authorities were hostile to minstrels and 'ballads and dancings and evil and wanton songs and such-like lures of the devil' (Power, p. 25).

But in Christian countries some of these minstrels were wandering scholars who frequented both tavern, hall or church; they could sing popular songs, carols and hymns, and they supplied a connecting link between folk song and church music – so that we find monks praising the Virgin in a style near that of love songs. The process of transmutation just exemplified was never ending; a work song became a tavern catch, a fertility chant lives on in a love song, and so on. Thus many medieval lyrics, secular as well as religious, embody elements from folk song, and so far as the tunes were concerned Cecil Sharp wrote: 'It would be very hard in the art music up to the end of the 16th century to find a single tune that was wholly the composition of a professed musician; and a very large proportion of the themes embedded in the music of the two following centuries were little more than free adaptations of folk airs.' In church again 'the hymns of the Office were not far removed from the stanzaic form of popular song'; G. B. Chambers has collected the evidence that plain-chant is firmly rooted in popular song; and possibly 'some plain-song hymns had currency as popular songs'. In addition, W. H. Mellers, writing of the impersonality of ballad poems, observes that

> the situation described in them is an essentially human one, but it is conceived in generalized terms, with reference to Everyman rather than Me. Both folk song and folkpoem have, of course, a more directly lyrical, rhythmic, and locally human appeal than the deliberately ritualized Latin chant; but the values latent in them have a closer affinity to the world view implicit in plainsong than one might superficially suppose; certainly there is no antagonism between them. Neither was interested in the conflicts of the individual with society or with its fellow creatures. The natural human instinct for the dramatic was absorbed in the wider context of the relation between God and man; into the ritual of the mass and into ceremonial pageantry.
> (Mellers 1946, p. 38)

Many collectors of folk songs have noted that the people they took songs from were courteous and civilised. Cecil Sharp for example found that in his dealings with the people of the Appalachians their

charm of manner was a constant delight; they had an easy, un-
affected bearing and the unselfconscious manners of the well-bred.
About the same time a British administrator, describing the extent
to which every activity of the Malays was accompanied by singing,
commented on the 'tone of quiet and humorous courtesy' in their
everyday songs. W. J. Entwistle found among the common con-
stants of ballad peoples that 'there is restraint and decency in the
ballads, however tragic or amusing the pieces may be. Criminal
themes and vulgar jesting are signs that a given ballad tradition is
on the wane'. Many folk songs handle sexual themes with candour
and delicacy; Willa Muir for example has recorded how the refrain
of 'Captain Wedderburn's Courtship' – 'We'll baith lie in ae bed,
an' you'll lie neist the wa'' – caused a faint ruffle of embarrassment
when sung to her as a girl by a young ploughman, 'but the un-
selfconscious directness with which Harry drove his way through
the song cured me of that'. The language of the people who pro-
duced the best folk songs was imaginative and expressive.

In one respect the history of folk song runs parallel to that of
'peasant' pottery; a thing of everyday utility attains the status of an
art form prized by critics and collectors. In the course of this
transformation folk songs served a variety of purposes. Associated
at first with every activity of living they eased and cheered the daily
round, from the dusty villages of India to the logging camps of
North America. They provided a vehicle for transmitting the
traditions of a community, and they were a steady influence for
conformity with those traditions – in some cases they institutional-
ised and provided a safety valve for dissent. They were the means
whereby the community shared its joys and offered consolation for
grief. To repressed and subject people folk songs gave a sense of
identity and an encouragement to preserve it. Near the beginning
of the first book of *The Excursion* the mature Wordsworth relates
the story of his Wanderer, who

> at my request would sing
> Old songs, the product of his native hills;
> A skilful distribution of sweet sounds,
> Feeding the soul, and eagerly imbibed
> As cool refreshing water, by the care
> Of the industrious husbandman, diffused
> Through a parched meadow-ground, in time of drought.

One of the fullest and most impressive accounts of the part played
by poetry in the life of a people is that given by Francis Mading
Deng in the Introduction to his translations of Dinka songs. The

singers are a Nilotic people of the Sudan, with an economy based on cattle rearing, so that cattle and pride in them are a pervasive theme of the songs, which are part of every aspect of individual and group life. They are the medium of their history, a support of the social structure and the means of maintaining the concept of immortality through posterity. They relieve conflicts between individuals and aggression generally, and they make for inner, as well as for social harmony:

> Songs are used as a means of turning experiences which are painful, shameful, or otherwise undesirable into a subject of art which enhances one's inner pride and recognition by society. The indignities of prison life, traditionally unknown to the Dinka, the insult of rejection by a girl, or of divorce imposed on a loving partner, the misfortune of illness and maybe of disablement...are examples of themes which it is better to sing about than brood over.   (p. 79)

Other examples of the place of songs in Dinka life are numerous. They are an established means of winning recognition and enhancing one's social position. Rich in parables and metaphor, they are the language of courtship and the road to marriage. They scrutinise the wielding of power and the working of justice; they serve to balance the interests of young and old. In religion they are a medium of communication with the spirits and their ancestors. 'By sublimating violent and otherwise destructive impulses, songs promote rectitude even though what is said in them would not be morally acceptable in a non-artistic context.' These are only a few of the purposes to which Dinka singing is applied.

Folk song is the product of a particular culture, and so far as England is concerned the erosion of that culture began with the printed broadside ballad. The poor quality of the composed material diluted the traditional poems, and printed versions even of the good ones hardened them into stereotypes. The destruction of English popular culture was continued by industrialisation, compulsory education and the decline of agriculture.

At this point we must recall the achievement of the Franciscans. St Francis had exhorted his followers to be minstrels of God ('joculatores Dei') and this inspired them to write songs in both Latin and the vernaculars. He had been quick to see the poetic and pictorial elements in the Nativity stories, and he obtained the Pope's permission to render stage versions of the story in churches; this also stimulated the making of carols. Thus in the thirteenth century thousands of these 'laude' – devotional songs – were produced; they were the work of individual authors, but they were aimed at a popular audience, and they were patterned on familiar songs. The greatest of the Franciscan singers was Jacopone of Todi, who wrote serious religious verse in both Latin and the vernacular, using dance forms for the latter, so that his poems were enthusiastically adopted and sung by companies of singers. 'The great merit of the "laude" poetry consisted in being the sole carrier of folk song and its spirit, warm humanity' (Lang, p. 113). The friars were welcomed in England, where they filled a gap left by the failure of the monasteries to carry out their responsibilities. They supplied a link between educated poets and the people, for they translated Latin poems into English and also tried (Davies, p. 13) to use secular lyrics for religious purposes. The attempts of the Franciscans to make Christmas revels more truly Christian seem to have been responsible for 'the emergence in the fifteenth century of a large number of refrain poems, hilarious but at the same time religious in character, which seem to have inherited alike the name and the metrical form of danced carols'. To sum up: 'When Chaucer mocked at the friars, he was biting the hand that fed him. They educated his audience' (Smalley 1960, p. 307).

4

Maid of all work

Integral with life

Some cultures have developed poetry as naturally as the earth produces heath or forest or steppe: and it is worth considering what qualities appear to make for this efflorescence. The societies have all been rural. There does not seem to be any positive reason why people in towns should not have produced poetry so readily, except that they are literate; and literacy inhibits the growth of 'natural' poetry, while it permits new kinds and opens a wider range of purposes and occasions to the poet. Moreover town life lacks some of the positive properties that make for creation in the country. Take the case of the ballad; this was the product of social conditions in the Middle Ages, and grew to maturity as the great migrations and crusades subsided and men settled down to cultivate the land (Entwistle, p. 91). So the ballad flourished from Spain in the West to Russia in the East, whereas France and Italy with their intensely developed culture were weak in traditional narrative poetry; which suggests that a complex society and a literate culture are incompatible with the growth of a ballad tradition. This is borne out by the British ballad, of which the best came, not from the Border, but from the settled agricultural conditions of north-east Scotland (Buchan, p. 5). Folk song (leaving out the Industrial Muse) was always part of the agricultural round, and so continued till it died out with the arrival of print, urbanisation and education, in that order. Where basic illiteracy persisted, as it did in the Aran Islands till the end of the last century, folk song lived on.

The link between poetry and agriculture has been observed in many parts of the world. In Korea the spring and autumn crop festivals from several centuries B.C. were the occasions for dance and song:

> The magical power of words was believed in to such an extent that poetry was supposed to please gods, help avoid natural calamities, bring rain and stop the winds, and promote recovery from diseases. Primitive society was tribal and patriarchal, and primitive life was carried on in terms of communal values. Hence poetry, music and

dance, the three vital elements in the religious services of the ancient Koreans, were inseparable and indispensable. The earliest Korean poetry...was closely connected with Korean religion and was mainly composed of sacred hymns. It was a folk art that grew naturally out of their agricultural life.

(Lee, p. 17)

Poetry has been part of the lives, not only of settled peasants, but also of nomads who lived by hunting and of cattle-grazers like those who used to pasture their herds in Uganda.

What Hardy wrote in 1879 about the life of the peasant points to some of the reasons for the vitality of poetry in communities close to the soil; he is considering the work of William Barnes:

Farm life as, regulated by the seasons, it varies from day to day through the year, is truthfully reflected; and we are at every step indirectly reminded wherein lies that poetry which, in spite of the occasional sting of poverty, is inseparable from such a condition of life. It lies less in the peasant's residence among fields and trees than in his absolute dependence on the moods of the air, earth and sky. Sun, rain, wind, snow, dawn, darkness, mist, are to him, now as ever, personal assistants and obstructors, masters and acquaintances, with whom he comes directly into contact, whose varying tempers must be well-considered before he can act with effect.

(Hardy 1967, p. 97)

Hardy was writing of people who though nominally Christian were in part pagan – like Synge's Aran Islanders, officially Catholic, but revealing their inner consciousness when keening at a funeral. 'In the presence of death all outward show of indifference or patience is forgotten, and they shriek with pitiable despair before the horror of the fate to which they are all doomed' (Synge 1906, I, p. 46). What Hardy says offers us a number of answers to questions about pre-literate people. They were intimate with nature; they sympathised with her; and they had to have a knowledge of her ways, if only to survive as farmer or herdsman or hunter. They had a lively eye for nature and a feeling for her abundant powers, whether regarded as supernatural or not – though for most there was no distinction. What they sought from nature and their feelings about her were expressed in verse in rhythms from the dance and from the sounds around them – in Synge's words 'the rude and beautiful poetry that is filled with the oldest passions in the world' (Synge 1966, p. 112).

The economy of pre-literate peoples was always at a subsistence level, and they were never rich. As the Chadwicks observed, 'Intellectual progress would seem to be not wholly governed by material civilisation; we may bear in mind what the intellectual activities of the Polynesians achieved with a material culture which was inferior to that of our own stone age' (1940, II, p. 900). There are still some peoples surviving in this century who lead a hard and exacting life in stone-age conditions, both in the Kalahari Desert and in Australia, and they have produced poetry that has delighted not only professional anthropologists like the Berndts, whom one would expect to be sympathetic, but also a classical scholar like C. M. Bowra, the product of a very different culture. Another example is that of the Russian peasants who, escaping serfdom through their remoteness, had a 'hard and healthy struggle for livelihood', which occupied all equally and permitted no great accumulation of wealth. Again, in Scotland the fine ballads of the north-east flourished where climate and soil were both inhospitable, and the land was 'forced into productivity by the hard work of generations' (Buchan, p. 13). In the Aran Islands, where tiny fields were artificially made by covering rock with sand and sea-weed, communications involved going into sea in flimsy curaghs, difficult to launch and land in a heavy swell; the danger involved and the skill required have made it impossible for 'clumsy, foolhardy, or timid men to live on these islands'. Many of the characteristics Synge noted in the islanders can be found also in other poetry-producing societies whose economy is based on primary production:

> It is likely that much of the intelligence and charm of these people is due to the absence of any division of labour, and to the correspondingly wide development of each individual, whose varied knowledge and skill necessitates a considerable activity of mind. Each man can speak two languages. He is a skilled fisherman, and can manage a curagh with extraordinary nerve and dexterity. He can farm simply, burn kelp, cut out pampooties, mend nets, build and thatch a house, and make a cradle or a coffin. His work changes with the seasons in a way that keeps him free from the dullness that comes to people who have always the same occupation. The danger of his life on the sea gives him the alertness of a primitive hunter, and the long nights he spends fishing in his curagh bring him some of the emotions that are thought peculiar to men who have lived with the arts.
> (Synge 1906, II, p. 13)

The societies we are considering were small, compact and homogeneous. The primitives, for instance, whose 'literature' C. M. Bowra studied, lived in groups of twenty to a hundred people, made up of a few families. The songs of the great period of Gaelic poetry, from the sixteenth to the eighteenth centuries, came out of a 'society which was close, kin-based, rural, independent and self-sufficient in the main' (D. Thomson, p. 58). A recognisable portrait of peoples who produced ballads over most of Europe can be drawn, with common constants: 'The community supposed by ballad poetry is small, stable and self-sufficient... These small communities are self-centred...attached to the soil by instinctive patriotism, and led by leaders who command their personal devotion. They have a lively intelligence, as their metaphors show...' (Entwistle, p. 7).

The homogeneity of the groups is characteristic, and when it is diluted their poetry declines. For example, the Scottish ballads already mentioned flourished in a 'non-literate, homogeneous, agricultural society...in remote, hilly or border regions' (Buchan, p. 47). Cautious, self-reliant, phlegmatic as they were, its members were blunt, truthful and endowed with a strong sense of the dramatic. Their social organisation was 'communal in spirit and co-operative in its activities' and provided conditions of working and living in which an oral culture throve naturally. David Buchan records that

> The old homogeneity of Scottish society that allowed Anne Far-
> quharson (wife of a minor laird) to learn her traditional ballads
> from rural nurses and old women at Allanaquoich, and the old
> homogeneity of taste that allowed both aunt and niece to delight in
> these ballads, had been superseded in 1802 by a new social concern
> for propriety, gentility and station.
> (Buchan, p. 72)

And when Cecil Sharp was collecting folk songs (of a higher quality than those of English collections) in the Appalachian mountains, he remarked that they were the expression of an innate musical sense, and added

> You must first understand the peasant, the sole survivor of a homo-
> geneous society, with few class distinctions; and what we think of as
> conscious arts were to him unconscious occupations...I should name
> his chief characteristics reserve, personal detachment, and dignity.
> He is gentle, unobtrusive, unassertive, both to his fellows and to
> cockneys like myself.
> (Fox-Strangways, p. 184)

Finally F. J. Child in 1893 on the conditions that produced the ballads he edited:

> The condition of society, in which a truly national or popular poetry
> appears, explains the character of such poetry. It is a condition in
> which the people are not divided by political organisation and book
> culture into markedly different classes, in which, consequently, there
> is such community of ideas and feelings that the whole people form

one individual. Such poetry, accordingly, while it is in its essence an expression of our common human nature, and so of universal and indestructible interest, will in each case be differentiated by circumstances and idiosyncrasies.

(E. K. Chambers, p. 175)

The society that produced oral poetry was rural, hardworking, small and close-knit. It tended also to be remote, and lacking much contact with other groups; it thus enjoyed some independence and had to be self-sufficient in nearly everything. Those of the Russian peasants who retained their freedom lived in a rough and primitive landscape; there were great distances between villages and obstacles between them in the way of swamps, lakes, rivers and tracts of rock. In autumn and spring the peasants were isolated for weeks together; in the winter fishing and hunting ceased and the people were driven into their houses. They were culturally as well as economically self-sufficient:

> The inhabitants have a natural sense of form and a ready invention, and they are thrown on their own resources for entertainment. Story-telling and singing are the delight of the peasants, few of whom (none of the good singers) know how to read and write. Schools are few; the nearest rail-head is sometimes hundreds of miles distant, and a vast forest sunders these regions from the rest of Russia.
> (Entwistle, p. 1)

A similar remoteness and hard struggle for independence and existence, allowing no time for a sheltered written literature, gave their character to the Yugoslav ballads. Inspiration was immediate and local; the local poet, 'often a blind fiddler on a single string', improvised praises of heroic deeds or laments for a disaster. 'The "guslar" was all the history and posterity that his leaders could expect. His gift of oral traditional expression was so highly cultivated that, in our own time, deputies of parliament have had a sufficient store of tags to put a whole debate into extempore verse' (Entwistle, p. 321). (In 1873–4 when the Yugoslav parliament was discussing the budget and a bill for introducing a new monetary system, the debates were reproduced by a peasant deputy in poetry to audiences outside the building.) A degree of isolation and independence contributed to the existence of oral poetry of many other cultures, such as the folk songs of the Appalachian farmers and the ballads of Scotland. Isolated communities have to make their own entertainment. In Iceland the hard conditions of life kept social units small, and the centres of European literary fashion were far away; so that the inhabitants, like the Russians mentioned above, had to rely on their own resources. In Yugoslavia epic poetry was till recently the chief entertainment of the adult male population in the villages and small towns, and in the country especially people came from a wide area to hear a singer at a gathering in one of the houses (Lord, p. 14). Instances could be multiplied; even in the grinding harshness of a labour camp, isolation from outside made negro convicts rely on their own poetry and song, not only to make the work easier but to make life tolerable at all.

Of course poetry in the societies we have been considering served a variety of other needs. At a humble level, there were the mnemonics which helped to transmit a knowledge of farming methods, managing horses and lore about the seasons and weather. Work songs made daily tasks more enjoyable and more effective, and there were songs for every event and interest in the lives of men and women. In some communities poetry was their means of understanding and coming to terms with the powers that gave them life and controlled the universe. In ancient Greece Agamemnon mustering his fleet at Aulis may have been compelled, E. A. Havelock suggests, to get his directives organised in rhythmic verse so that they could remain unaltered. Genghis Khan also is said to have sent his battle orders in rhyme. So essential was verse to this society that 'all public business depended on it, all transactions . . . The poet was in the first instance society's scribe, scholar and jurist'.

Every man a poet

Shakespeare, as F. R. Leavis has insisted, did not invent the language he started with. Brought up in the country, he was equipped with the experience of hundreds of years' battling with the elements, coming to terms with the seasons, and wresting food from the soil, all expressed in a vivid vernacular. According to Hardy the agricultural civilisation was natural to the farmers and everyone else, and the people were in harmony with their civilisation (Hardy 1957, p. 165). When there was bread to eat, people knew the fields and the farmer who grew the grain, the mill that ground it and the baker who made the loaves. The men who made wooden vessels and carts knew whence came the right timber for their needs. All had to be able to tell good from bad, in people as well as in things. Thus the language of the Elizabethans was more than a medium for exchanging information; it was part of a way of life.

Consequently the language Shakespeare inherited was not a literary one but a rich poetic and imaginative speech. It included many Anglo-Saxon words, driven out of court circles by the Norman conquerors. It had a wealth of expressive idioms, drawn from agriculture and the life of animals, keenly observant and full of energy. It was the vehicle for sayings and proverbs – shrewd, sceptical, stoic, resigned. They kept to the middle way and supported their users by a philosophy of common humanity – 'it will all be the same in a hundred years' time' (Taylor, p. 168). Elizabethan English drew its sap from the soil, and that is one of the reasons for its long life in the plays of Shakespeare, who was near his audience because he had so much in common with it. As Henry Williamson noted in 1930:

> Some of his phrases, the plain common phrases of the country, I wrote down in my notebook at the time, and later was astonished, and delighted, to find the same phrases in Shakespeare. (He had not taken them from the book Shakespeare; but the living Shakespeare had taken them from common speech.) Sometimes in talk, when meeting a friend in the lanes, I would ask for a phrase to be repeated; and almost invariably the speaker would hesitate, deprecate his own language, and explain, 'That's how us says it; the rough way, you know; it ban't the educated way of saying it, no doubt.' Also with what is called dialect words – they hid them sometimes from strangers, believing them inferior: some of them probably in English use before the Norman conquest, others as old. *Fitchey* (stoat), *dreshel* (flail), *weest* (dreary), *dimmity* (twilight), etc. *He was as proper a man as ever trod ground. Wait until the ground's in temper*; (i.e. the garden soil warm and loose for digging) *it's no use mucketting.*
> (Williamson, pp. 68, 9)

Whatever statistics of minimal literacy may suggest, many of the audience at a sixteenth-century theatre were essentially illiterate, with a use of and attitude to language comparable to those of some pre-literate peoples. Education was orally imparted; sermons in church were listened to and remembered for subsequent discussion; the finest literature of the day was to be found in Shakespeare's plays, but it was not at the time thought of as literature. Elizabethans wrote and read with difficulty; and Shakespeare came at the end of an oral tradition. The end can be seen in several aspects. The rise of capitalism tended to devalue poetry as an unprofitable activity, except in so far as it became a commodity. The balance between town and country tilted in favour of the towns, and literacy became important because the management of towns requires a good deal of writing. Thus the part played by schools increased and a split developed between the literate and non-literate. Books and reading reduced learning by heart and the habits of attention and retention that are part of a tradition of oral literature. With writing came rules and grammars, 'and words and idioms are judged, not by their expressive power, but by their "correctness"' (Smith, p. 162). In the end the normal relation between speech and writing is inverted, the eye becomes more important than the ear, and language loses the vigour and directness imparted to it by its connection with human actions and emotions.

Finally, Edwin Muir records just in time something of what it was to be brought up at the end, the non-creative end, of an oral tradition:

> In our farmhouse in one of the smaller Orkney islands, there were not many books apart from the Bible, *The Pilgrim's Progress*, and the poems of Burns. Except for Burns, we had no poetry books, but we knew a great number of ballads and songs which had been handed down from generation to generation. These, sometimes with the airs traditionally belonging to them, were known in all the farms; there must have been hundreds of them. They were part of our life, all the more because we knew them by heart, and had not acquired but inherited them.
>
> I am trying to describe what poetry meant, all those years ago, to an uncultivated but in a real sense civilized community, or more civilized one that you will easily find now. What did we think of poetry? We did not *think* of it at all...
>
> Now this treasure of poetry had been preserved by many generations of peasants in Orkney, in Scotland and England, and the countries of Europe, for hundreds of years. The fact that it had been preserved shows how much of it was prized, and also that poetry was taken to be a natural thing: an exercise of the heart and the imagination.
>
> (Edwin Muir 1962, p. 9)

Poetry has flourished wherever it has had a vital function to perform, as we have seen in examples from ancient Greece and Judaea and elsewhere. It still has a place in the traditional life of Africa. For example, 'Poetry occupies a large and important part in Somali culture, interest in it is universal, and skill in it something which everyone covets and many possess. The Somali poetic heritage is a living force intimately connected with the vicissitudes of everyday life' (Andrzejewski, p. 3). The same is true of many Indian tribes and aboriginal peoples; among the Uraons, for example, poems were linked with dancing, marriage and crop cultivation, so that till recently at least a poem was as essential a piece of equipment as an axe and plough. Even today

> The poems (of Yiddish poets) are occasional verse in a way most English poems no longer are. Yiddish poets write for the daily newspapers, some of them publish a poem a week. If a friend dies, you write a poem for him. If there is an event of great political importance, you write a poem about it. If a child has a birthday or it

is the anniversary of an artist's death, you write a poem. Even if you read a new book, or reread an old one, you write a poem about it. (Betsky, p. 31)

The medieval Church was fed by popular song. Minstrel tunes were used in monastic music; there is little difference between the musical character of sacred and profane melodies, for the wandering scholar was equally at home in ale-house, hall, market-place or cloister, and could sing equally well a love song, a glee, a carol, a hymn or a lament on the instability of life or the fickleness of riches. At least one tune served a double purpose, as a nativity carol and a drinking song. The church tunes, when effective, came from folk songs; the Reformers wanted intelligibility, so they used the metres and rhythms of popular song (Stevens 1961, p. 93). The old love songs were turned into psalms, on a hint from Luther himself; and Rowland Hill is said to have remarked that there was no reason why Satan should have all the good tunes.

The way in which poetry was taken for granted in the Middle Ages is illustrated by some surviving commonplace books. One from the fifteenth century in the library of Trinity College, Cambridge, contains a satirical carol, miscellaneous Latin verses, medical recipes, short English religious and political verses, forms of indentures, instructions for setting a harp, theological extracts, and a moralised version of 'Come over the burn, Bessy, to me'. Another at Balliol College, Oxford, consists of material deemed useful to a household, and contains a variety of poetry, religious and secular, narrative and lyric, together with prose treatises, recipes and prescriptions, puzzles and riddles, and business notes.

The split between poetry that was a popular possession and 'art' poetry written for a section of the community, distinguished perhaps by its literacy, was always pronounced in societies, like that of Athens, which were based on slavery. The art which had originally been of great practical value now diminished to a pursuit engaged in for its own sake; its social function vanished and it became a hobby for the individual. In England too there developed in the later Middle Ages a poetry for the few – the literature of the court. It was directed at a cultivated audience; its range was far beyond that of ballad and folk song; its technique was more resourceful and it produced new developments. Apart from Shakespeare, who in any case was not a literary figure, since plays were entertainment competing with such sports as bear-baiting, the main stream of English poetry has ever since taken the course which has appealed to a restricted audience. The new bourgeoisie of the sixteenth century may have followed some of the court fashions, but by the time of James there was a marked gap between the attitudes of the middle class whom Shakespeare catered for and a court that was despised as effete and immoral. With the Restoration the split, prefigured in the plays of Jonson, was complete so far as the theatre was concerned; the upper ranks of society filled the stalls, their servants went in the gallery, and the citizen was driven out. Another aspect can be seen in the history of printing. Caxton and his successor Wynkyn de Worde produced beautifully printed versions of texts with a very limited appeal, while the populace was soon catered for by the cheap and nasty printed ballads of the sixteenth century, ridiculed by the satirists of both that and the seventeenth century. Literary writers and academic critics regarded poetry as unfit for common ears and pens; they wished poetry to be the preserve of privileged initiates.

The split also appeared in the history of the newspapers, which after the Restoration were adjusted to the tastes of the gentry and the well-to-do merchant. Early in the eighteenth century any page of Addison's *Spectator* shows that what Samuel Johnson called 'the common reader' was a minority, well-educated or taking its standards from its cultivated superiors. The division was an economic as well as a cultural one, in the making of which inflation played its part. To acquire the *Dunciad* in 1743 at the price of seven-and-sixpence (37p) would have taken almost a full two weeks' salary of a schoolmaster paid ten pounds a year; whereas an unbound copy of *Hamlet* sold for sixpence (2½p) at a time when a master craftsman earned one-and-fourpence (6½p) a day. (The mention of *Hamlet* brings to mind what happened in September 1607 when the ships of William Keeling and William Hawkins stood off Sierra Leone. The crew of Keeling's ship, the *Dragon*, played *Richard II*, and later *Hamlet*, for their own pleasure and that of Hawkins' crew. Keeling permitted these performances 'to keep my people from idleness and unlawful games, or sleep'.)

As the industrialising of the country proceeded in the early nineteenth century, the cultural split between the common people and the privileged classes was almost institutionalised, and the contrasting picture of the Middle Ages became unrecognisable:

> Every Sunday the peasant at the Mass was (as it were) irrigated from the mainstream of European society. Its benefits to him were not only spiritual. His eyes rested on lovely craftsmanship. He heard Palestrina's music. He learned unconsciously something of the standards of art and music and oratory which were the pride of Europe. (Ashby, p. 88)

This may be a somewhat idealised version; certainly by the middle of his century there was not much going to Mass in the country, as Kilvert's *Diary* attests. The medieval villagers taking communion may not have known very clearly what it meant, but they took communion. 'Their descendants in the slums of London in the 1830s, 40s and 50s did not do so; they already looked on Christianity as belonging to the rural world which they had lost. It was something for their employers...' (Laslett, p. 72). Then came elementary education for all and the swift exploitation by the Northcliffe press of the masses of the newly half-educated, whose tastes were soon developed and seemingly consolidated by the other media at the level we are familiar with today. However this apparently monolithic block of bad taste, of indifference and sometimes hostility to good art and literature is probably nothing like so secure as the tycoons of the entertainment world would like it to be. The individuals who make up the deprived masses are not the contemptible morons envisaged by newspaper peers.

The further back we pursue inquiries into the origin of language, the more poetic do we find it to be. Analogies in aid of the inquiry, taken from still surviving primitive peoples, cannot be pushed far, but it is worth noting that poetry comes naturally to them. 'Since all primitive peoples are trained in song from childhood and practise it continually, there is nothing astonishing in their ability to burst into it without notice' (Bowra 1962, p. 34). That is certainly the impression given by such ancient history as the Old Testament, which includes some excellent pre-literate poetry. The reports of travellers from the eighteenth century onwards record, for example, that all Red Indians had the gift of improvising in verse; and Mungo Park, exploring the interior of Africa in 1796, describes the kindly welcome he received at one stage. The women were spinning cotton, and

> They lightened their labour by songs, one of which was composed extempore; for I was myself the subject of it. It was sung by one of the young women, the rest joining in a sort of chorus. The air was sweet and plaintive, and the words, literally translated, were these:
>
> The winds roared, and the rains fell.
> The poor white man, faint and weary,
> Came and sat under our tree.
> He has no mother to bring him milk;
> No wife to grind his corn.
> > *Let us pity the white man;*
> > *No mother has he*, etc.
>
> (p. 152)

According to the Chadwicks the same facility was to be found in most parts of Africa. In Abyssinia, for instance,

> the composition of oral poetry among men and women of the middle and lower classes...is universal. The soldiers recite extempore verses on the march, one member composing a couplet, and the rest of the party joining in the refrain. The women compose at their household tasks, and indeed one gets the impression that this is almost their only form of intellectual exercise. (1940, III, p. 529)

With the Northern Bantu (the people of Uganda) the commonest form of poetry was extempore, recited at recurrent social ceremonies, or at work; and all Tuareg, men and women alike, used to be poets, with a love of poetry and song a characteristic feature of their social life. Among the Yoruba people of Nigeria 'everybody becomes a bit of a poet himself' in the absence of a written language, and even now poetry comes more naturally to them than prose. In Russia up to about a hundred years ago wakes and weddings were marked by extempore poetry; travellers reported that the peasants frequently composed songs about their past experience or present situation – a groom for example encouraged his horses not to flag, in verse, addressing each one separately. In Montenegro (now Yugoslavia) minstrelsy used to be a more or less general accomplishment and poetry was improvised even when fighting was going on. Instances could be multiplied from all over the world.

Speaking in verse has been part of the social life of many cultures. It was a common practice among the Tartars to introduce general observations in couplet form into their ordinary conversation; and the way of asking a person's name was to say

> Every wild beast has hair,
> Every person has a name,
> What are you called?

Such social formulas by themselves may not tell us very much about the poetic ability of the users; they are not creative. More positive however is the fact that in some African societies it is a social grace or diplomatic skill to manipulate proverbs successfully (Achebe, p. 4). This is nearer the more poetic use that has been noted among the Polynesians, who would move almost involuntarily from prose to poetry in moments of emotion and on occasions of formality; and in their prose sagas poetry was used at points of emotional intensity. Similarly (as K. Rasmussen noted, p. 320) 'Songs are thoughts, sung out with the breath when people are moved by great forces and ordinary speech no longer suffices.' In southern India among a pastoral tribe, the Todas, the art of song is highly developed, and every member can and does compose songs. So far as England is concerned, Cecil Sharp has presented evidence that till about a hundred years ago 'every country village in England was a nest of singing-birds'.

Moreover there were occasions on which to sing or compose poems was obligatory. Bede has told us how Caedmon would evade this compulsion: 'Whenever all those present at a feast took it in turns to sing and entertain the company, he would get up from table and go home directly he saw the harp approaching him' (p. 245). It was common in medieval England for people at Christmas to contribute carols which they could sing from memory:

> Therefore every man that is here,
> Sing a carol in his mannere;
> If he can not, we shall him lere
>   So that we be mery alway.
>
> If that he say he can not sing
> Some other sport then let him bring
> That it may please at this feasting
>   For now is the time of Christmas.
> (No. 168, R. T. Davies, *Medieval English Lyrics*)

Australian aborigines have to contribute songs for ritual or magical purposes, 'for a man cannot withdraw from his responsibilities as an ordinary member of the community' (Berndt, p. 307). In Africa there are 'times when every member of a society (or every member who falls into a certain category) is expected to have some competence in certain types of verse' (Finnegan, p. 104). Men seem to have been required to show some skill at composing panegyrics; every Akan woman is expected to be competent in the dirge, and every woman mourner must sing or run the risk of criticism; 'thus they perform as part of their general social responsibilities' (Finnegan, p. 103). This obligation to take part in ritual lament at a funeral is world-wide. In Polynesian Mangaia each male relative of the deceased must chant a song, and those who cannot must pay a substitute; and in Greek villages till recently lamentation at a funeral was a social duty for the whole community (Alexiou, p. 50).

J. R. Firth has remarked that 'Whenever a man speaks, he speaks in some sense as a poet.' This was true of the best period of the ballad, when everyone was a minstrel. The audience consisted of the majority of the local community and it conditioned the singer's performance as reciter and creator. Everyone knew the content, and anyone who might do better could have a try. 'The art', Entwistle wrote, 'is greater than the artist'. The art was that of a language

which sprang from a way of living. And it was not merely the folk
singers who drew on these resources; a great writer cannot exist in
isolation but must draw on the common stock, so that Shakespeare
and Bunyan owed much to popular speech, thus confirming for
their time at least Yeats' belief that all good poetry presupposed an
unwritten tradition. This basic language was that of a people in
touch with the earth and the seasons, speaking of what they could
see and know. Nothing was really inanimate:

> Once every people in the world believed that trees were divine, and
> could take a human or grotesque shape and dance among the
> shadows; and that deer, and ravens and foxes, and wolves and bears,
> and clouds and pools, almost all things under the sun and moon, and
> the sun and moon were not less divine and changeable. They saw
> in the rainbow the still bent bow of a god thrown down in his
> negligence; they heard in the thunder the sound of his beaten
> water-jar, or the tumult of his chariot-wheels; and when a sudden
> flight of wild ducks, or of crows, passed over their heads, they
> thought they were gazing at the dead hastening to their rest.
> (Yeats, p. 174)

As contact with their physical environment and its changes was
close, so their experiences came to them unprocessed. If the impact
was lessened and the shock made tolerable, it was by poetry and
ritual, supplying a framework of accepted behaviour, a measure of
explanation and consolation. Synge declared that the Aran islanders
keening at the side of a grave were mourning for themselves – 'the
inner consciousness of the people seems to lay itself bare for an
instant, and to reveal the mood of beings who feel their isolation
in the face of a universe that wars on them'. Edwin Muir found that
the Scottish peasants he knew in his youth still grieved over the loss
of Sir Patrick Spens, hundreds of years before, when they sang or
heard the ballad; and he added:

> The collective mourning gives a more adequate idea of the original
> nature of poetry than we have ever had since poetry has been
> understood more and more as an art. The immediate participation
> of the audience in the poetry makes the strangeness of the poetic
> experience immediate and palpable, and restores to it something
> which it has lacked, except in dramatic tragedy, perhaps ever since
> the invention of printing.

The language of pre-literates, as we noted earlier (Edwin Muir
1962, p. 28), was poetic in diction, imagery and cadence. The names
given to places, animals and plants are often beautiful: heart's ease,
love-in-a-mist, forget-me-not, ladies' tresses, fox-glove – and their
quality is vividly evoked by Edward Thomas in his poems 'Lob' and

'Words'. The imagery was drawn from their own observation and experience; they felt connections between things and found the right words. The peasants of Chattisgarh in India were all poets, in the sense that the commonest device in their poetry is symbolism. 'When a man has daughters to marry he tells his friends that he has kodon (millet) in his house; when he goes to ask for a girl in marriage he says that he has come for a gourd in which to put his water or for a flower to put in his hair' (Elwin 1946, p. l). Irish has many images from the countryside; these are (probably genuine) examples from *The Playboy of the Western World* and *Deirdre*:

> (of an old man sleeping)...there'll be no old fellow
> wheezing, the like of a sick sheep, close to your ear.

> I have put away sorrow like a shoe that is worn out and
> mouldy.

And in their imagery an early Chinese poem and an English folk song are close to each other:

> The cloth-plant grew till it covered with thorn-bush
> The bindweed spread far over the wilds.
> My lovely one is here no more.
> With whom? No, I sit alone.
> (Chinese)

> I leaned my back against an oak,
>   I thought was a trusty tree.
> But first it bent and then it broke;
>   My true love has forsaken me.
> (English) (Elwin 1946, p. xiv)

It has often been noted that the speech of pre-literate peoples is rhythmic, probably because rhythm was developed as an effective means of communication; and the sense of rhythm may have been encouraged by the natural sounds the speakers heard. Yeats commented on the dialect speech of Kerry and Aran that 'The cadence is long and meditative, as befits the thought of men who are much alone, and who when they meet in one another's houses ...listen patiently'. When an old Aran woman repeated a poem that had just been spoken, she 'recited the verses with exquisite musical intonation, putting a wistfulness and passion into her voice that seemed to give it all the cadences that one sought in the profoundest poetry' (Synge 1906, I, p. 102).

There is thus some force behind Shelley's 'In the infancy of society is necessarily a poet, because language itself is poetry.' The language started as poetry and continued thus because it met deep and lasting human needs. When one surveys the stream of poetry, from surmises about its early source to the present, one can see how it passed from being the possession of a whole people to the care of specialist and eventually professional poets. As long as poetry took its life from popular speech it enjoyed the strain of health and strength, and suffered the limitations, that characterise an uncultivated plant; and in turn it gave back life to that speech in the form of new associations and changes of meaning from the context of the poets' work; the difference between poet and people was quantitative, not qualitative. But poetry moved away and lost its integration with daily life; and with the coming of print and education it passed beyond the reach of all but specialised performers and a literate audience.

The oral poet and his audience

The men and women who made syllabic noises to mark the rhythm of their dancing were the first oral poets. Their successors in this country thrived in the Middle Ages, and still exist among a few remote peoples. Their work includes heroic and epic poetry, some drama, ballads, work songs, folk songs and a great range of mnemonic verse; and the characteristics of all this oral poetry have been identified and its mode of composition described in the pioneer studies of Cecil Sharp, the Chadwicks, Milman Parry and others.

The first poets shared a poetic language with their hearers, because, as Macaulay noted, the vocabulary of a 'half-civilised people' is poetic. Their language dealt realistically with what they knew: human beings and their activities, the natural world of plants and animals and the powers behind it, the seasons, night and day, the heavenly bodies. Voice and gesture combined to express emotion:

> The emotions did not exist before the mimic and vocal expression of them, but...songs, dances, and love arose out of the festivals of which they formed the various ceremonial phrases. Thus they reveal a state in which thought is concrete and direct, in which syntax cannot be separated from rhythm, and in which metaphorical associations have not yet replaced spontaneous connections.   (Granet, p. 144)

This is an account of early Chinese poetry, but it can be applied generally, for in all languages before the invention of print there was this direct relationship between word and thing. If a story or myth were to be told, the outline would be familiar to the hearers; if a song of joy or grief were called for, the occasion would be known; so that when the poet came to compose, his need was to clothe his

theme in language that would both hold the attention of the audi-
ence and be readily intelligible to it. There was never a set text,
except in the case of poems like the Vedas: the concern of a
specialised priesthood, not of the oral poet we are considering here.
The language of 'primitive' poetry may seem to us beautiful, but
all the poet aimed at was efficiency; he had a clear aim and
economical means. The beauty we appreciate is proof that the poet
had succeeded.

The oral poet could express only the generally accepted ideas for
which he had words and phrases available. Thus the language he
used consisted largely of formulas, which (in Milman Parry's
definition) are 'a group of words which is regularly employed under
the same metrical conditions to express a given idea'. The poet, or
rather the singer – because it was after thousands of years of being
sung or chanted that poetry was separated from music – built up
his recital by using phrases and formulas from his memorised stock
that he knew would make their impact on his hearers. If he was
inventive he would alter some of these or light on new ones that
seemed more effective, and these might go into circulation. This
would depend on their being approved by the community, just as
nowadays neologisms are tried out in the form of slang or technical
jargon to pass, if accepted, into the vocabulary permanently or for
as long as they fill a need. The individual invents words and
phrases; society tests them, and adopts or drops them. The expert
poet would build up a large store of these building blocks for use
when required; memorising such material and instruction in its use
were part of the training given to apprentice poets in bardic schools
in places as far apart as pre-Christian Ireland and Rwanda in Africa.

The style of oral poetry was much influenced by the audience.
With a modern book many of the steps leading up to its actually
being read are planned by the publisher in the form of advertising,
reviews and an attractive jacket; once the book has been chosen and
opened the author has only to hold the reader's attention. But the
oral poet has an unstable audience, on which he must concentrate
energy to get silence and stir interest; and to keep it attentive he
must be an actor and even a dancer, bringing into play every jot
of narrative skill and dramatic ability. Owing to the lack of these
elements in cold print the modern reader of old epics, for example,
may find them tedious. The expert reciter had to be firm with his
listeners, drive home his points with emphasis, repeat his state-
ments, vary his diction; he might enlist their co-operation in refrains
and in bodily movement, from stamping and clapping to dancing.

poet is bringing the lost sheep back to the fold: 'Ultimately it is the community that cures....Behind the shaman...stands the great community as the ultimate corrective of personal disorders' (Rieff 1966, p. 68).

Oral poetry was one means whereby the culture of a people was transmitted from one generation to another, in general acting as a brake upon sudden change. In many places it helped to create and sustain a sense of nationhood (discussed in the next chapter), as did the ballads of Bulgaria, Greece, Spain and elsewhere; and in Ethiopia wide cultural uniformities are traceable to a long history of wandering poets. Oral poetry transmits, but not (except in the case of religious texts like those mentioned above) with literal accuracy. In the telling of a historical legend each link is the opportunity for creating new variants, changes are made every time the tale is repeated, and as a result the original testimony sometimes disappears altogether.

The method of transmission often determines the nature of what is transmitted. With everything depending on memory, oral cultures tended to conserve and employ standardised forms, shaping their knowledge and wisdom into proverbs and commonplaces and mnemonics. This affected content as well as style; only the memorable was handed on; 'in formulas thought lived and moved and had its being' (Ong 1971, p. 275). The fact that the poet had to arouse the interest of his hearers made some distortion likely. The medium favoured drama, myth, epic, and a sequence of aphorisms and adages rather than lineal, logical thinking; only certain kinds of thought and literature could flourish in an oral culture, so that for example any form of science could not get very far without the brick-upon-brick structure of print that it needs. The poetry which an oral culture produced naturally had been largely used for spiritual rather than material concerns. With so much thought and knowledge existing only in the memory, the content of a culture was small, compared with the vast amount of wisdom and information available in thousands of libraries today; and it seems likely that a high proportion of it must have been actively possessed by ordinary men and women. In a pre-literate society people were not classified by their degree of literacy.

Literal accuracy (as we have noted) is not a characteristic of oral transmission. The substance handed on is selected, because it is expressed by those interested and able to transmit it, and sieved by their minds. Jack Goody has described what happens when the whole content of social tradition is held in the memory. What the individual remembers tends to be what is of critical importance in his experience; in each generation the individual memory 'will mediate the cultural heritage in such a way that its new constituents will adjust to the old...and whatever parts of it have ceased to be of contemporary relevance are likely to be eliminated by the process of forgetting' (p. 30).

Those who listened to oral literature must have followed the words with an intensity that we can hardly grasp, much less share. To start with, there has always been an attitude of respect for the word, from the days of magic when words seemed to exist in their own right and to exert a control over things; there are vestiges of it today. Speech was delivered with great penetrative power by the poet's whole body to the hearers who directly confronted him and reached their feelings more immediately and more deeply than the written word. Being delivered to an assembly of people, it encouraged group feeling, and tended to transmit mainly material that was suitable for addressing to a group. All this sets up a division between literature, and hence attitudes, before and after the invention of printing, for many of the forms of expression in poetry and many access-roads to modes of thought and feeling we are familiar with through books could not exist in an aural culture. The difference however is not between deprivation and full enjoyment, for

> illiteracy has its compensations. It is good for the memory and strengthens the imagination. People who depend entirely on oral tradition will tend to cultivate an ear for the memorable and a taste for figures of speech. They will share in a folk literature and play their part in perpetuating and enlarging it. They will feel themselves to be participators in whatever art they have access to. Though they may not have access to the greatest literature, at least they will be custodians of an art that comes home to their business and bosoms, and within the limit of that they will recognize and encourage integrity and vitality.
> (Daiches, p. 20)

The earliest poetry expressed the common consciousness of a small group. Their songs voiced strongly felt emotions like joy and grief or the wish to communicate with the supernatural, and took the singers out of their ordinary selves. When performers emerged, they and their audience represented both more and less than themselves. The professional reciter Ion claimed for his recitals of Homer that God himself was the speaker, addressing men through the poetry. At critical points he was transported by feeling: 'At the tale of pity my eyes are filled with tears, and when I speak of

horrors, my hair stands on end and my heart throbs.' And he agreed
that he produced similar effects on his audience: 'I look down on
them, and behold the various emotions of pity, wonder, sternness,
stamped upon their countenances' (Plato, *Ion*). When St Augustine
preached, sometimes employing poetic devices, we note the same
closeness between speaker and audience: 'The audience was far
from passive...they would be following the preacher intently,
registering their grasp of what he said, and their approval, with sighs
and exclamations, shouts and tears, hand-clappings and breast beat-
ings, so that he never had any difficulty in telling whether he had
made his point' (Hill, p. 19). Though the performer did separate
out from his audience, he was for centuries still very much of it. He
was dependent on its co-operation, and this might mean that pre-
sentation was as important as the content itself. In fact in an oral
tradition, as we have noted above, the poem does not exist till it is
performed. As Ruth Finnegan reports of African oral literature,
'Printed words alone represent only a shadow of the full actualization
of the poem as an aesthetic experience for poet and audience' (p. 2).

In this face-to-face encounter the poet could exploit the interest
of his audience and rely on its contributing to the narrative and the
choruses, and joining in a dance when he wanted them to. Poet and
audience were almost identical. The pre-Moslem poets of Arabia,
for example, aimed at stimulating the imaginative response of their
audiences so that the poem became a dialogue between them, in
which the listeners were 'alert to grasp the hints and allusions...and
to complete his portrait or thought for themselves'. Moreover:

> The poet had not only to play up the tribal sense of pride or his
> patron's self-importance; he was obliged even more to keep within
> the range of themes which his audience understood, trying to touch
> their feelings and captivate them by an allusive and pictorial evocation
> of subjects with which they were familiar and on which they were
> ready to back their judgment. He could not, even had he wished,
> strike out on fresh paths and introduce a new or wider range of ideas;
> had he done so, he would have outstripped their comprehension and
> lost contact with them.
> (Gibb, p. 18)

Later, in England, there is evidence of the medieval reciter's need to
hold an audience among 'a fluctuating crowd, perhaps in some pub-
lic place' (Speirs, p. 192): in the opening lines of 'Havelok the Dane':

> Herknet to me, godemen,
> Wives, maydnes, and alle men,
> Of a tale that ich you will telle,
> Wo-so will here and ther-to duelle... (linger)

Performance made verse that seems tedious to us come alive by bringing out much that a reader cannot feel and hear. *The Song of Roland* for example had

> a vigorous martial beat that could have an almost hypnotic effect on the listener . . . The effects of sound and vision should combine to shift the hearer's reactions from a state of intellectual observation to one of sensual participation, with the exaggerations, simplifications and repetitions of the narrative helping to increase rather than inhibit his involvement.
> (Owen, p. 23)

The emergence of individual poets, the prevalence of writing, and then of print changed the relationship between artist and audience. The medieval writer of carols kept in close touch with his public by using as the burden of his piece 'some common moral or prudential saying suited to his purpose and at the same time accepted by the people to whom he addressed his song'; and the poets who complained about the corruption of the church were men of the people 'writing for an essentially popular audience, for the poor' (Peter, p. 93). This is evident in Alexander Barclay's (b. 1475?) opening lines, which leave no doubt about his wish to keep close to his readers:

> My speche is rude, my termes comon and rural
> And I for rude peple moche more convenient
> Than for Estates, lerned men, or eloquent.
> (*Ship of Fools*)

The medieval sermon in the vernacular, sometimes in verse and rhymed, was very much at the level of the people to whom, homely in style and matter, it was delivered, but it *was* a sermon, addressed to people from a pulpit. In Europe too a new relationship developed between writer and audience; 'the author no longer curried favour, but admonished, preached, and instructed' (Auerbach, p. 298). Of the new attitude Dante was an example – by no means the voice of the people, but striking out a new line, representing his own will as God's will, and creating a public for himself. Chaucer perhaps is another example of the self-conscious author, supplying art to a chosen section of the population; a fifteenth-century illustration shows him in the grounds of a castle, reading his poems to a courtly audience, mainly of women. At the same time the peasants at the lower end of the scale enjoyed the stories of Robin Hood the Outlaw, while the country squires and squireens above them reproduced in miniature the royal household. Their literature was *King Alisaunder*, Robert Manning's *Story of England*, and a story of the siege of Troy.

'All three point to the existence of an unlettered or half-lettered audience. The rhymes, which could be recited and memorised, brought them within reach of persons who either could not read or who preferred to listen' (Smalley 1960, p. 26). Thus in England the artist-poet began to emerge and the spokesman-poet to recede; and it may be that the use of printing put a premium on literacy that can be seen as socially divisive.

Collectors of unwritten poetry have often noted the difficulty experienced by performers when trying to dictate poetry without the stimulus of a listening crowd. This influence showed itself in several ways. The third stage in the apprenticeship of a Yugoslav singer, for example (after he had learned the formulas and the special language), was to perform before a critical audience. He had to concentrate intently and use the best of his narrative skill and dramatic ability to hold a shifting audience. In different parts of the world the audience participated with laughter, assent or dissent, running criticism or encouragement of the narrator, singing, dancing, or acting out parts in a tale. In Ireland a good audience was essential, to make comments or interjections, to encourage the singer after each stanza, or help him go back to the rhyme when he lost the thread. In sea shanties, after a stereotyped opening, the shantyman improvised, with intimate and personal allusions and criticism of the food and conditions; and the audience of an Eskimo singer not only joined in the refrain but provided replacements the moment the singer tired. And a final example is that of the Tartars, with whom the rank and temper of the audience were a material influence on the content of a poem. The singer won the sympathy of his audience by alluding to distinguished members of the circle of listeners, and success here would spur him on to fresh efforts. The Russian collector, V. V. Radlov, reported that after a recital by a Kirghiz minstrel among Tartars he saw one of the sultans spring up suddenly during a song, tear off his silk overcoat and fling it, cheering, as a present to the minstrel (Chadwick 1940, III, p. 184).

In their day Shakespeare and other Elizabethan dramatists were popular providers of entertainment. There is hardly a play of Shakespeare's that fails to disclose a recognition of his audience's demand for clowning, pageantry, dancing, word-and-sword-play, and music – as well as his success both in supplying what was wanted and in turning it to artistic advantage. In *Richard II* the concluding note sounded the popular theme of the invincibility of England, so long as she remained free from internal strife. The *Henry IV* plays provided Falstaff for the groundlings, for the citizen the tale of the king who had put down Richard II, and for his wife the romantic figure of Hotspur. In *King Lear*, the clowning of Edgar is at the heart of the play. And in *The Merchant of Venice* he presented familiar types against the background of Venice, the city so much admired and emulated by Londoners, with a stock figure of fun in the money-lending Jew, but at the same time wrote a near-tragedy that sheds undiminished light on xenophobia and the clash of race and religion. The Elizabethan play and its actors were close to the audience in every sense; all (whatever their social level) shared a set of medieval ideas, some racial attitudes, an acceptance of religion and a sense of right and wrong. The spectators contributed their language, their goodwill and their co-operation to the dramatist. The plays did not exist till they were presented by the performers, acting in an accepted convention, and aided by sound, music, movement, processions and a collaborative audience.

Shakespeare and his audience supply the last notable instance of a symbiosis which had been the normal relationship between poet and listener, at a time when poetry filled a clear social need. After him, though there is no very sharp dividing line, we find that poets are not closely related to a homogeneous audience, and that their work is acceptable to a section of, rather than to the whole, community. Not of course that subsequent poets have not needed an audience; and as their public has diminished they have been vocal about it. Representative expressions are those of W. B. Yeats: 'You must always remember your audience, it is always there and you cannot do without it'; and T. S. Eliot: 'A poet should normally be glad to feel able to feel that the entertainment or diversion is enjoyed by as large and various a number of people as possible' (1933, p. 30). On the other hand poets are good for society; it needs to see itself and take its bearings, and to preserve its language and human consciousness. The lack of interaction between poet and audience is a loss, for (as R. G. Collingwood eloquently contended) the poet, not as mystagogue to the dark paths of his soul, but as spokesman for his audience, says the things it wants said, but cannot express without his aid.

However, there is now no audience for poetry. It has been replaced, in Edwin Muir's words, by an 'alarming, vast, shapeless something, deaf and blind to a once recognized and accepted part of life, and a human inheritance. That something is called the public, and it is quite unworried, does not know what it has lost, and goes its way'. So the modern poet writes for the few – a solo performance before a passive public. Even by the middle of the last century John Stuart Mill could say, 'All poetry is of the nature of a soliloquy'. Apart from the special case of Blake, the rift opened with Keats and Shelley, both of whom suffered from a lack of intelligent criticism and understanding in their readers – in contrast with Burns, who found an audience ready for the poems of a considerable talent shaped by traditional forms. In this discussion Tennyson is an important figure. His work sold enormously, he became a member of the establishment, and was ahead of his time only in being a sort of media figure for the half-educated masses. He could not walk in London without being recognised, even by a tramp in Covent Garden – 'I've been drunk for 6 days out of 7, but if you will shake me by the hand, I'm damned if I ever get drunk again'. In the north of England a poor weaver learned his poems by heart to avoid buying them; at Tintagel an old woman rushed out of her cottage and started reciting the 'Idylls'; and a boatman at Killarney exclaimed, 'So you're the gentleman who brought the money to the place!' (Altick, p. 2). The quickest gauge to the level of his popularity is to be found in 'Rifleman Form' and other poems he wrote for the press to stimulate recruiting (to meet the threat of a French invasion, 1859). Much worse, Kipling's crude and brutal imperialism brought him also popularity and sales on the Tennysonian scale. But by the turn of the century the day of bestselling poets was over, and the middle-class public looked for the tepid products of the Georgian poets.

Now that poetry is rarely spoken aloud there is less opportunity for it to make an almost physical impact on the reader. Conversely the poet's voice is no longer immediately influenced by the size and quality of the audience he is addressing, or by the actual or imagined acoustics of the place he is speaking in. Francis Berry has described how modern auditoria do not allow verse to be heard properly, with the microphone deleting certain frequencies and the amplifier distributing what is left, thus preventing 'effective realisation in sound of all that poetry where inward resonance and outward reverberation are substantial' (Berry, p. 21).

Finally, an essential in a satisfactory relationship between poet and reader is lucidly indicated by D. W. Harding. Near the end of his essay 'Reader and Author' he discusses the causes of an author's unsure control of the reader's response, and the consequent risk of 'a chaos of idiosyncratic readings':

> Some individual differences in reading will necessarily occur owing to diversities of individual experience and private associations to words and events. But unless a large nucleus of the poem is public

> property, with an intelligible meaning agreed about by those readers whose capabilities bring the poem potentially within their reach, we shall have lost the bond between author and reader and between one reader and another. And these bonds are vital, for – as the history of Blake's poetry, for instance, shows vividly – a literature is not just a sequence of authors but a growing social structure of which readers form an integral part. (Harding 1963, p. 108)

There are several conditions there that the poet may find no longer obtaining; he cannot be sure that there will be much of a bond between himself and his reader. He cannot for certain rely on the power of words to set going in the reader's mind the overtones acquired over hundreds of years; nor can he be confident that the reader will share with him the experiences and attitudes that give the 'right' content to abstractions like 'wisdom' and 'honour'.

Education

It is a human trait to hand on knowledge, wisdom and manners to the next generation by word of mouth. This is the oldest form of education; the other is more specialised, with professional teachers and special buildings. Both used poetry as a medium of instruction. In classical Greece boys were expected to learn a large amount of poetry by heart, and some early poets have survived solely through this practice. At about the same time the ancient Chinese anthology, *The Book of Poetry*, became a book of instruction in school. The early Christians employed verse extensively both for religious and secular education. For teaching purposes Commodian wrote eighty acrostic poems and the Spaniard Juvencus versified the Gospel story. Later, in the eighth century, Paul the Deacon wrote 'grammatical hymns' for memorising in school. The Gauls and the Brahmins of India carried on their instruction in the form of traditional poems orally transmitted; and in the sixth-century Ireland the bards played as a big a part in education as the clergy themselves (Hyde, p. 167).

Recently we have learned much about the use of poetry for education in Africa. The northern Bantu (in what is now Uganda) taught the young with verse descriptions of animals and narratives of hunting and military expeditions. Gnomes – sententious sayings in verse, in which an older member of the family gives advice to a younger one – included sayings of observation and of obligation, and were part of the education of boys in Basutoland; the Anglo-Saxon equivalents are the gnomic verses found in the *Exeter Book*. Moralistic fables about animals are included in the education of children among the Chaga people of East Africa to secure conformity with accepted patterns of behaviour; songs of praise are also sung to indicate social approval of those who conform. Some of the verbal instruction given during the initiation ceremonies of boys and the preparation of girls for marriage takes the form of songs; and in later life songs of ridicule are important as a means of censuring misbehaviour. Here as usual folklore ensures continuity from generation to generation. It was much the same even in the very different civilisation of Greece; poetry was the core of the educational system and gave society the continuity and coherence it needed. In Africa again the poet Okot p'Bitek sums up what poetry still does for Acoli children in northern Uganda:

> The lullabies, the games and the songs accompanying them form a most important introduction to the cultural and moral education of the Acoli child. As he participates in these enjoyable activities, he learns to express himself through his bodily movement, in his voice as he sings, and in the poetry. He develops his sense of rhythm as he keeps time with the rest – a very significant training for the complex dances, music and poetry of the adults. The child is plunged right into the core of poetry which is the song that arises from the tensions of human reaction. (p. 2)

Verse was the means of memorising when information, rules of conduct and special linguistic skills had to be imparted. Elizabethan emblems, for example, were not only well established as part of social life, but were also much valued by schoolmasters, because their pictures and improving verses helped with style and syntax and supplied a stock of themes and commonplaces (Freeman, p. 88). The founders of Elizabethan schools built the study of literature into the constitutions of their foundations, in which the acting of plays was a chief recreation; and in 1582 Richard Mulcaster insisted on the power of the drama to teach 'good behaviour and audacity'. Poetry was established as a normal part of life, and the mind was trained beyond our capacity today, when the development of logical power and the nominal availability of so much printed matter have weakened the memory. It is worth recalling too, especially when a purely vocational view of education is advanced, that the writing of verse is one of the shortest ways to writing good prose.

No education has ever been purely vocational; even modern technical training cannot help being something else as well, if only as a chart which omits certain areas of interest. In the play-acting that was part of a vocational education the actors took over the feelings and attitudes of characters different from themselves, and in some cases at least their imagination must have been stimulated and their sympathies widened. The traditional poetry that children absorbed tended to be conservative; it acted as a mirror of adult life and handed on to the young the mores of their society. For instance the words that used to be sung to their children by mothers among the Euahlayi of Australia may have been a lullaby, the words of which the children could not understand. But the words, chosen by the mother in her desire to implant the best tradition of behaviour, would eventually be understood and drop into the mental place prepared for them:

> Be kind,
> Do not steal,
> Do not touch what belongs to another,
> Leave all such alone,
> Be kind.
> (Parker, p. 54)

Another example is the idea of death received by children, one very different in other times and places from that now current in the west; 'a society's image of death reveals the level of independence of its people, their personal relatedness, self-reliance and aliveness' (Illich 1975, p. 122). The accepted image among some peoples has been that of the falling leaf, the vegetation dying when the familiar round of the seasons required it. This attitude of acceptance towards death is soon learned by children in parts of Africa. 'To the Acoli, the death of a very old person is not considered a terribly sad thing. In "Dini-dini ye" we hear the children making fun of the death of one such old woman who had overstayed her welcome in this world:'

> Dini-dini ye,
> Otoo ber;
> Dani ma yam otoo te layata,
> Otoo ber;
> Dini-dini ye,
> Otoo ber,
> Dani ma yam otoo te laywee,
>
> Otoo ber;
> Lamanya-manya!

> I hit you hard, I hit you hard, oh,
> It is good that she died;
> Your grandmother who died among the potato-heaps,
> It is good that she died;
> I hit you hard, I hit you hard, oh,
> It is good that she died,
> Your grandmother who died under the broom bushes,
> It is good that she died;
> I close your eyes completely.
> (p'Bitek, p. 30)

This brings to mind the mock-lament recited by children in England:

> Poor old Peggy's dead,
> She died last night in bed.
> We put her in a coffin
> And she fell right through the bottom,
> Poor old Peggy's dead.

The poetry that children heard from adults or from their own traditions amounted to an education in how to live. It seems to have had some advantages over the formal and obligatory schooling of English-speaking countries. In England at least compulsory education went wrong from the start. The system of paying for elementary schools by results inspired a hatred of the printed word. The introduction of 'English literature' into the elementary schools of 1871 took the form of memorising a passage of poetry; in the training colleges too there was a great deal of memorising of mere information – the place of reading was never learned. Thus it is not surprising that from the beginning there was a 'gap between the public literate tradition of school and the very different and indeed often directly contradictory private oral traditions of the pupil's family and peer group' (Goody, p. 59). What the children missed is eloquently presented by Willa Muir, discussing the children's singing games of her youth at the turn of the century. These games formed a habit of mediating the children's 'energies into artistic expression, which with any encouragement could have been continued and developed in later life'. What they lacked most were stories about grown-up experience, stories which the children's forebears had enjoyed in the Scottish ballads. Their parents did not supply the need, nor did the printed word, since for Willa Muir's contemporaries stories in books did not exist. 'To my friends, reading was a hated school exercise, performed aloud in class, slowly, unwillingly and with apparent incomprehension' (Willa Muir, p. 28).

Education sharpened the dichotomy of speech from writing and widened the gap between literate and non-literate. Both the educated and the partly educated suffered from the split, as we can see from the anaemic poetry of the one and the poverty of non-existence of poetry for the second group. It can be perceived too in the decline of language, noted early on by Thomas Hardy, writing in *Longman's Magazine* in July 1883; a visitor to the home of a Dorset farm worker would find, he said, that the language

> instead of being a vile corruption of educated speech, was a tongue

with grammatical inflexions rarely disregarded by his entertainer, though his entertainer's children would occasionally make a sad hash of their talk. Having attended the National School they would mix the printed tongue as taught therein with the unwritten, dying Wessex English that they had learnt of their parents, the result of this transitional state of theirs being a composite language sans rule or harmony.

(Hardy 1967, p. 170)

The culture of the country, instead of being absorbed willy-nilly in the intervals of grubbing a living from the soil, was recorded in print in its finest and most memorable forms and put on the shelf, where for many it has remained. Children no longer acquired culture from the cradle onwards; they were offered it in a packet which they could either take or leave, and most of them left it. (Though we must not forget the admirable struggles of the Victorian poor to educate themselves.) So far as poetry is concerned, what has got into print survives as an academic study, and provides set-books. The education of the emotions, which the arts can carry far, does not appear on the curricula of today, and all the statistics of gallery-going and the sale of good records cannot conceal the truth that the arts are no more than tolerated.

Branches of knowledge

About a thousand years after Homer's epics took their final shape, the Christians in their zeal for interpreting mythology and literature turned their attention to the *Iliad*. The search for hidden meanings led them to make Homer 'the founder of science, history, philosophy, poetics, music, rhetoric, siege-works, astronomy, medicine, gymnastics, surgery and painting' (Halliday, p. 81). Their discoveries reflected the many-sidedness of early poetry; the same poem might contain both technological and religious matter. Myths diminished men's fears by making things more intelligible, providing cosmology, theology, history and science, as well as lore about the seasons and weather, crops and animals. These elements began to be distinguished in the Vedas, in which cosmology was a favourite subject; and spells – love-charms, against disease, for the recovery of cattle – separated out at an early stage. The ancient poetry of Europe also combined such elements as information, antiquarianism and prophecy. About 800 B.C. Hesiod, for example, supplied his countrymen with a mixture of agricultural advice, information about lucky and unlucky days and hints from general experience. Even so, *Works and Days* is still a poem, with its sympathy for animals and its enthusiastic descriptions of summer joys and winter hardships. He also introduced a grumble about his brother's meanness, and the first social criticism in his complaints about the 'crooked judgments' of the local kings. Thus we can see in *Works and Days* a poem at the crossroads, containing literature, philosophy, religion, practical advice, and protest.

The longest epic in the world, the Sanskrit *Mahabharata*, of about 900–500 B.C., includes elements of philosophy, religion, astronomy, cosmology, polity, economics, sociology and other didactic matter. The Arabs developed the sciences of philology and lexicography as a by-product of studying the ancient poetry used in interpreting the Koran; exact shades of meaning were defined by reference to the pre-Islamic poets, collected and memorised for the purpose. The Finnish medieval epic, *Kalevala*, offers advice to brides and inculcates respect for in-laws, as well as instructions for lighting fires, bedding cattle, feeding animals, baking, spinning, brewing and so on. The early Welsh poets dispensed heroic poetry, speculative and didactic theology, antiquarian lore and philosophy. Even in the comparative barbarism of Saxon England, poetry was used for higher things; Bede records that when Caedmon was found to have poetic talent he was ordered to use it for versifying sacred history.

Myths rendered the universe less formidable by explanations that served their purpose perhaps as well as modern science serves us, but they were not exactly scientific. We can however discern the beginnings of science in the elementary systematisation of men's knowledge of nature in gnomic poetry – statements of general truths and observations based on experience. Here are some gnomic verses from the Anglo-Saxon in the *Exeter Book*:

> Frost shall freeze, fire consume wood;
> Earth shall grow, ice form a bridge;
> Water shall wear a covering, wonderfully lock up
> The sprouts of earth. One shall unbind
> The fetters of frost, God very mighty;
> Winter shall depart, good weather come again,
> Summer brightly hot...

The first scientific poem was by a Greek, Ananius, of the sixth century B.C., listing foods according to the seasons; and a number of others on astronomy and geography of about the same time have been lost. With the growth of speculation in the fifth century, one might expect that the Greeks, who have supplied us with the roots of today's scientific vocabulary, would have developed a prose style for their profuse writing on science. But no, the philosophers of the Ionian school, like Xenophanes, continued to write in verse, perhaps because the strength of their convictions needed poetry to express it. Some of this didactic poetry is thin stuff, but the 350 surviving lines of Empedocles' (c. 493 – c. 433 B.C.) *On Nature* are impressive; the naturalist and philosopher, the preacher and the poet were still one. The next century produced a quantity of didactic poetry on geography, astronomy, history, medicine and other subjects. They included Epicurus (c. 340 – c. 270 B.C.), who gave an account of an atomic theory. The main surviving exposition of this is Lucretius' (94–55 B.C.) *De Rerum Natura*, an intelligent and powerful work which rejected as foul superstition the terrorising omens and taboos of Roman religion. The splendid sweep of the exordium to Venus that opens his first book reveals him as a religious poet from the start.

> Mother of Aeneas and his race, the delight of men
> and gods,
> Life-giving Venus: under the wheeling constellations
> of the sky,
> It is through you that nature teems with life –
> The sea that bears our ships, and the earth that
> brings forth fruit.
> Through you all living creatures are conceived, and look
> upon the sun.
> Before you flee the winds, and at your coming the
> clouds vanish.
> For you the dappled earth flings up sweet flowers.
> For you the tracts of ocean laugh, and the sky gleams
> With wide-spread radiance...

By contrast Manilius' *Astronomicon* (about A.D. 10) is profoundly dull; a compilation of already known lore running to 4,200 lines, it is the earliest known treatise on astrology. An isolated oddity are the Latin hexameters on the moon's eclipse, written in Spain by Sisebut, King of the Visigoths, early in the seventh century.

Versified science was a feature of medieval writing, especially in England, where with the switch from Latin and French to English in the late fourteenth and early fifteenth centuries there appeared medical treatises in quantity, many in verse. The ordinary medical man remembered his professional knowledge in the versified Latin rules of the school of Palermo, but an untrained village leech, John Crophill of Wix near Harwich, wrote a popular rhymed poem on rosemary, containing a recipe for gout. As late as 1657 Abraham Cowley wrote up in Latin verse the results of his inquiries into the medicinal properties of plants and herbs; and the poet Thomas

Gray (1716–71) turned some of the botanist Linnaeus's work into Latin hexameters. Of all this material the *Ordinal of Alchimy* of Thomas Norton (*fl.* 1477) is one of the most interesting; in this tract on chemistry, expressed in tolerable English verse, Norton stated his belief, quite advanced for his era, in the value of experiments. Also under the heading of science we may include geography, from a brief Irish poem of the tenth century to Michael Drayton's (1563–1631) enormous *Poly-Olbion*, a county-by-county survey of England.

Between the early forms of science and history there is no dividing line. The cosmology with which we start our survey of history in verse might equally well be classified as science. Under this heading appears one of the oldest surviving pieces of writing, the *Babylonian Creation*, which opens with a cosmogony, a provisional hypothesis that gives a foothold to the speculating mind. This Sumerian account of the creation tells us that, before the gods came into being, there was a primeval sea or chaos from which the earth and its oceans developed; the ancient myth sounds rational and like many others seems close to modern ideas about the origin of the world. The conclusion of the epic, 'The Hymn of Fifty Names', contains an early form of history in its mention of man's advances in the arts and skills of life. Another very ancient and appealing piece of speculation, the original of which took shape somewhere between 1000 and 800 B.C., is the 'Hymn of Creation' from the tenth book of the Rig-Veda; its mood of philosophic doubt seems timeless. The simplest of the translations, by Juan Mascaró, is given:

> There was not then what is, nor what is not. There was no sky, and no heaven beyond the sky. What power was there? Where? Who was that power? Was there an abyss of fathomless waters?
>
> There was neither death nor immortality then. No signs were there of night or day. The ONE was breathing by its own power, in deep peace. Only the ONE was: there was nothing beyond.
>
> Darkness was hidden in darkness. The all was fluid and formless. Therein, in the void, by the fire of fervour arose the ONE.
>
> And in the ONE arose love. Love the first seed of soul. The truth of this the sages found in their hearts; seeking in their hearts with wisdom, the sages found that bond of union between being and non-being.
>
> Who knows in truth? Who can tell us whence and how arose this universe? The gods are later than its beginning: who knows therefore whence comes this creation?
>
> Only that god who sees in highest heaven; he only knows whence comes this universe, and whether it was made or uncreated. He only knows, or perhaps he knows not. (Mascaró, p. 64)

Huizinga notes that in its poetical structure the hymn retains vestiges of question-and-answer, the riddles that were asked in competitions on the subject of cosmogony. (There is a creation riddle in the pre-Conquest *Exeter Book*.) How near to the Veda in its wisdom is this Maori cosmogony, recorded a hundred years ago:

> From the conception the increase,
> From the increase the swelling,
> From the swelling the thought,
> From the thought the remembrance,
> From the remembrance the consciousness, the desire.

> The word became fruitful;
> It dwelt with the feeble glimmering;
> It brought forth night;
> The great night, the long night.
> The lowest night, the loftiest night,
> The thick night, to be felt,
> The night to be touched, the night unseen,
> The night following on,
> The night ending in death.

> From the nothing the begetting,
> From the nothing the increase,
> From the nothing the abundance,
> The power of increasing, the living breath;
> It dwelt with the empty space,
> It produced the atmosphere which is above us.

> The atmosphere which floats above the earth,
> The great firmament above us, the spread out space dwelt with the early dawn,
> Then the moon sprung forth;
> The atmosphere above dwelt with the glowing sky,
> Forthwith was produced the sun,
> They were thrown up above as the chief eyes of Heaven:
> Then the Heavens became light,
> The early dawn, the early day, the mid-day. The blaze of day from the sky.

> The sky which floats above the earth,
> Dwelt with Hawaiki...
> (Trask 2, p. 106)

Polynesia yields perhaps more cosmogonies of interest than any other field, as one might expect from a culture with so highly developed an intellectual life; in them 'we have a process which resembles in many respects the act of Creation by the simple effort of divine will which is found in the Book of Genesis' (Chadwick 1940, III, p. 400).

Cosmogonies came to fulfil needs other than that of telling people how the universe began:

It was always good to begin a religious text with a cosmogony; it fixed the ceremony or spell or healing, or whatever the occasion was, into the order of eternal things. It tapped the spiritual power stored and latent in the surrounding world and gave extra potency to whatever followed. A charm for curing toothache was introduced by one well-known cosmogony, and the whole of the Adapa myth was preserved into the seventh century as an incantation against disease. (Sandars, p. 24)

When poetry was maid of all work the making of history came to be one of her duties. The myths acted as a kind of history, in giving people a sense of the past, of order in the universe, and of man's place in it. They may, some of them, even be historical, for the legend of a Golden Age is an improved version, perhaps, of a distant past when man had achieved homeostasis in his environment; and accounts of the creation may contain vestiges of the facts. The poets have also turned history into myth. One example is *The Song of Roland*; originally the narrative of Charlemagne's defeat at the Pass of Roncevaux in A.D. 778, it developed by the year 1000 into a great epic poem. Transformations of this kind were normal when the memory of the oral poet selected from the past such material as met the need of the present to create its own version of the past.

From remote times clans and courts have attached to themselves poets whose duty it was to compile eulogies on their ruler and his ancestors; and the genealogies and catalogues they produced are a world-wide element in ancient poetry. They deal with the origins not only of princes but also of mankind, the gods and the world; places and their names; buildings, personal names, customs and institutions. They are important as the first attempts to collect and classify knowledge, not just as at first for propaganda or entertainment, but for its own sake. The Polynesians – once again – preserved long and accurate genealogies that served as charters, letters patent, and books of reference in practical and legal matters; and their catalogues formed a record of migrations. From India comes an example of a tribe of wandering minstrels in the Chattisgarh who specialised in genealogies; and Africa offers us a royal family tree of twenty-three generations, many poems on tribal history, and riddle contests that provided a knowledge of history. An example from Palestine accessible to us all is recorded in 2 Samuel 23. Like the Gauls, the early Irish Christians were keen antiquarians, inclined to specialise in explaining the origin of place-names by means of stories in prose or verse; and the Welsh bards kept their genealogies going even during the eleventh and twelfth centuries, when literature was subdued throughout the Norman attempts to consolidate their power. In England the first poem of a genealogical nature was an Anglo-Norman piece of about 1333, called *Des Grantz Geanz*, which tried to account for what happened before Brutus the Trojan conquered the giant inhabitants of Britain. Narratives liked to place themselves in history by starting with a genealogy; the Anglo-Saxon *Beowulf* begins with the hero's parents, and the fourteenth-century *Sir Gawayne* opens with the descent of Arthur from Aeneas.

Primitive history was commonly employed to serve interests. Genealogies were invoked to shore up a dynasty or support claims to territory. About 600 B.C. Athens staked her claim to the island of Salamis, citing the *Iliad* (2, 557–8) as authoritative history. An extreme example is recorded in Mexico, where there were two versions of history. The Inca rulers reserved a secret general history that was taught in schools only to an élite, but for the general public there was a popularised version for recitation in poems, publicly performed. The poets had no choice of subject matter for, after the death of each Inca, officials met to choose themes that could be popularised (Vansina, p. 35).

After genealogies and eulogies came heroic poems. The earlier panegyrics and laments and narratives tended to contain elements of magic; the very words of a panegyric were designed to strike fear into the hearts of the foe and were believed to be capable of inflicting injury. But heroic poetry, emerging all over the world where conditions were right, as in archaic Greece or the Dark Ages of Europe, was the product of a more man-centred consciousness that admired the individual hero out for glory; its range over space and time shows that it met a real need (Bowra 1961, *passim*). The aim of the heroic poet was to provide entertainment by telling stories of adventures sought by members of an aristocracy. Courage, loyalty and generosity were the values upheld, in an ambience of eating, drinking and fighting; dramatic appeal was more important than historical accuracy, though the poetry seems to have been regarded as true both by ordinary people and by historians. As Bowra has written, heroic poetry gives dignity to the human race by showing of what feats it is capable; it extends the bounds of experience and enhances appreciation of life.

In early times we can discern two main classes of poet: the entertainer, especially at court, who recited heroic poetry; and the didactic poet, concerned with prophecy, philosophy and antiquarianism. The second class replaced the first, and history became a little more historical. Two Anglo-Saxon poems, *The Battle of Maldon* and *The Battle of Brunanburh*, describe Danish and Norse raids on the English coast with a fair measure of accuracy. In Ireland, after the dream of a Danish kingdom there had been shattered by the Battle of Clontarf in 1014, there was a revival of learning, and Flann, head of a bardic school, wrote a history of ancient times from Assyria to Rome, and summarised it as a class book for his pupils in a poem of twelve hundred lines. In England after the Conquest we start with poems in French: one of 1172–4 was on the life of Thomas à Becket, and another told the story of William, regent of England. Lives of the saints were put into verse, and with the tolerance at least of the authorities were recited by jongleurs, perhaps in church, perhaps outside, independently of divine service. This is evidence of a strong popular demand for versified history that lasted into the sixteenth century. Another sign was the translation into English verse by a Gilbertine monk, Robert Manning, of Langtoft's *Chronicle*, because he thought it right that the English should know their history in English. People had begged him to tell his story in easy rhyme, so he wrote it

> Not for the learned but the lewd
> For those that in this land wone,
> That neither Latin nor French cone,
> For to have solace and gamen
> In fellowship as they sit samen.

> (*lewd*, uninstructed.
> *wone*, live
> *cone*, know
> *samen*, together)

The popular appetite for ancient tales was such as to oust men's interest in religious history, so the church engaged a priest to write a competing poem, *Cursor Mundi*, which presented the Christian 'gestes' as an exciting and romantic story (Smalley 1960, p. 24).

Of all this material one item is both more historical and more literary: *The Bruce*, a creditable piece of history in verse by Archdeacon John Barbour of Aberdeen (d. 1395). Conscientious and indignant and patriotic, it reflects the Scots struggle for independence; the apostrophe 'Ah! freedom is a noble thing' has been anthologised:

> Ah! Freedom is a noble thing!
> Freedom makes man to have liking;
> Freedom all solace to man gives;
> He lives at ease who freely lives!
> A noble heart may have nane ease,
> And nothing elles that may him please,
> If freedom fail; for free liking

Is yearned for owre all other thing.
Nor he, that aye has livyt free,
May nocht knaw well the property,
The anger, nor the wretchit doom
That is couplit to foul thraldom.
But if he had assayit it,
Then all by heart he should it wit,
And should think freedom mair to prize
Than all the gold in world that is.
(*The Bruce*, II, 225–40 slightly altered)

It is far superior to contemporary English verse in the same field, such as the historical poetry of Lawrence Minot (*fl.* 1350) on the wars of England against the Scottish, French, Spanish and others. He is xenophobic and jingoist; 'look for no strict fairness here, no compassion for the fallen foe; brutality, vengeance, and silence about English reverses, are the rule in Minot' (Cottle, p. 61). In the next century the nationalist spirit developed the wish to know more about the origin and history of England, so that Lydgate (c. 1370 – c. 1451) in his *Troy Book* once again traced the line of English kings back to Brutus. Finally in the sixteenth century the demand for history was met, first in the simple broadside ballads which compressed the reigns of kings into a single sheet, and then by way of various popular historical ballads up to more ambitious efforts, such as the history plays, John Sharrocks' *The Valiant Actes and victorious Battailes of the English nation* (1585), and poems by other versifying historians.

These verse chronicles catered for the literate. For the non-literate there were a few historical ballads, though they do not seem to have circulated widely or to have lasted long when they did. Sometimes they were romantically inaccurate, like *Queen Jane*, who according to the ballad produced Edward VI by caesarean after nine days' labour; in fact she bore him naturally (Lloyd, p. 151). However an element of fact sometimes persisted in romantic circumstances. In 1919 a sea captain, born at Porlock in north Somerset, produced a ballad from the family repertoire, *The Three Danish Galleys*, in which raiders came to Porlock and stole a newly-wed bride. She refused to marry the Danish king, and was thrown overboard. The basis of fact is that about a thousand years ago there were Danish raids on Porlock recorded in the Anglo-Saxon Chronicle (Tongue, p. 57). And Douglas Hyde, in favour of the limited reliability of oral history, recorded an example of the Celtic memory for poetry: 'I have heard from peasants stanzas composed in the thirteenth century; I have recovered from an illiterate peasant, in 1890 in

Roscommon, verses which had been jotted down in phonetic spelling. . .in the year 1512.' Ballad singers themselves thought that their tales were true, and would identify the places where they occurred; an old man was sure that *The Douglas Tragedy* had taken place 'way back in Mutton Hollow' (Entwistle, p. 115). In some countries – Spain for example – ballads seem to have explained to people the main outline of their history; and perhaps Fletcher of Saltoun (1655–1716) was thinking on these lines when he observed that 'if a man were permitted to make all the ballads, he need not care who should make the laws of a nation'.

In fact the laws of a nation have often been put into verse, mainly no doubt because they were thus easier to remember, but also because they were serious matter calling for the most highly esteemed medium. Examples come from all over the world. In Ireland St Benignus is said to have drawn up in verse a complete statement of the various rights, privileges and duties of the high king, the provincial kings, and the local chieftains. Monastic rules were sometimes versified; the community at Bangor in Northern Ireland provides this brief example:

> Benchuir, bona regula,
> Recta atque divina,
> Stricta, sancta, sedula,
> Summa, iusta et mira.

In the East the Galla people of Abyssinia handed down their laws in metrical form. The best known example of the widespread medieval practice of utilising verse and proverb form for laws is the Friesian code, the first to be written down in any Germanic language.

Akin to laws was the didactic material that kept up a steady flow in the service of the church. At one end of the scale were John Mirk's instructions for parish priests in a versified translation from the Latin, of about 1400; at the other, a 'popular' summary of medieval theology, *The Pricke of Conscience*, running to nearly ten thousand lines. But the great didactic medium was the vernacular sermon, which at times followed the example of St Augustine, who used rhyme to bring out passages of feeling or pathos, and St Bernard, whose sermons had rhyming sentences that could be recast as hymns. The sermons used whole poems, popular jingles, and an Anglo-Saxon diction that was already poetic; thus 'the impassioned speech of responsible persons in the Church's midst. . .passed into the current coin of popular rhyme and song' (Owst 1933, p. 285). There were metrical homilies and sometimes complete sermons in

verse; and the preachers used rhyming mnemonics, like this one
from John of Grimston's sermon note-book:

$$\text{Pecunia} \begin{cases} \text{maket wrong rith.} \\ \text{maket day nith.} \\ \text{maket frend fo.} \\ \text{maket wele wo.} \end{cases}$$

The sermons influenced most of the political verse satire of the
Middle Ages, and even George Herbert in the seventeenth century.
In 1665 Evelyn recorded in his diary (24 February) that Dr Fell
'preached...a very formal discourse, and in blank verse...how-
ever, he is a good man'.

In addition to the religious there was a large volume of merely
moralising verse. As the reading public widened in the fifteenth
century there seems to have been a great thirst for improving
literature; and poetry was employed by those who sought to incul-
cate manners, instruction, popular wisdom and so on, in palatable
form. Social behaviour rather than religious belief was the theme
of much of this minor verse. The moralising strain persisted into
the sixteenth century, when the needs of the middle class were met
by a variety of hortatory handbooks.

The great mass of historical poetry does not offer us records of
fact. Though the poets believed in the truth of what they were
saying, their cultures determined what they wrote; to the Eskimo
for example the world has always been as it is now. Again, the
Polynesians held their history in high esteem and trained specialists
to maintain it, with the result that they have one of the finest oral
historical literatures in the world; but their sense of time is different
from ours, because their language has no tense system like that of
Indo-European languages. Similarly the Dinka people of the Sudan,
when retelling events from the past in their songs, 'continually fuse
past, present, and future tenses. In doing so they vividly link the
present to dramatize them and increase their significance for the
future...the past is seen in continuous relationship with the present
and as influencing the future' (Deng, p. 58). The oral history of the
Greeks was as selective as any other of its kind; they remembered
what they needed to remember for the life of their time, and forgot
what was irrelevant.

However unreliable as an accurate record versified history may
be, it is valuable for its accounts of what people thought and how
they felt. Heroic poems for example are a source of information
about the light by which life was conducted rather than a narrative
of real events. *Roland* reveals the working of the crusader mentality;

Anglo-Saxon battle poems display the heroic code in action; *Beowulf* shows what the introduction of Christianity meant and the difficulties of adjustment it caused. The ballads in particular are informative, for as Macaulay (discussing the England of 1685) wrote of working people, 'a great part of their history is to be learned only from their ballads'. Examples are the practice of foreign embassies in London in the sixteenth century of studying the printed broadsides and reporting back to their governments, and the poverty of Irish street ballads. The latter, clumsy, trivial, incongruous, show vividly 'to what the Irish people, kept in misery and deprived of their own culture, were reduced in the greater part of the last century' (Zimmerman, p. 9). It is impossible to understand the Yugoslavs or Russians or the Armenians without studying their heroic poetry; for it 'enshrines a mass of human experience which is excluded from polite letters and may indeed be beyond the ken of publicists and spokesmen' (Bowra 1961, p. 531). From the Balkans too have been gathered the Greek folk songs which tell us what the people really felt about the traitorous agreement of the British with the Turks in selling Parga in 1817–19, or about the German occupation in the 1939 war. Popular poetry can inform us about men's attitudes to historical events; and strictly official poetry throws light on the attitudes and patterns of behaviour that the rulers of a society seek to impose on its members.

At this point Peter Laslett's question obtrudes itself: 'Why is it that we know so much about the building of the British Empire, the growth of Parliament and its practices, the public and private lives of English kings, statesmen, generals, writers, thinkers and yet do not know whether all our ancestors had enough to eat?' (p. 127). Part of the answer would be our failure to use, where it would be most telling, the evidence from poetry, especially popular poetry, that is available over most of our history. What an excellent text (for example) is supplied for a history lesson by the toast which the fishermen of Lowestoft in a successful herring season drank to the Pope, as head of the church which encouraged the eating of salt fish in Lent:

> Here's to his Holiness
> The Pope with his triple crown,
> And here's to nine dollars
> For ev'ry cask in town...

– nine dollars being the hoped-for price of herrings in Italy.

5

Patriotism and politics

Eulogies

An early type of poem was the eulogy. The aim was to strengthen the position of a tribal leader by celebrating his deeds in war, glorifying his ancestors or listing the allies on whom he might rely. The supply of eulogies tended to become the duty of an official poet attached to a princely court or important house. Some of the poems provided a kind of history, when they took shape as genealogies; they placed the chief in his line of descent, shored up his authority and described his home and household and demesne. Eulogies had to be as quickly available as a roll of red carpet when asked for, so they depended more than most types of verse on the poet's ready skill in finding the right selection of formulas. Specialists in panegyric, glorifying the tribe, buttressing the prestige of the chief and arousing the patriotism of his people, have been reported from all over the world. In Wales for instance the traditional function of the poet was to support authority and an ordered mode of existence. This dated from the time when the tribe's well-being depended on the skill and bravery of the chieftain, and 'when the poet's eulogy was the whole community's tribute, a genuine expression of gratitude and an incentive to further deeds of valour and deliverance' (Parry, p. vii). Eulogies existed in Wales in the sixth century A.D. and persisted till the twelfth century.

So much early Hebrew literature has survived that we can find most types of writing in the Bible. We are told in the first book of Samuel 18, written in the tenth century B.C., that when David returned from killing the Philistine champion Goliath he was welcomed by women dancing and singing antiphonal chants of praise. There are more examples of praise poems in the second book of Samuel 23; and, much later, in the poem of Job each of the three friends who offer him conventional comfort delivers a panegyric on the God who persecutes Job without justification or explanation. And then (in chapter 12 of the book) Job ironically replies:

No doubt but ye are the people, and wisdom shall die with you. But I have understanding as well as you; I am not inferior to you; yea, who knoweth not such things as these?

and then goes on to deliver a panegyric of his own on the destructive, negative power of God. In the translation of the Revised Version:

With him is wisdom and might;
He hath counsel and understanding.
Behold, he breaketh down, and it cannot be built again;
He shutteth up a man, and there can be no opening.
Behold, he withholdeth the waters, and they dry up;
Again, he sendeth them out, and they overturn the earth . . .

In Greece panegyrics began to be heard when barbarian invaders from the North displaced the Minoan culture, and a ruling class of military adventurers established itself. They need a special type of poet, so minstrels were attached to their households to turn out the new kind of poetry required, celebrating the prestige and military exploits of their employers. In historic times Pindar (518–438 B.C.) was hired by a number of towns and individuals to produce odes celebrating such achievements as those of athletes, on their return home. His surviving work has been enthusiastically praised by classical scholars, but the modern reader is likely to find the odes tedious, and to agree with Lesky, who comments sharply on Pindar's 'pomposity, inextricable sentence structure and strained and strutting language' (Lesky, pp. 118 ff). Professional poets supplying praise for pay were a feature also of the heroic age (A.D. c. 500 – c. 622) of Arabic literature. In return for gifts they performed at poetic tournaments, when different tribes assembled for fairs or pilgrimages. Their duty was to play up their tribe's sense of pride and their patron's self-importance; and as this was for the poet a matter of acquiring the appropriate technique there was, as so often with products of the kind, a loss of spontaneity. Arabic philologists looked down on these 'slaves of poetry', contrasted with the 'poets by nature'.

Readers of Camara Laye's *The African Child* will recall the beautiful account of how his father, a blacksmith and goldsmith, would sometimes make trinkets out of gold dust brought to him by young women. Since they usually needed the ornament for a particular date or occasion, 'to better their chance of being quickly served, and the more easily to persuade my father to interrupt the work he had in hand, they would request the services of an official praise-singer, a go-between, and would arrange with him in advance what fee they would pay for his good offices'. Then:

The praise-singer would instal himself in the workshop, tune up his cora, which is our harp, and would begin to sing my father's praises. This was always a great event for me. I would hear recalled the lofty deeds of my father's ancestors, and the names of these ancestors from the earliest times; as the couplets were reeled off, it was like watching the growth of a great genealogical tree that spread its branches far and wide and flourished its boughs and twigs before my mind's eye. The harp played an accompaniment to this vast utterance of names, expanding it and punctuating it with notes that were now soft, now shrill. Where did the praise-singer get his information from? He must certainly have developed a very retentive memory stored with facts handed down to him by his predecessors, for this is the basis of all our oral traditions. Did he embellish the truth? It is very likely: flattery is the praise-singer's stock-in-trade! Nevertheless, he was not allowed to take too many liberties with tradition, for it is part of the praise-singer's task to preserve it.   (p. 23)

This twentieth-century example is one of many thousands from all periods and most parts of the African continent. As elsewhere it was common form for the courts of kings and nobles to include a specialist poet, whose duty was to glorify his patron and the patron's ancestors. And again as in other parts of the world the bards were at times something of a pest, being objects of fear as well as of admiration, for example when they took their stand in a market-place and blackmailed those who would not pay protection-money against their satire. As one might expect, the court poetry tended to over-elaboration, developing an obscure and allusive style for official praises. The hired poets sang of the cattle-raiding prowess of their high-born employer, but commoners sang their own praises at festivals and weddings and ceremonials (Finnegan, p. 141).

In Europe we have an early account from the historian Priscus. In A.D. 448 he was a member of an embassy to Attila, king of the Huns and heard his warlike deeds chanted. The bards

recited the verses which they had composed to celebrate his valour and his victories. A profound silence prevailed in the hall and the attention of the guests was captivated by the vocal harmony, which revived and perpetuated the memory of their own exploits; a martial ardour flashed from the eyes of the warriors who were impatient for battle; and the tears of the old men expressed their generous despair that they could no longer partake of the danger and glory of the field. (Chadwick 1932, I, p. 448)

The name of Attila appears also in the heroic poem *Widsith*, the oldest Anglo-Saxon verses we have (probably seventh century A.D.), in which a typical wandering minstrel tells with pride of the rulers and peoples and heroes he has known. These catalogues take up most of the poem, but it ends with a passage on the life of a poet and his value to men:

> Thus the minstrels of men go wandering,
> As fate ordains, through many lands.
> They speak their needs, they say the word of thanks.
> South or North, they always meet one
> Wise in measures, liberal in gifts,
> Who wishes to exalt his glory before the warriors,
> To perform valorous deeds, until light and life fall in ruin together.
> He gains praise, he has lofty glory under the heavens.
> (cf. Gordon, p. 67 and Alexander, p. 33)

One of the best-known early hymn writers, Venantius Fortunatus (A.D. 540–609) Bishop of Poitiers, started as a court poet, among whose duties it was to deliver eulogies on the bishops who at various times were royal guests (Raby, p. 86). Several of his hymns are still in use: 'Pange, lingua, gloriosi proelium certaminis' (Sing my tongue, the glorious battle) is written in trochaic tetrameters, the metre of Roman soldiers' marching songs, and 'Vexilla regis prodeunt' (the royal banners forward go) was composed for a procession of relics at Poitiers, to become the favourite hymn of crusaders. Praise poems were much employed in support of Welsh, Irish and Scottish princes. Among the oral traditions of Welsh bards were sagas which they used to recite in the halls of their chieftains, with songs of their own in praise of their patrons. War with the Normans from 1169 onwards arrested the development of Irish literature for centuries; it was thus limited to tribal genealogies, eulogies and elegies for the dead. Fragmentary panegyrics are among the earliest remains of Irish poetry, and in Ireland as elsewhere the bards in the seventh century were too numerous and too parasitic, demanding money to buy off satirical attacks (Hyde, p. 488). In Scotland praise poetry was the commonest form of bardic verse, but England can produce little of interest. The accession of Henry VI evoked a number of poems, flattering verses written on the occasion of royal visits to loyal towns; and a dull poem intended for recitation ('A Ballet of the King's Majesty') was a feature of one of the pageants arranged on the route of Edward VI's coronation procession (Greene, No. 438). Even in the sixteenth and seventeenth centuries in England public eulogies were still being produced; Spenser's *Daphnaida* was written at the request of a chance patron about a lady he had never seen, and Donne addressed verses to the bereaved father of Elizabeth Drury, a lady probably unknown to the writer.

A weapon of war

The earliest poetry hardly ever exalts individuals, and if primitive peoples ever produced war songs these were incidental to their main concerns and routine. It was more developed societies, obsessed with vigorous and violent action, that adopted the heroic stance, and employed poetry to rouse the common people to kill and die for their masters. War songs – so great was the belief in the power of the word – could also bring destruction and shame on enemies by means of spells and curses. Since 'to the view of ancient people, war was always in the last analysis a sort of psychological contest, psychic weapons, i.e. words uttered in verse forms, were of greater importance than stone or iron. Among them a piece of poetry could work at any time as a real, dangerous weapon' (Izutzu, p. 130). The Arabs excelled at this, and there are Hebrew examples also; David delivered a powerful verbal assault (1 Samuel 17: 45–7) before he knocked out Goliath with a skilful sling-shot. Deborah's song of exultation (Judges 5: 19–31) was probably a camp-fire number with Hebrew warriors for centuries; it was a regular procedure for military bards to inflame their men against the foe by singing songs of their great past. The best-known lines run:

> The kings came and fought,
> Then fought the kings of Canaan
> In Taanach by the waters of Megiddo;
> They took no gain of money.
> They fought from heaven;
> The stars in their courses fought against Sisera.
> The river of Kishon swept them away,
> That ancient river, the river Kishon.
> O my soul, thou has trodden down strength.
> Then were the horsehoofs broken
> By the means of the prancings, the prancings of their mighty ones.

One of the earliest mentions of war songs in Europe is that of Tacitus, writing his *De origine et situ Germanorum* about A.D. 98, in which he mentions the 'concentus' of German soldiers as they moved into battle to fight for their aristocratic chieftains. A large number of the latter are catalogued in the early Germanic *Widsith*, mentioned above. Much later we have records of a battle-song of which the words are known; it appears that before the battle of Hastings, William the Conqueror's minstrel, Taillefer, begged permission to lead the charge, and did so, singing from the *Song of Roland* till he was killed. William of Malmesbury wrote that the purpose was 'that the warlike example of man might inflame those who were about to fight'. Once more Scots, Irish, Welshmen and Arabs combine, this time to provide examples of versified war-whoops. Of Ireland, Tom Moore (1779–1852) provides a romantic picture:

> The minstrel boy to the war is gone,
> With his wild harp slung behind him;
> His father's sword he has girded on,
> In the ranks of death you will find him...

Like the pre-Islamic Arabs, the Irish regarded as indispensable the menaces and insults they hurled at their enemies in battle, and the type also existed in the Gaelic poetry of Scotland. Robert Burns records the tradition that the song 'Hey, now the day daws' was Robert the Bruce's march at the battle of Bannockburn in 1314.

The oldest surviving poetry to have been used in and before battles is that of the Psalms, none of which is later than 150 B.C., while some may date back to 1000 B.C. In France the Huguenots made a great battle hymn out of Psalm 68, in Theodore Beza's version; and the same Psalm ('Let God arise, let his enemies be scattered') was started before the Parliamentary troops attacked Leeds in 1643. This is only one of many records of the psalm-singing habit of the Roundheads on starting a fight (Winstock, pp. 12–15).

Songs of battle have smitten the air over most of the African continent. Some were designed to stir up a people to the point of declaring war and to prepare them for battle; others were an expression of high morale among the tribesmen; and yet a third group took the form of challenges for use in the field. As usual war was often a glorified form of cattle-raiding; and in the Abyssinia of the early nineteenth century poets were accustomed to ride before their chief when he went into battle, chanting loudly to encourage the troops (Chadwick 1940, III, p. 510). No glorification of war is cause for optimism about the future of humanity, but at least in this battle hymn from Uganda the motive is not disguised with patriotic paint:

> We are poured on the enemy like a mighty torrent:
> We are poured like a river in spate when the rain is in the mountains.
> The water hisses down the sands, swirling, exultant, and the tree that stood in its path is torn up quivering.
> It is tossed from eddy to eddy.
> We are poured on the enemy and they are bewildered.
> They look this way and that seeking escape, but our spears fall thickly about them...
> Let their villages be desolate, let them echo with the cry of mourning.
> We shall return rejoicing; and the lowing of cattle is in our ears.
> The lowing of innumerable cattle will make glad our hearts.
> (Trask 1, p. 101)

It is hundreds of years since the composers of patriotic songs themselves took up arms, and they have proved enough of a blight for real poets (like Siegfried Sassoon in 'Blighters') to wish them shot into silence. The most famous patriotic song in Sassoon's war was a music-hall number of 1914, 'Tipperary'; it achieved instant popularity, but by the end of the year the new armies were nauseated by it, and it was howled and whistled down by the soldiers themselves. Towards the end of the Second World War there was produced a song called 'M-O-N-T-G-O-M-E-R-Y, Montgomeree!' but its sentiments were far from those openly expressed about their commander by the rank and file.

Nationhood fostered

A tradition of poetry has aided the development of many small countries. When, in about 1200 B.C., over-population led the Greeks to emigrate to the islands and the Anatolian coast, Homer, 'their tribal encyclopaedia', preserved their identity and maintained continuity for them. Poetry also strengthened the Greek city-states in their resistance to the expansion of the Persian empire in the fifth century B.C., and it contributed to the cultural efflorescence of Athens in the same era. And later 'the national propaganda of the small nations of Europe has been largely in anthologies of poetry as the media best designed to protect them from the influences of "products of pure intelligence"' (Innis, p. 123). The Greeks lived in small units that allowed (for those who were not slaves) meetings of men for discussion, and we can read the result in the scanty remains of polemical verse by Alcaeus (following c. 620 B.C.), Tyrtaeus (seventh century B.C.) and Solon (c. 640 – c. 560 B.C.). But in northern Europe the inhabited areas were too large, the towns too small and few, and the distances too great to permit a rapid political development, with the result that it was the personality of the ruler himself that attracted fidelity and devotion. A cult of the leader took the place of local patriotism, and the poets who voiced the tribal loyalty had not the independence that was enjoyed by the Greeks. The kind of poetry engendered by the heroic code is exemplified in *The Battle of Maldon*, celebrating a defeat of the English by Danish invaders in an engagement that took place in Essex in August 991. The English leader is killed, and his warriors avenge their lord, lying dead beside him; death-or-glory loyalty is central to the poem. In another Anglo-Saxon verse-history, *The Battle of Brunanburh*, there is less emphasis on leaders and perhaps a hint of group feeling (Crossley-Holland, p. 40).

The words of the early Hebrew prophets, especially Isaiah, contributed to the Jewish sense of nationhood, and there are signs of national feeling in a poem like Psalm 18. But it is in Arabia that we have the most notable case of linguistic unity being attained, through poetry, before political unity. Arabic verse of the sixth century presented to its hearers an image larger than life; 'the passions and emotions and portrayals were idealized in content and expression – in content because it presented the Arabs to themselves as they would have liked to be, immeasurably bold and gallant and openhanded...' (Gibb, p. 25). The poetry preserved the memory of the past and thus provided a base for a new consciousness of Arab nationhood. As we have seen, the bards of Ireland helped to preserve the idea of freedom, and as a result they were the targets of severe acts passed by Elizabeth I. They were also the object of malignant attacks by Edmund Spenser, who brought against them quite unfounded charges of 'wickedness and vice'. In Wales too the poetic prophecies of the thirteenth and fourteenth centuries kept alive native traditions and exerted a tremendous influence over the minds of the people. English kings realised that these bards were a menace to them, and passed oppressive acts in the attempt to destroy the belief in the return of Arthur to liberate Wales. Edward I made a statute against 'Westours, Bards, Rhymers and others, Idlers and vagabonds lest by their invectives and lies they lead the people to mischief and burden the common people with their inquisitions' (Griffiths, p. 215); and later Henry IV made a similar law against the wandering minstrels, who by their 'divinations and lies were the cause of insurrection and rebellion in Wales' (Jusserand, p. 113).

Serbia was another small nation that found and fostered its sense of independence in oral poetry. The Kosovo cycle of ballads begins with a report in verse of a national disaster in a battle in 1389 against the Turks:

> They report an event of breath-taking importance to the Serbian folk. But they also insinuate remoter and immediate causes, interpret character, and view the event 'sub specie aeternitatis'. In the moment of overwhelming disaster they fortify the national spirit. They make it invincible since it is pure spirit, independent of places and persons, of strength or weakness, but living in words and rhythms that could not be forgotten. It is in these ballads that the Serbian nation truly lives...
> (Entwistle, p. 325)

A struggle that lasted five centuries allowed no scope for a written literature, and the simple ballad was the best medium for impro-visation. The spirit of resistance was embodied in chieftains and the outlaws who held the mountain passes, and 'beside the chief stood the poet, often a blind fiddler on a single string, able and ready to put deeds into words, to praise a hero, condemn a traitor, and lament a disaster'. In Greece too the mountain guerillas – 'klephts' – played a decisive part in winning the Greek war of independence, combining a life of plundering with resistance to the occupying Turks. Their ballads were hardly more than news bulletins about details of the struggle, but as long as they circulated the Greeks could taste freedom. 'The Greek klepht led a life of wild exhilaration in summer and bitter privation in winter; it was sure to end on the gallows, probably after torture; yet his "tragoudia" let him believe that Olympos and Kissabos talked of his exploits and convinced him that freedom is a glorious thing' (Entwistle, p. 14). In Finland the national poem *Kalevala*, predominantly handed on by oral tradition till it was written down in 1835 in its final form, was one of the most powerful of national epics and had great influence on nineteenth-century Finland. The Danes and the Swiss also nour-ished their feelings for independence on poetry, and in this century there is a late example in Somaliland. The most successful leaders of the Somalis have been poets such as Sheik Muhammad, who led the national uprising of 1900–20 to free his people from Christian rule. 'His brilliant success as a leader was closely connected with his consummate powers as a poet. He made extensive use of poetry as a political weapon...' (I. M. Lewis in Goody, p. 267).

Though the national imagination of England has found expres-sion more fully in poetry than in any other way, no specifically patriotic verse is worthy of note. Anglo-Saxon poetry may have instilled a feeling of respect for ancestral achievement, and the fifteenth century saw a heavy crop of nationalist verse. But poetry did not contribute much to the nationalism that we hear in the Agincourt 'carol' ('Our king went forth to Normandy') and in Shakespeare's *Henry V*; in fact the latter may be taken as a highly critical account of the events it is supposed to celebrate. Philip Sid-ney (1554–86) admired the border ballads, and Alexander Fletcher of Saltoun made his well-known remark about the influence of ballad-writers, but patriotic poetry has mattered little in England. The hymns of Isaac Watts praise the success of British arms in the defence of Protestantism; and Charles Dibdin (1745–1814) wrote patriotic songs to encourage recruitment in the Navy, for which Pitt rewarded him with a pension of two hundred pounds a year.

Propaganda

The aim of most of the poetry we have mentioned in this chapter
has been general – to induce a mood rather than attain an imme-
diate objective – and the poet could usually feel that he was speaking
for the community. He could even believe what he was saying. But
specifically propagandist verse shows some differences from the
poetry of eulogy, war and nationalism that we have been discussing.
It has a fairly short-term purpose, such as a change of government
or the relief of a wrong; the poet does not necessarily believe in what
he is saying – as often as not he is a hireling; and he is probably
working for an individual or group that is trying to win support,
rather than voicing popular feeling. Of course the division between
the kinds discussed above and the propagandist poetry we are now
to consider is not clear-cut.

The earliest propaganda – or at least politics – appears in frag-
ments of Greek verse, from a time when the poets' interests centred
on state or city. Solon (c. 640 – c. 560 B.C.), 'archon' of Athens, used
his verse to publicise views and policies which today would be fed
through the media or party literature. Eight lines survive of an elegy
in which he urged the Athenians to capture the nearby island of
Salamis; he is said to have disguised himself and recited it in public
at Athens. Other fragments attack the presumption of the ruling
class and explain his own policies. One such fragment runs:

> From men of power comes a city's ruin; so it falls under
> A despot – by their folly its folk to bondage go.
> Once a man is exalted, hard he grows to restrain.
> Already the time is on you to see that issue plain.

Solon may have been influenced by the example of the Spartan poet
Tyrtaeus, who was also a general; the burden of his fragmentary
verse is 'Go forward into battle and wager life for victory.' The
Spartans are said to have sung his songs on the march.

The conditions that helped Solon to produce his poems have not
recurred. His voice was that of an individual to whom verse was the
only way of saying something of importance to a small population.
The climate was genial; men had leisure to listen because slaves
did the work; leaders were expected to be skilled in verse. His
craftsmanship as a poet made him an effective politician, whose
policies were carried out because they were clearly impressed on
the memory of his hearers. Certainly Northern Europe produced
no parallel, though political propaganda in verse has had a long
history there. It flourished in Wales for hundreds of years from the

fifth and sixth centuries A.D., when the Welsh felt that their Christianity distinguished them from the Saxon savages. A bardic prophecy about the fate of the ancient races that once ruled Britain ran:

> Their God they shall praise,
> Their language they shall keep,
> Their land they shall lose except wild Wales.
> (Trevelyan, p. 53)

For centuries most of the prophetic material in Welsh poetry was political, and the ancient trust in magic and divination served to influence the minds of people in political crises. Long after the sixth-century prophets, Myrddin and Taliesin, had died, forged prophecies were attributed to them and used as a weapon in the long struggle against the English, for

> A bard composing a *darogan*, or vaticination, to foretell the victory of the Cymry in the war against the Saxons, had no more scruples about lying than the propaganda department of a modern state at war. The *daroganau* were essentially propaganda, and had tremendous influence on the course of history, because men believed in them, and acted on them.
> (Ifor Williams, p. 125)

Later, a twelfth-century poem supported the claim of St Davids to be independent of the see of Canterbury.

After the Dark Ages in Europe a new kind of oral poet appeared, in the troubadours. Musicians and poets, often well-born, they exercised their art, apparently for its own sake, from the end of the eleventh century to the end of the thirteenth. We know of four hundred of them, and two thousand six hundred of their songs have survived (Lang, p. 102). Though they performed for the entertainment of the ruling class they started with popular poetry in the vernacular, and they sent out jongleurs (performers rather than composers) to present their compositions to a particular person, court or district. Thus their songs of love and religion popularised the two ideas of the equality of men and of the nature of the nobility. In addition they produced 'sirventes', poems constructed like a love song, but concerned with social or political satire. These songs were useful to the noble employers of the troubadours, for broadcast by jongleurs and circulating from mouth to mouth they influenced general opinion. 'The patron therefore regarded the jongleur or minstrel as something more than an expensive luxury. He could make or mar a reputation; he could spread the fame of his employer' (Chaytor 1945, p. 132). Bishop Longchamp, for example, Chancellor of England during the absence of Richard Coeur de Lion, hired jongleurs to sing his praises in public; and in France of the thirteenth century the new middle class followed the feudal lords in hiring troubadours to sing their own praises. As well as acting as public relations officers, troubadours themselves took an interest in English politics to the end of the thirteenth century. The warlike Bertran de Born was a troublemaker and the evil genius of Henry II's time. Savaric, a fighter troubadour, was active for much of John's reign, and took part in war as well as writing. Another, Amoros dau Luc, urged Henry III to recover his lost territory in France. Jongleurs were also used sometimes as messengers where tact was needed.

Chivalry was the code of the courts at which the troubadours and others provided entertainment, and in the revival of chivalry in Europe after 1300, poets played a leading part imagining that they were returning to antiquity. We hear a good deal of the ideals of loyalty, courage and self-control said to have been contributed to civilisation by chivalry, and doubtless they were the fuel that impelled men to good deeds. At the same time, as Huizinga observed, they were a cloak for a whole world of violence and self-interest, and the actual contemporaries of Malory (d. 1470) 'would, at close quarters, have seemed to us singularly deficient in "chivalry" according to modern notions'. It is against this background of black and white and gray that we must consider the greatest poet of the Middle Ages, Chaucer. In *The Canterbury Tales* he describes the social changes of his time in concrete terms with humour and sympathy; the *Tales* present a lively picture of his day; the pilgrims from all levels of society, and their relations with each other, are portrayed with vigour. It is therefore arguable that 'in thus representing much lower classes (than those in *The Decameron*) as endowed with awareness and judgment, Chaucer communicates a much sharper and more political picture of the country' (Auerbach, p. 325). It is just this cognisance of classes below their own that was lacking in the court set for which Chaucer wrote, and whose 'élitist' philosophy he accepted, like other medieval story-tellers. The ethical qualities and the style of living which the poets celebrated were those that could be afforded only by the rich and well-born. In spite of this, 'it is the great achievement of Chaucer...in his *Wife of Bath's Tale* and *Franklin's Tale* to have extended and deepened the courtly concepts involved in the definition of a "gentil" man until their class-basis, their narrowly conceived aristocratic tenor, becomes irrelevant. Chaucer's courtliness...is Christian at root' (Stevens

1973, p. 58). On the other hand in a particular piece of glamorising in *The Knight's Tale* (lines 2495–2515) Chaucer seems to have been a trifle too enthusiastic about the equipment of fighting men, and it is difficult not to agree with the view that the verse is unfelt and that 'a poet such as Chaucer should have seen beyond – and seen through – this costly tinsel to its awful implications for his own generation' (Cottle, p. 52). At least one other poet of his time, his friend John Gower (?1330 – 1408), was much more critical; his poem *In Praise of Peace* shows us war as 'the source of all wrongs: the priest slain at mass, the virgin violated, the city ruined, the law nullified, poverty, toppled fortunes, the best endeavours forced to begin all over again' (Cottle, pp. 67, 8).

The Middle Ages produced a quantity of dissenting and protesting poetry, but it was not in general directed to a political or revolutionary end; it is much more interesting than propagandist verse. There are a few political efforts that come under this last head, following the form of the 'sirventes'. There is a poem of 1265 denouncing those who supported Henry III against the barons. Eleven poems by Laurence Minot (writing about 1352) have survived; all are war songs, savagely partisan but competently written for their purpose. He celebrated the triumphs of Edward III against the Scots in *The Battle of Bannockburn*, and other verses against the French and Spaniards give vent to his hatred and scorn for all foreigners, without a trace of what we call chivalrous feeling. There are also elegies on the deaths of Edward I and Edward III; the latter, neither ranting nor violent, has more claim to being a poem than the others just mentioned. In Brian Stone's version it begins:

> Ah dear God, how can it be
>   that all things waste and wear away?
> Friendship is but vanity,
>   And barely lasts the length of day.
> When put to proof, men go astray.
>   Averse to loss, to gain inclined:
> So fickle is their faith, I say,
>   That out of sight is out of mind.
> (*Medieval English Verse*, p. 114)

However the most substantial piece is *The Libel* (little book) *of English Policy*, which was written in 1436–7 and runs to 1,200 lines. It makes out the case for promoting overseas trade, fisheries and sea-power, especially in the Channel, and it is said to have influenced later naval developments. In one place at least it reads like a Navy League plea for spending more money on warships:

The end of bataille is pease sikerly (surely)
And power causeth pease finally.

The travelling entertainers, including minstrels and jongleurs, were always welcome in the Middle Ages; no feast or occasion of rejoicing was complete without them, and they performed at inns as well. Popular movements were the opportunity for satirical songs against the great, songs which were soon known by heart among the people; one such song encouraged the peasants of Kent when they rose against Henry VI. Moreover the minstrels showed their sympathy for liberal tendencies in their remodelling of romances recited in noble houses, as well as by their own songs. It looks as if the poets had some influence on social movements, to judge by the official repression they provoked:

> The authorities had other reasons for watching over singers and itinerant musicians...sowing sometimes strange disquieting doctrines under colour of songs. These were more than liberal and went at times so far as to recommend social or political revolt. The Commons in parliament denounced by name, at the beginning of the fifteenth century, the Welsh minstrels as fomentors of trouble and causes of rebellion. Their political songs encouraged the insurgents to resistance; and parliament, who bracketed them with ordinary vagabonds, knew well that it was not simply cut-purses whom it sent to prison...
> (Jusserand, p. 112)

Printed ballads, poets and popsongs in politics

With cheaper printing in the sixteenth century the wandering minstrel was replaced by the seller of broadsides (printed on one side) and broadsheets (printed on both sides), and verse as a political weapon began to be widely exploited. The ballads of which Autolycus gives a good account in *The Winter's Tale* were superficially loyal and conformist, in order not to fall foul of authority and its barbarous punishments, so that 'A most strange and trew Ballad of a monstrous child born in Southampton' concludes with this tacked-on petition:

> Lord save our gracious soverayne
>   Elizabeth by name,
> That long unto our comfort
>   She may both rule and raigne.

But in fact there was a political strain in these poems from the start and through their four hundred years of existence; hacks could be hired to lampoon your opponent, and both printers and writers tended to support the popular cause against authority, sometimes at risk to themselves. Many political ballads were printed, because they provided the best means of making some political or religious view known to the common man. For example, a poem against a profiteering landlord, who had turned out a widow to use her house as a corn-store, included this verse:

> And filled it full in harvest time
> With good red wheat and corne,
> To keep it safely from the poore
> Until there came a yeare,
> That farmers might oppress them all,
> And make all victuals dear.
> (*Shakespeare's England*, 2, p. 522)

Except for his education, Thomas Deloney (c. 1543 – c. 1600) was typical of the Elizabethan ballad-maker, selling his wares to tradesmen, journeymen and apprentices. He wrote on many subjects, but when in 1596 he lamented the shortage of corn (in a lost ballad) he was summoned to appear before the Mayor, because the poem was thought capable of provoking a breach of the peace. As a strong patriot and Protestant, he had a virulent hatred for Spain and the Catholic Church, and was not above cooking up an atrocity or two in his

> A new Ballet
> of the strange and most cruell Whippes which the Spanyards
> had prepared to whippe and torment English men
> and women: *which were found and taken*
> *at the overthrow of certain of the*
> *Spanish Shippes*, in July
> last past, 1588.

With sixteen lines on the whips for men, and another sixteen on those for women, the ballad is thin stuff compared with the offerings of the media today, but it was a beginning. The social, psychological and industrial conditions which Northcliffe exploited three centuries later did not exist, and in his *The Winning of Cales* Deloney could write a patriotic poem that is lively and inoffensive.

As well as for political and nationalist propaganda the printed ballad served commercial interests, as a useful means of influencing the public, like the financial columns of a newspaper. Thus there were ballads aimed at investors, about commercial ventures overseas, and trade with the New World and the East. A broadsheet of 1612, called *London's Lotterie*, offered the chance of winning riches, though the main fund was to be spent on exploiting Virginia.

(Similarly in the eighteenth century there were ballads urging investment in overseas trade, and at least one denouncing the South Sea Bubble.)

Only occasionally can we be sure that a political ballad achieved its purpose. One example, though, of a poem, or at least a song that, like 'The Marseillaise', made history is *Lilliburlero*, called in its day *A New Song*, and with words by Thomas Warton. In 1686 James II had assembled on Hounslow Heath an army of thirteen thousand to over-awe London, and began to put Catholics into key posts in England. James then sent the troops into the country and introduced Irish Catholics into English regiments, in order to secure enforcement of his Declaration of Indulgence. The song was enormously popular with English soldiers, and when it spread all over the country James escaped abroad, so that the author could boast that with it he had 'sung a King out of three kingdoms'. The verses are imagined as being spoken by an Irishman who congratulates a fellow-countryman on the coming triumph of Popery, so they attempt to reproduce an Irish accent. The words are poor and nearly everything depends on the catchy tune (Pinto and Rodway, pp. 115, 610).

Few political ballads have been given such strong testimonials as those just cited, and we cannot be sure how much influence the ballads in general exerted. That their power was feared by the authorities is clear from the laws passed and oppressive measures taken against them. In the middle of the sixteenth-century religious struggle the inflammatory potential of the songs caused the Act of 1543 to be passed against them, and it was much invoked while it lasted, because 'forward and malicious minds, intending to subvert the true exposition of scripture, have taken upon them, by printed ballads, rhymes, etc., subtilly and craftily to instruct his highness' people, and specially the youth of this his realm untruly'. And in Scotland in 1579 two men were hanged for writing satirical ballads. In the next century, under the Commonwealth, the singing of ballads was prohibited, though the poets were evidently pleased by Cromwell's dismissal of the Rump of the Long Parliament:

> Brave Oliver came to the House like a sprite.
>   His fiery face struck the Speaker dumb;
> 'Begone,' said he, 'you have sate long enough,
>   Do you think to sit here till Doomsday come?'
> (Trevelyan, p. 311)

As late as the middle of the nineteenth century, in Ireland, the printers of ballads were still being imprisoned, and the singers harassed and jailed by the police when a situation deteriorated.

Verse has continued as a propaganda medium to our own time, with its sordid television jingles, but probably with less efficacy as the audience split. It was most exploited for political purposes in the seventeenth century, when poetry was read, respected and had not entirely lost its place as maid of all work. Writers like John Cleveland, John Taylor and Sir John Birkenhead wrote poems as political weapons against Parliament; so did the leading writer of broadsheets, Matthew Parker (d. 1656). The death of Cromwell in 1658 sparked off an explosion of spiteful ballads, and there were plenty of election ballads in the Stuart period, written by established poets rather than journalists. On the other hand Andrew Marvell (1621–78) is said in his later years to have written anti-royalty poems that 'were powerful instruments in the struggle between the "country party" and the court'. These are lively, if of no great merit, such as *A Dialogue between the Two Horses* (in statues of Charles I and II); however, Marvell's most recent editor has expelled the whole lot from her edition.

But (if we leave out Milton, who died in 1674) the greatest poet of the late seventeenth century was John Dryden (1631–1700), of whose work all that is still admired was undertaken for political ends. He experimented with a political play (*Amboyna* in 1673) and continued with others of the kind and an opera, *Albion and Albanius*, the latter a tedious glorification of Charles II. But it was this king's alarm at the resurgence of anti-Romanism that gave Dryden his chance as a political propagandist, just at the time when the theatre had ceased to be profitable and his pay as Laureate was interrupted. Having attacked the Catholics with the *Spanish Fryar* in 1681, Dryden now changed sides and wrote the anti-Whig *Absalom and Achitophel*, an extremely clever show-piece, with brilliant character sketches like that of Buckingham:

> In the first rank of these did Zimri stand,
> A man so various that he seemed to be
> Not one, but all Mankind's epitome;
> Stiff in opinions, always in the wrong,
> Was everything by starts and nothing long;
> But, in the course of one revolving moon,
> Was chymist, fiddler, statesman and buffoon;
> Then all for women, painting, rhyming, drinking,
> Beside ten thousand freaks that died in thinking.
> Blest madman, who could every hour employ
> With something new to wish or to enjoy!
> Railing and praising were his usual themes,
> And both, to show his judgment, in extremes;
> So over violent or over civil

That every man with him was God or Devil.
In squandering wealth was his peculiar art;
Nothing went unrewarded, but desert.
Beggared by fools, whom still he found too late,
He had his jest and they had his estate.
(I, 544–62)

The poem was an immediate success, 'for while Dryden unhappily
pandered too slavishly and too completely to the taste of his time,
he had the redeeming merit of carrying to perfection every literary
style he attempted...Without models, without precursors, he cre-
ated the political poem, and at the first attempt produced a mas-
terpiece' (Beljame, p. 169). Also to order Dryden wrote *The Medal,
a Satire against Sedition* and a Part II of *Absalom and Achitophel.*
Another propaganda piece, the pro-Catholic *Hind and the Panther,*
was less successful. Dryden was a more competent writer than the
literary hirelings of his time, and so was very effective politically,
and correspondingly well rewarded. It may be that the tasks he was
set brought out the best in him; he never showed signs of employing
his talent to less ignoble ends than those set by the demands of a
fashionable circle and its leader.

In the second half of the seventeenth century pamphlets were
beginning to oust printed ballads, and the demands for the latter
continued to lessen in the eighteenth century, though the oral
tradition of song and ballad still flourished. It is significant that
though Swift (1667–1745) wrote both political verse (in the popular
style) and political prose, it was the latter that he relied on most and
proved the more effective. His essays in ballad form ('To the tune
of...') are vigorous but hardly incisive. Two of Swift's contempor-
aries, John Gay (1685–1732) and Matthew Prior (1664–1721), were
among the century's poets who gained advancement by their politi-
cal poems and dedications to political figures. This in fact was the
poet's progress most characteristic of the period; apart from Pope,
the first author to make a handsome living solely on the sales of
his poetry, those eighteenth-century writers who attained a position
in society managed this by their political activity and not as in the
past by securing the patronage of the court. Beljame gives the
reason. The eager haste to attract and hold the loyalty of authors
was fuelled by powerful political motives; it was urgently necessary

> for the very existence of any Government after the Revolution, to
> ensure the support of public opinion, to keep in touch with the nation,
> and to influence it from day to day...It was imperative that the work
> of discussion, already accomplished in Parliament, should be carried
> on in the world outside...The influence nowadays exerted by Par-

liamentary speeches then belonged solely to the Press, which meant not only newspapers and pamphlets but every literary work, and even verses handling political ideas. It has been justly said that Addison's *Campaign* is merely a rhymed *Gazette*.
(Beljame, p. 324)

But things were different by the end of the century. The functions of prose and verse were sharply differentiated; prose itself had been improved according to the prescription of the Royal Society, while verse in the form of the heroic couplet, orderly, precise and almost simple in its habitual balancing of opposites, reflected the rational movement of contemporary thought. As the nineteenth century advanced, the industrial era destroyed the conditions in which poetry of a popular kind was readily produced and enjoyed; no one could now usefully employ the printed ballad as a means of getting a political message across to a wide public. No taste for poetry could survive among an over-worked and half-starved proletariat of slum-dwellers, deprived of health, leisure, traditional entertainment and rewarding work by the mines and factories. Long hours of depressing toil and sub-animal living conditions had their brutalising effect. The taste for violence and atrocity, already evident in the Elizabethan broadsheet, was now developed at the expense of other preferences. In the middle of the century Henry Mayhew, as so often, supplies the evidence; his interview with a 'running patterer' – one who sold lurid ballads by shouting their titles in the street – throws light on the trend. The man, who was born about 1812, said, among much else:

> There's nothing beats a stunning good murder, after all. Why, there was Rush – I lived on him for a month or more.... On the morning of the execution we beat all the regular newspapers out of the field; for we had the full, true and particular account down, you see, by our own express, and that can beat anything they can publish; for we gets it printed several days afore it comes off.   (Quennell, p. 25)

He sold to the gentry as well as to the poor, and found anti-papal ballads profitable, though his staple was accounts of 'horrid and inhuman murders', committed by 'fiends in human form'. The sales of some of his lines – he started with the first on our list – are said to have been:

1828	Corder ('Maria Marten')	1,166,000 copies
1840	Greenacre	1,650,000 copies
1840	Courvoisier	1,666,000 copies
1849	the Mannings	2,500,000 copies
1849	Rush's murder	2,500,000 copies

With a reduced readership and a beginning of stratification in taste, there was little opening for political verse. Shelley himself said in the Preface to *Prometheus Unbound*, 'Didactic poetry is my abhorrence; nothing can be equally well expressed in prose that is not tedious and supererogatory in verse'; and his finest political writing – among the most moving of the whole century – is his prose *An Address to the People on the Death of the Princess Charlotte, 1817*. He may have discounted his own near-political poetry – the sonnet 'An old, mad, blind, despised and dying king', *The Masque of Anarchy* ('I saw Murder come this way/He had a mask like Castlereagh') and *Song to the Men of England* – but he could not help being an influence on the Chartists, who flourished from 1837 to 1848, setting out their demands in the six points of the People's Charter. Like the Ranters of the seventeenth century who sang hymns at their convivial meetings, they adopted some of the forms of Christianity; thus there was a Chartist church and Chartist hymns. When a young member died in prison there was a huge attendance at his funeral and a hymn by one of the Chartist poets, J. H. Bramwich, was sung. The first verse ran:

> Great God! Is this the patriot's doom!
> Shall they who dare defend the slave
> Be hurled within a prison's gloom,
> To fit them for an early grave...
> (Gammage, p. 214)

When Dickens attended a strike meeting at Preston in 1854, the proceedings opened with this hymn:

> Assembled beneath thy broad blue sky,
> To thee, O God, thy children cry.
> The needy creatures on thee call,
> For thou art great and good to all.
>
> Thy bounty smiles on every side,
> And no good thing hast thou denied;
> But men of wealth and men of power,
> Like locusts, all our gifts devour.
>
> Awake, ye sons of toil! nor sleep
> While millions starve, while millions weep;
> Demand your rights; let tyrants see
> You are resolved that you'll be free.
> (*Household Words*, 11 Feb. 1854)

This was evidently written by an admirer of Shelley who had read a great many hymns, and while it might do for singing at meetings of the faithful it would hardly make converts.

The street ballad as a medium for political matter was dead; the attempts of the reformers to provide their own poetry used literary signposts (Burns, Byron, Shelley, Cowper) that led nowhere. When we come to the specifically political verse of established poets, most of what we find is best forgotten. Tennyson (1804–92) for example published three patriotic poems (e.g. *Hands All Round*), when there was talk of a French invasion; and again when anti-French feeling was running high he published *Rifleman Form!* in *The Times* of 9 May 1859. The third of its four verses runs:

> Let your reforms for a moment go!
> Look to your butts, and take good aims!
> Better a rotten borough or so
> Than a rotten fleet and a city in flames!
> Storm, Storm, Riflemen form!
> Ready, be ready against the storm!
> Riflemen, Riflemen, Riflemen form!

Hopkins (1844–89) needed readers badly, and his anxiety to escape from solitude must excuse his 'a patriotic song for soldiers' ('What shall I do for the land that bred me') in which the conventional sentiments of 1885 are conveyed in a style almost of self-parody. About the same time William Morris wrote his very different 'March of the Workers' but it was already old fashioned, tired and at the end of the literary cul-de-sac. W. S. Blunt (1840–1922), an upper-class diplomat, was strong-minded and clear-sighted within a short range. He campaigned against imperialism and industrialism, when they were being extolled by the poets of the establishment, in a quantity of political verse that deserves a second reading. About 1900 he wrote (in *Satan Absolved*):

> These Lords who boast Thine aid at their high civic feasts,
> The ignoble shouting crowds, the prophets of their Press,
> Pouring their daily flood of bald self-righteousness,
> Their poets who write big of the 'White Burden'. Trash!
> The White Man's Burden, Lord, is the burden of his cash.

The poet referred to was Kipling (1865–1936), whose emotionalism and loud-mouthed imperialism were extremely popular; and the poem concerned was *The White Man's Burden*, an effusion of nauseating smugness. (For sheer viciousness though, he never surpassed his anti-suffrage *The Female of the Species*.) Lastly in this section on nineteenth-century propagandist poetry we should mention *The Ballad of Reading Gaol* by Oscar Wilde (1844–1900). It was not a political poem, but it seems very likely that it was effective in opening the eyes of society to the horrors of its penal system, and it suggests that if Wilde had been able to transcend rotting ideas of life and art he might have become the poet of the social consciousness of his age.

Kipling's poems had a large circulation, because they expressed so well the mood of the mob; his large sales were not evidence of a poetry-reading public. This had begun to decline somewhere about 1880, when leather-bound editions of the established poets began to decorate middle-class bookshelves, and it has never recovered. As for the literature of the masses: folk song was destroyed by industrial civilisation, and by the end of the century was not much more than a memory, as we gather from the work of Cecil Sharp and novels such as *Adam Bede* and *Under the Greenwood Tree*. The printed broadsheets, originally developed from the oral ballad, finally petered out, to be replaced for a time by music-hall songs which, with their realism, often sardonic humour and closeness to their audience, were good entertainment value as long as the theatres lasted. They did not express impossible aspirations; and if the voice of the singers was sentimental their feet were on the ground. Writing over half a century ago about Marie Lloyd, T. S. Eliot made the point that her superiority was a moral superiority: 'It was her understanding of the people and sympathy with them, and the people's recognition of the fact that she embodied the virtues which they genuinely most respected in private life, that raised her to the position she occupied at her death' (Eliot 1932, p. 406). And after some acute and prophetic observations on class and music-hall comedians, in whom the lower class found 'the expression and dignity of their own lives', he foretold that all classes would 'drop into the same state of protoplasm as the bourgeoisie'. For all the brilliant expertise that goes into the slick and shiny package in which our entertainment is brought to us, the performer and writer cannot have a finger on the pulse of the audience, which in its turn can no longer supply its own essential participation in the performance. The content of entertainment is now made up, not of what is wanted by an audience, but of its third and fourth preferences, representing the widest range of material that it can tolerate without switching off.

A branch of commerce which conducts operations to secure and maintain willing purchasers of its offerings, by influencing thought, feeling and behaviour, is propagandist. It is from this viewpoint that we must consider pop culture. This is the section of our consumer civilisation which provides a culture for children, and shows teenagers how to hand over their billion a year spending money. The process starts early; in the States 'even five-year-olds sing beer commercials over and over again with gusto...moppets not only sing the merits of advertised products but do it with the vigor displayed by the most raptly enthusiastic announcers, and do it all day long "at no extra cost to the advertiser"' (Packard, p. 159). The life and character of the teenager are settled by the goods, services and processed experience he is induced to buy, all requiring a minimum of effort – Wendell Johnson noted that some of his clients in a university speech clinic would 'do no drills, perform no exercises, read no books, carry out no recommendations' (Rosenberg and White, p. 394), because they seemed to expect that having come to the right speech clinic their stuttering would somehow magically go away. Charles Parker has shown how difficult it is for the teenager to break out; he is self-enslaved, because pop culture manipulates what is there, controls what is real in people's response, so that this becomes the very opposite of what they intended, in a way it is hard for them to perceive (Abbs, p. 141).

What is offered we can see readily in the pop lyrics. First and last, sex in the idealised, romantic, mendacious pop style:

> Dream, dream, baby;
>> Dream, dream, baby;
>>> How long must I dream?
>> Dream, dream, baby;
>>> You can make my dreams come true.

and

> Some day he'll see
> That he was meant for me.

The difficulties of adjustment, earning a living and making a home do not enter the magic world, where there are always

> Blue skies, shining on me;
> Nothing but blue skies do I see...

and romantic landscapes and occupations:

> The whispering pines of Nevada
> Are whispering 'I love you'...

> Shepherd of the hills, I hear you calling...

Things sometimes go wrong:

> I thought that I was yours and you were mine,
> But you were someone else's all the time,

and disenchantment is the result:

> Now, since my baby left me
> I've found a new place to dwell,

Down at the end of Lonely Street
At Heartbreak Hotel.
I'm so lonely,
I'm so lonely,
I'm so lonely,
That I could die.

Reality is distorted; problems are disguised; solutions are false. This irrelevant and partial picture arouses expectations that can lead only to frustration, instead of an accommodation with and a grasp of life. The adolescent is offered no help with growing up, no notion of the duties and responsibilities that love brings. In fact the move into adulthood seems to be thought of like death, since mention of it is avoided. The poetry of pre-literate people on the other hand helped young people to make the passage to adulthood; the delicacy of feeling and the good sense found in English folk song are paralleled in the songs of primitive Indians and many other peoples. In early China antiphonal songs by girls and boys were sung at the seasonal festivals of peasant communities; people emerged from the monotony of private life for these solemn occasions and introduced their young to public and sexual life simultaneously. Moreover pop and its parasitic magazines make things more difficult by creating and fostering family tensions:

People try to put us down
Just because we get around
Things they do look awful cold
Hope I die before I get old

Why don't you all f-f-f-fade away
Don't try and dig what we all say...

The argument that songs of protest have appeared in the popularity charts carries no weight; the pop operators never fail to exploit and defuse anything with life in it. A sympathetic observer of pop writes: 'Perhaps the operators' biggest crime is just this: that by their refusal to discriminate, their reluctance to criticise, they have helped create a shock absorber between a cosy, comfortable pop scene and a rather different world' (Mabey, p. 131). But of course no serious protest could survive processing by the pop medium; diversity would not pay, for it is much easier and more profitable to sell fifty thousand discs by one group rather than five thousand each by ten groups. Moreover a discriminating audience would be a threat to profitability. Radio Luxembourg's Station Policy is explicit:

(The following are not permitted.) References, jokes or songs con-

cerning any reigning Monarch, Members of Parliament, the Cabinet or any branch of Her Majesty's Government or any other government, politics or political figures, subjects that may be regarded as having an indirect political significance nationally or internationally, religion, other advertisers, physical deformities or any other reference, joke or song considered to be in questionable taste.
(Mabey, p. 117)

It does not matter much, therefore, whether one believes that the output of pop culture is conditioned by the innate conventions of the media or sees in it a deliberate measure of social control – as does Charles Parker in the eloquent chapter already cited. The result is the same: powerful propaganda is emitted, accepted, and absorbed. One cannot help recalling the part played by popular singers in the emancipation of the people in the Middle Ages.

Tennyson, W. E. Henley and Kipling in the nineteenth century all published political poetry, and the result in each case was the same: the poems were the worst they ever wrote. On the other hand Goethe refused an invitation to write anti-French propaganda. In this century we have the example of Mayakovsky, who carried on poetry purely as a trade, announcing that he had established a 'word workshop' and so could supply 'promptly and on easy terms' revolutionary poetry in any quantity desired. He wrote poems which he recited in public, and it is said that his large build, resonant voice and command of rhythm made them splendid propaganda. But the conflict between the desire to write real poetry and the compulsion to write public pieces for the benefit of the Russian state was too much, and he committed suicide (Bowra 1966, p. 110). As Brecht wrote:

> Art is not capable of turning artistic ideas dreamed up in offices into art. Only boots can be made to measure. Moreover, the taste of many people who are highly educated from the political point of view is perverted and therefore of no importance whatsoever... It is not the business of the Marxist-Leninist party to organize poetic production the way it would set up a chicken farm. If it does so, poems will all be as much alike as one egg is like another.
> (Arvon, p. 109)

6

Dissent and protest

Ancient China, Greece and Israel

When the poet was the mouthpiece of his society there was no outlet for dissent, and protest could be voiced only against the gods. And then it would be the complaint of the group; oral poetry, even when it sounds a clear individual note, is not marked by self-absorption. When leaders and classes and warfare were evolved and became institutions, causes of protest were generated, and the sound of it has never been silenced since. As early as the tenth century B.C. the unknown Jewish writers of the book of Samuel deemed kings to be a dispensable luxury, to judge from the words they put into the mouth of the aged patriarch. In reply to the insistent requests of the Israelites for a king: 'We will have a king over us, that we also may be like all the nations; and that our king may judge us, and go out before us, and fight our battles,' Samuel warned them plainly that a king would conscript their sons as soldiers and servants, exact forced labour from men and women ('he will take your daughters to be confectionaries, and to be cooks, and to be bakers'), confiscate their farms and give them to his favourites, and extort tributes and service of every kind; 'and ye shall cry out in that day because of your king which ye shall have chosen'. Thus resentment against military service and forced labour was felt and recorded early in the history of civilisation. A soldier of the Chou dynasty in China expressed his feelings (about 500 B.C.):

> When we went away
> The millets were in flower.
> Now that we are returning
> The snow falls and the roads are all mire.
> The king's business was very difficult
> And we had not leisure to rest.
> Did we not long to return?
> But we were in awe of the orders in the tablets.
> (Woolley and Hawkes, p. 818)

Later, during the building of the Great Wall, the emperor Tsin Chi Huang was hated and feared by the pressed labourers; people died,

were executed, lost their families. In the third century B.C. a widow
protested in a folk song:

> With flowers blooming and birds singing,
> Spring is here calling us to visit friends far and near.
> Other women are accompanied by their husbands and sons,
> Poor me, I shall go to the wall where my husband's bones bear.
> Great Wall! Great Wall! If you can save us from enemies,
> Why not save first our dear ones?
> (Dundes, p. 311)

As we have seen, kings and tyrants realised the value of poets in
maintaining their authority, disseminating edicts and propaganda,
and whipping up their subjects to kill and be killed. Thus we have
an enormous volume of poor quality verse, produced for favour
or reward, and directed to specific ends. On the other hand we have
the complaints of individuals, roughly divisible into satire, in which
a writer reprimands the evils of his day by reference to an ac-
knowledged standard, and purely personal protests, which may also
voice the feelings of many of the poet's fellow-men. Of course
dissenters and protesters have often met with difficulty in making
themselves heard, and with trouble when they succeeded; as Jesus
said, when he returned to preach in the synagogue of his own
village and met with an indignant reaction, 'A prophet is not
without honour, save in his own country.' In the early days of many
countries writing was reserved to priests and the ruling class, and
even when there was no ban on writing, the people with leisure and
writing material were the clergy, who were not always disposed to
criticise the order of things in which they flourished. Cheap printing
eventually supplied the means of expressing complaints at large, but
it frequently evoked repression by the authorities; and this is still
with us. A popular ballad like *Lilliburlero* could spread with enor-
mous rapidity and precipitate the fall of an unwanted king; Swift
could influence public opinion with no more material resources than
a back-street printer could lay on; but today, to achieve a comparable
impact, the protester would need more hours and space on the
media than millions could buy, even if his message could survive
the normal processing. The conditioning of output and audience
at present makes the world safe for the entertainment industry and
its nitwit personalities.

The class of verse we are discussing includes some of the world's
finest poetry from most periods and places. The Greek Hesiod
(probably eighth century B.C.) was one of the last poets to write
all-purpose verse: myth, moral precept, philosophy, religion all in

one poem. In his *Works and Days* he gave advice for each season of the farmer's year, but his main purpose may have been to complain of his brother's conduct over the unfair division of his father's farm. His work reflected the struggle of small peasants to make a living from the soil; he urged them to work hard and fill their barns, and he opposed the ideas of justice and honest toil to the pride of status shown by the local aristocrats. He was no radical, and his solution was conservative. He did not wish to change the social structure of his day, but to reform it according to moral standards. This concern with justice as the central problem of existence puts him at the head of a line to Aeschylus and the other writers of tragedy (Finley 1962, p. 164). Other elements in his work persisted; in the seventh and sixth centuries he was followed by other protesting poets, some of them expressing the complaints of the privileged against nouveaux riches and the discontent of the people; and the versifying of agricultural technology went on for two thousand years and more.

Hesiod today is of historic rather than literary interest; he is not a rewarding poet. But the book of Job (about 450 B.C.) is a very different matter, especially if we accept W. B. Stevenson's view that the poem of Job is enclosed in the two halves of a prose folk tale. In this way we can more clearly see that the author was a great poet, using ideas and attitudes then in circulation and traditional methods to present the moving and powerful complaint of a suffering, helpless individual against a cruel and arbitrary god – who for all his boasted omnipotence seems to need the worship and admiration of men. In his protest against the evils of life on earth Job stands for the human race; in several places he mentions the misfortunes of others. The poem is too long for much quotation, but for those who wish to read a coherent version, this is how Stevenson presents the Authorised Version, in three cycles of dramatic dialogue between the protagonist and his friends. (Though the speeches of Job are of much greater interest than the replies, his friends are not just aunt sallies; see chapter 4: 12–17 and chapter 22.)

Cycle 1: chapters 3–11

Job curses his birth (note his mention of prisoners and captives), makes clear the reasons for his bitter complaint, and addresses himself to God as the great destroyer.

Cycle 2: chapters 12–20

Job shows that all is not well with the world; God's power is shown in destructive and subversive acts. He challenges God to come before an imaginary court.

Chapter 19 is a 'climax of wonderful power and pathos'; Job is a wronged and deserted man, who expresses his supreme desire (which is not fulfilled) for a redeemer.

Cycle 3: chapters 21–7, 29–31 (note the description of the happy pagans in chapter 21)

Job speaks for the downtrodden and wretched, who cannot speak for themselves, and in chapter 31 states his claim to goodness (in the form of a negative confession like that in the Egyptian *Book of the Dead*). Job's sufferings have not ended; he is still a victim of the wicked; his claim to happiness has been rejected and the evil of the world has not been explained. But he is no longer a rebel.

Shelley's words (in *A Defence of Poetry*) may be applied to Job: 'A man, to be greatly good, must imagine intensely and comprehensively; he must put himself in the place of another and of many others; the pains and pleasures of his species must become his own.' The poem is of even intensity, so it is not readily quotable by way of illustration; and other passages might serve as well as this extract from chapter 3:

> For now should I have lain still and been quiet;
> I should have slept, then had I been at rest:
> With kings and counsellers of the earth,
> Which built desolate places for themselves;
> Or with princes that had gold,
> Who filled their houses with silver:
> Or as an hidden untimely birth I had not been;
> As infants which never saw light.
>
> There the wicked cease from troubling;
> And there the weary be at rest.
> There the prisoners are at ease together;
> They hear not the voice of the oppressor.
> The small and great are there;
> And the servant is free from his master.
>
> Wherefore is light given to him that is in misery,
> And life unto the bitter in soul;
> Which long for death, but it cometh not;
> And dig for it more than for hid treasures;
> Which rejoice exceedingly,
> And are glad, when they can find the grave?

Why is light given to a man whose way is hid,
And whom God hath hedged in?
For my sighing cometh before I eat,
And my roarings are poured out like the waters.

For the thing which I greatly feared is come upon me,
And that which I was afraid of is come unto me.
I was not in safety, neither had I rest, neither was I quiet;
Yet trouble came.

The book of Job stands by itself. Greek literature has nothing to compare with it, for however much we may admire Athenian tragedy we can never forget that the plays were chosen by the state for performance on official occasions at public expense. The conditions were restrictive, even if they were not felt to be so. Euripides is a possible exception: 'It is difficult to read [his] portrayal of the pitiful aftermath of the fall of Troy in the *Trojan Women* (415 B.C.) without connecting it with the brutal Athenian conquest of Melos in the previous year' (Baldry, p. 78). There were Greek satirists, but apart from the comedies of Aristophanes their work has not survived in quantity. Roman satire developed from the original 'satura', a disjointed series of action songs and musical sketches without a plot, but not enough of the earlier satirists, Ennius and Varro, is extant to make it considerable. It is different with Juvenal (*fl.* A.D. 100), whose sixteen satires have survived and were profoundly influential in the Middle Ages. They are excellent documents for the rottenness of imperial Rome, and they pull no punches, but they are the bitter products of personal rancour. Dryden translated five of them, and the third and fourth satires gave Samuel Johnson the models for his two great poems, *London* and *The Vanity of Human Wishes*.

Christian and medieval

For its first four hundred years or so Christianity was a working-class movement, consciously puritanical in opposition to the luxury and grossness of the pagan ruling class, and attaching importance to work as an honourable occupation – there was a long list of trades prohibited to Christians. When it became the official religion of the empire (after A.D. 313), these attitudes began to change; there was less hostility to the arts, and the first great writers of hymns, like Prudentius and Paulinus, wrote their still-current poems. But in England it was not till the fourteenth century that Christian verse sounded the notes of protest which were maintained for hundreds of years and became a characteristic of English poetry. The popular and indigenous character of English literature in that century is reflected in a practical sense of what is right in men's dealings with each other; and the moralistic satire of the time had an instinct for what was socially desirable:

> Though Christian and even Biblical in origin, this ethical feeling adapted itself readily to actual experience and had nothing in common with a theoretical system...such as we find in Dante. The view of social conditions that emerges from the English literature of the time is at once practical and Christian, and often the two aspects converge in the application of Biblical object lessons to current situations. This was the first appearance of a morality both Christian and social, aimed at an earthly society that would thrive in justice and freedom.
>
> (Auerbach, p. 326)

Justice and freedom being very scarce commodities, it was natural that the gap between the ideal and the actual should give rise to complaints – about corruption, lawyers, and church, money-lenders, wealthy people. The complaints were shaped largely by men who had emerged from the poor and lowly, and they wrote for a popular audience of peasants in an endless struggle with their lords. The poor were becoming more vocal and perhaps a little more literate. When Robert Manning translated Langtoft's chronicle into English, early in the fourteenth century, he said he was writing for the uneducated. And later in the century manor houses were broken up and the retainers discharged, so that the minstrels found a new audience that welcomed their severe criticisms of the establishment (Lloyd, p. 114). At the same time folk songs became a vehicle of protest, so that while the nobility and gentry enjoyed 'gestes' and *Sir Gawayne* the lower orders preferred stories of robbers and rebels such as Robin Hood. Two of the ballads about the latter, the *Litel Geste of Robin Hood* and *Robin Hood and the Potter*, are mentioned in Piers Plowman and are therefore of great antiquity. This folk hero and his idealised community were the subject of many ballads which from the closing decades of the fourteenth century expressed the feeling of rebelliousness against feudalism; and his popularity may be judged from what Latimer related in his sixth sermon before Edward VI. He had waited for half-an-hour outside a church where he was to preach, when a man came up to him and said, 'Sir, this is a busy day with us, we cannot hear you; it is Robin Hood's day.' Another righter of wrongs who took to the woods was Gamelyn, whose deeds are related in *The Tale*, of about 1350. Summoned to court, he throws the judge over the bar, and has judge, sheriff and jurors hanged. Then he wins the king's approval, makes a good marriage and lives happily ever after. Such a romance would have fulfilled the wishes of the poor, suffering from the Black Death, the Hundred Years' War and the exploitation and repression that led to the Peasants' Revolt of 1381.

The sermons, Piers Plowman and Robin Hood

But the great channel of complaint in the Middle Ages was the vernacular sermon, a powerful influence on English literature even up to the seventeenth century. J. W. Blench gives this example of the way in which a poet echoed a sermon; Latimer's expansion of John 7: 47 ran: 'What, ye brain-sick fools, ye hoddy-pecks, ye doddy-pouls, ye huddes, do you believe him? Are you seduced also?' From its early days the Christian sermon seems to have used popular poetry and homely examples; both St Augustine and St Bernard are said to have used rhymes. At the beginning of the thirteenth century Stephen Langton found that his hearers liked popular proverbs and little jingles that impressed some pious thought upon the memory, and Latin sermons had often used small sets of rhymed verse as mnemonics. The vernacular sermon and the rhymed homily offered much more than religious instruction: 'at a time when the ability to read with understanding and to write much more than a personal letter was confined for the most part to the ruling minority, in a society which was otherwise oral in its communications, the preaching parson was the great link between the illiterate mass and the political, technical and educated world' (Laslett, p. 9).

The sermons in English were racy and colloquial, bringing abstract truths to light with vivid concrete examples and enlivened with proverbs and snatches of verse. 'The pulpit... was quite unable to escape a general contagion which involved alike the song of the minstrel, the cries of the street, and even such prosaic necessities as medical receipts' (Owst 1926, p. 271). There were also completely rhymed sermons, which were much to the taste of congregations. Though these were attacked, notably by Pierre de Baume in the first quarter of the fourteenth century, they fitted in with the persistent English metrical tradition in the vernacular literature of religious instruction; on feast days and Sundays metrical lives of the saints and expositions of the gospel were read out in churches. An attitude of complaint against injustice, oppression and the luxury of the rich was common; and the preaching friars, Franciscans and Dominicans, were always critical of the worldliness of some priests. A metrical *Sermon on the Feast of Corpus Christi* denounces the whole-salers who exploit the poor by making a corner in grain to push up the price:

> He buyeth corn again the year
> And keepeth it till it be dear.
> 'Thereof he doth wysliche,
> If he depart it skilfulliche.'
> Nay forsooth thinketh he nought
> To poore men parten ought;
> Bought he never so good cheap
> He reweth nought the poore weep;
> He reckoned not how all the world gode,
> So that his owne profit were goode.
> (Scattergood, p. 333)

The most eloquent of protesting voices was that of William Langland in his *Vision of Piers the Plowman*, a poem immensely popular in its day, to judge by the extent to which it supplied catchwords to the political movements of the time, and by the survival of no fewer than forty-five early manuscripts. In it the poet has a marvellous dream, and sees a field full of folk in which all classes are busily engaged in their ordinary occupations. But corruption is rife among them, and most, especially the numerous representatives of organised religion, gain their living by lying and fraud. Only the ploughmen, the hermits, and the singers who provide entertainment unquestionably earn an honest livelihood. Various abstractions – Bribery, Reason, Conscience, Repentance, for example – are embodied in characters, most graphically presented, and play their parts; and 'a thousand of men' decide to seek St Truth. Piers offers to guide them, if they will help him to plough his half-acre. Some shirk this; and there follows a discussion of the labour problems of the day. It is not possible to give a brief account of a long poem, of which there are several versions with additions by different hands, but among the author's concerns are the corruption of the church, the merits of poverty and the value of love. However Langland was not a radical; he had no new system and no practical reforms to suggest, for what he wanted was that all men should conform to the teaching of Christ. What strikes the modern reader is that he was the first to affirm the sanctity of productive labour at a time when the deep-rooted contempt of feudal lord for villein had not yet died out.

Two other points are noticeable. First, his poem was described by Owst as 'the quintessence of English medieval preaching gathered up in a single metrical piece of unusual charm and vivacity'.

Langland introduced many of the topics and employed all the devices of the preachers, but he had clearer insights, was moved more deeply and gave consistency to his work by his search for love through truth. One gets the impression that the God of Piers was much more the God of love than the vengeful Old Testament tyrant of contemporary writers. He followed the preachers precisely in bringing home to hearers the truth of abstract qualities by putting them into human, concrete forms that everyone could understand. For example, Glutton is on his way to church to make confession, but is persuaded to stop at an ale-house. There he meets a range of other characters, stays the whole day, and has to be carried home, drunk and incapable. The poet characterises the remaining Deadly Sins with the same force and vigour; this is how he describes Avarice:

> And thanne cam Coveitise,   can I him nought descrive,
> So hungrilich and holwe   Sir Hervey him loked.
> He was bitelbrowed   and baberlipped also,
> With two bleared eyen   as a blind hagge;
> And as a letheran purs   lolled his chekes,
> Wel sydder than his chin   they chiveled for elde,
> And as a bondman of his bacon   his berd was bidraveled.
> With an hood on his hed,   a lousy hat above,
> And in a tauny tabard   of twelve winter age,
> Al to-torn and baudy,   and ful of lys creping;
> But if that a lous coude   have lopen the better,
> She shulde nought have walked on that Welch,   so was it thredbare.
> (lines 188–99, *passus* v, ed. C. D. Pamely)

(And then came Avarice – I know not how to describe him, he was so gaunt and hungry-looking. Also he was beetle-browed and thick-lipped, with two bleary eyes like a blind hag. His cheeks hung out like a leather purse; they shivered with age, much lower than his chin; and his beard was beslobbered, as a bondman is with bacon. He had a hood on his head and a lousy hat on top, and wore a short tawny coat, twelve years old, all tattered and dirty, and full of crawling lice. Though if a louse could have been better at jumping, it would never have stayed on that Welsh cloth, it was so threadbare.)

Langland's vigorous use of the language resembles that of the preachers; there is a minimal gap between word and thing, so that if read aloud the words transmit half their meaning before the brain takes in the intellectual sense. Thus all his listeners could immediately feel and know what each of the Sins meant, in an actuality that could almost be seen and touched. The diction and movement of Langland's verse were close to that of everyday rustic speech, and the metrical form may have been familiarised by what was heard in church services; J. M. Gibbon has observed that the rhythm of the Anglo-Saxon metre came naturally to a poet (Langland was a clerk in minor orders and earned a precarious living as a chantry priest) who was steeped in the rhythm of ecclesiastical Latin. Since he was so occupied with church music, his lines with their caesuras slid easily into any of the eight tones specified for the psalter, making them readily acceptable to his hearers.

Secondly, for all its conservatism *Piers Plowman* must be included in the revolutionary literature, disseminated all over the country, that was a major cause and an immediate provoker of the Peasants' Revolt in 1381. So close is Langland to the sermons, in aim and content and style, that he cannot be dissociated from the wandering English preachers who (Owst prophesied) would eventually be given their due by every textbook as pioneers of the literature of popular freedom. When John Ball delivered his famous sermon at Blackheath in 1381 he took as his text the lines from a popular song:

> When Adam delved and Eve span
> Who was then a gentilman?

– the sort of versicle that was in circulation at the time, and was much used by the preachers. It even found its way, as the burden, into a carol on the Fall of Man:

> Now bethink the, gentleman,
> How Adam dalf and Eve span.

R. L. Greene tells us that 'it was apparently an established practice for a carol-writer to utilize as the burden of a piece some common moral or prudential saying suited to his purpose and at the same time accepted by the people to whom he addressed his song' (Greene, p. clxiv).

In the fifteenth century *Piers Plowman*, the Robin Hood ballads and the sermon continued as the mouthpieces of protest. But a new mood prevailed after the Peasants' Revolt, and can be detected in much topical verse. Despite the reasonableness of the peasants' claim and the fact that Ball's protest was as much moral criticism as political propaganda (his *Letter* 1 is only a version of an 'abuses of the age' poem), the Revolt was savagely put down, with none of its demands met and with no improvement in the state of the people. What did change was the climate of opinion; and the Langland view of the lower classes, as important and deserving of respect, came to be generally held in the century. The Franciscan notion of poverty as something admirable gave way to the new feeling that poverty was a social evil and not an apostolic virtue. Some of the

Twenty-six Political and other Poems of the period that J. Kail edited in 1904 are marked by a democratic tendency; they stress the importance of the commons, strive to protect the lower ranks against the encroachments of lords and officers, and call on judges, officials and the nobility to be just.

Though they are called political and though like many monitory verses of the age they shade off into the near-political, these poems now appear to be much more in the nature of moral protest. They extol virtue, warn men against worldly folly, and always set a high value on the works of a man, but none on his words. They frequently recommend righteousness for practical reasons – a note that was to sound more loudly in the sixteenth and early seventeenth centuries. 'In fact it is often impossible to separate moral and religious complaints from political ones, principally because their authors did not distinguish them' (Scattergood, p. 299). There were many poems of protest about the decadence of the age and its various abuses, the list of the latter stemming from the Twelve Abuses of the early Christian fathers. There were complaints in verse about the lack of truth, the power of money, acquisitiveness, materialism and luxury. With such topics we approach more specific grounds for discontent, falling under two heads: poems about the church and poems about the rich and powerful. A preacher could always win the attention of his congregation by a piece of stirring invective against ecclesiastical worldliness; people seemed never to weary of listening to indictments of clerical vice, inefficiency and materialism. Many of the complaints were well founded; among the clergy there were absenteeism, pluralism and neglect of duty. Often too there was good ground for the numerous complaints about the luxury and laxity of monastic houses.

The second group of complaints also was amply justified by the prevalent lawlessness, injustice and distress. At the outbreak of the Wars of the Roses in 1455, the grievances of a quiet people were summed up in a poem:

> In every shire with jacks and salads clean
> Misrule doth rise and maketh neighbours war.
> The weaker goeth beneath, as oft is seen,
> The mightiest his quarrel will prefer.
>
> They kill your men alway one by one,
> And who say aught he shall be beat doubtless.
> For in your realm Justice of Peace be none
> That dare aught now the contesters oppress.
>
> The law is like unto a Welshman's hose,

To each man's legs that shapen is and meet;
So maintainers subvent it and transpose.
Through might it is full low laid under feet.
(Trevelyan, p. 196)

('Maintenance' was the protection afforded by a noble to his client against the consequences of illegal action; verdicts of juries rarely went against the friend of a great man.) Other poems stressed particular elements in the verses just quoted. For example, some lines quoted in a sermon of 1434 suggest that bondmen resented their servitude:

Thy father was a bond man,
Thy mother curtesye non can.
Every beast that liveth now
Is of more freedom than thou.

And even during the war with France poets spoke out and urged that hostilities should be ended and peace made.

The last example of a particular fifteenth-century complaint to be cited here is *London Lickpenny*. The author strongly criticises the social and economic abuses of his time, attacking especially the impossibility for a poor man of getting just treatment under the legal system. A Kentishman goes to London for legal help to put right a wrong done to him when he was defrauded of some property. At Westminster Hall he appeals to lawyers, judges and clerks, humbly presenting his petition, but though the justice of it is recognised, no one will help him because he is too poor:

before them I kneeled upon my knee
showed them mine evidence, and they began to read.
They said truer things might never be –
but for lack of money I may not speed.

His hood is stolen, but he cannot get it back when he sees it for sale; he cannot buy anything, or get food and drink, because he lacks money. So he returns to his ploughing in Kent without gaining redress for his grievances, bitterly felt but stated with good humour. In subject and style, in its feeling and lively descriptiveness, the poem has all the marks of a street ballad, and that probably 'it is the only surviving example of an English street-balladry of the Middle Ages that existed before the introduction of printing' (Pinto and Rodway, p. 148). The poem certainly looks forward to the printed sheets of the next century, but it is distinctly superior to the general run of the later product.

In fact the difference in quality is such that one cannot regard *London Lickpenny* as a close relative of the usual printed ballad, which appeared in quantity in the sixteenth to reach a peak in the seventeenth century. It is distinctly the work of an individual moved by strong feelings about injustice, but preserving a balance and expressing himself with skill – the variations on the refrain show this. Few of the printed ballads equal it. Most of these were occasional poems, restricted by the needs of the moment and the ability of the writer to meet them. Anyone who reads a collection of them for pleasure is likely to find that they grow tedious; the level is not high and oustandingly good work is rare.

Ballads and broadsides

The better broadsides and broadsheets of the sixteenth and seventeenth centuries were often in the form of complaints, less limited than most of the ballads by topical and immediate demands. Characteristic themes were the state of society and the decay of morals, which supplied the writers with plenty of material. The medieval society of status and obligation, based on primary production, was giving way to one of urban capitalism; such familiar components as the raising of capital for interest, production for profit rather than for use ('he had what his hands earned not') and conspicuous expenditure were well developed; and inflation gathered momentum, making the rich richer and the poor poorer (Knights, p. 112). All this the poets saw, described and lamented. From *The Poore Man Payes for All* come these lines:

> Even as the mighty fishes still
>   doe feed upon the lesse;
> So rich men, might they have their will,
>   would upon the poore men seize:
> It is a proverbe old and true –
>   that weakest goe to th' wall,
> Rich men can drink till th' sky looke blue,
>   *but poore men pay for all.*
> (Pinto and Rodway, p. 158)

One of the most deeply felt injuries involved by the change was the decay of 'house-keeping' – the maintenance of a big country house and its dependents. The great house in its day was a self-sufficient economic unit in which centred the agriculture of a district and all its related activities. It employed many people; it sheltered relations and retainers; it fulfilled some of the functions of a welfare state, and helped to maintain education and general culture. The loss of all this was resented, and described in ballads about the good life that had ended; with their circumstantial detail they still carry conviction three or four hundred years later. A ballad first printed in 1660, called *The Old and the New Courtier*, tells us that the old-fashioned gentleman maintained a large number of people, relieved the needy, and entertained generously; the first stanza runs thus:

> An old song made by an old aged Pate,
> Of an old worshipful gentleman, had a wealthy estate,
> That kept an old house at a bountiful rate,
> And an old Porter to relieve poor people at his gate,
>   *Like an old Courtier of the Queen's*
>   *And the Queen's old Courtier.*

The second part of the poem presents the new courtier:

> With new titles of honour bought with
>   his Grandfather's old gold,
> For which most of his father's manors were sold,
> And that's one cause housekeeping is grown so cold,
> Yet this is the new course most of our new Gallants hold,
>   *Like new Courtiers of the King's,*
>   *And the King's new Courtiers.*

Another good poem of protest is *The Map of Mock-Begger Hall*; and *Christmas Lamentation* also describes the life of the poor tenant once the master has moved to London. The house is empty and the land has gone to ruin too:

> Houses where music was wont for to ring,
> Nothing but Battes and Howlets do sing;
> Welladay! Welladay! Welladay!
> Where should I stay?

> Christmas beefe and bread is turned into stones,
> Into stones, into stones, into stones
> And silken rags;
> And Lady Money sleeps, and makes moanes,
> And makes moanes, and makes moanes, and makes moanes,
> In Misers' bags.

There were numerous religious ballads, Protestant and Catholic, by turn, as either party was on top in the ghastly fight between them. In addition, there were ballads which complained of the evils of the time and exhorted their hearers to repent. They satisfied the ancient demand for moral and religious literature, continuing the medieval tradition of lamenting the transience of life, and stressing the dread judgments that awaited the irreligious. An accomplished poem, *To Pass the Place Where Pleasure Is*, was intended for publication in *The Stationer's Register* of 1561–2; this is the second stanza:

The lives that we long livèd have
   in wantonnesse and jolitie,
Although they seeme and show full brave,
   yet is their end plaine miserie.
     Let us therefore, therefore,
     now sinne noe more,
     but learne this lore:
     all remedie gone
     except in Christ alone, alone.

But by 1600 the hellfire sermon (of which Chaucer's Parson provides
a small example) was losing its power to impress; the complainants
of the broadsheets were out of touch, and the gap between them
and their audience was steadily widening. Moreover there were
signs that literary stratification was setting in; the ballads were
ridiculed by satirists as food for the uneducated.

Though the main aim of the jongleurs (first heard of in England
in 1150) was to entertain by singing troubadour songs, they also sang
satiric verses, and were thus at the head of a line of protest in
vernacular poetry that continued for hundreds of years. For a time
the Robin Hood and other outlaw ballads were the main channel
of dissent. They were not revolutionary, but they fulfilled the wishes
of the poor and oppressed by tales in which the rich and powerful
were humiliated, and they kept alive the spirit of resistance. Com-
parable stories in verse circulated all over Europe. They flourished
in Wales, for example, where one such poem complains about
excessive taxes, bribery, perjury and oppression by petty officials.
In Ireland also, people were legally deprived of any chance of
improving their condition and were denied education, so that
poetry was their only solace and outlet; even a rather late and
literary complaint, *The Wearing of the Green*, is charged with resent-
ment at years of harsh repression. In the seventeenth century,
Russian folk poetry that had earlier related heroic deeds sounded
a note of criticism; the 'boyars' were now regularly depicted as
wicked, with a reckless freedom that disregarded censorship.

In England the printed broadside added many new poems of
protest to the Robin Hood stories, and continued right up to the
time of Wordsworth, as the eighteenth century closed. A ballad in
circulation at the beginning of that century, *All Things be Dear but
Poor Men's Labours*, is yet another complaint about the price of food
and the heartlessness of the rich; it ends on a pious note that is
far from revolutionary. The wealthy are also castigated in *The Red
Wig*, a Nottingham ballad about a self-made man who profiteered
and exploited his workpeople. But the great age of the printed

ballad had been the seventeenth century, and in the eighteenth we find that the form, and some of the functions, were being taken over by literary poets like John Gay and Matthew Prior. Jonathan Swift (1667–1745) deliberately copied the ballad form, even to specifying a tune, for anonymously published verses that include some of the most effective protests of the period. Examples are *An Excellent New Song Upon His Grace Our good Lord Archbishop of Dublin*, which attacks the debased coinage supplied to Ireland by the contractor William Wood, and *An Excellent New Song on a Seditious Pamphlet*, written in support of Swift's campaign on behalf of Irish goods.

The earlier songs of protest were successful when they voiced the complaints of groups or the people at large about poverty and repression in general or particular cases of injustice or swindling. The established poets of the eighteenth and nineteenth centuries may, like Byron and Shelley, have supported popular causes, but they did more to heighten their stature when they wrote on topics about which public feeling was unformed and unenlightened; and in the eighteenth century at least the lucid idiom and favourite couplet of the age were an admirable medium for news and attitude that in later times would have been set down in prose: even the mild Cowper (1721–1800) observed that 'There is a sting in verse that prose neither has nor can have.' One thinks of Pope (1688–1744) as a social poet, rather than a dissident, and one who embodied the best culture of his day; but in his two moral essays *Of the Use of Riches* he brought the good sense of civilisation to bear upon the vulgar ostentation of some country-house projects, and the distortion of Nature by the artificial treatment of trees and landscape:

> The suffering eye inverted Nature sees,
> Trees cut to statues, statues thick as trees...

In the prophetic *Dunciad* he warns his readers against the coming of a reign of Dullness, with what seems clairvoyance to those who live among the realisations of some of his forecasts.

The eighteenth-century poets who protested against cruelty to animals probably helped to modify our consciousness and contributed to the modern feeling of responsibility and respect for non-human life. In a superb page or two of the *Idler*, No. 17, the poet Samuel Johnson (1709–84) describes examples of contemporary vivisection, delivers a rational judgment on its practitioners, and condemns cruelty to animals because it is bad for humanity:

> I know not that by living dissections any discovery has been made by which a single malady is more easily cured. And if the knowledge

of physiology has been somewhat increased, he surely buys know-
ledge dear who learns the use of the lacteals at the expense of his
humanity. It is time that universal resentment should arise against
these horrid operations, which tend to harden the heart, extinguish
those sensations which give man confidence in man, and make the
physician more dreadful than the gout or stone.

James Thomson (1700–48) in *Spring* condemned the caging of birds;
and Cowper devoted pages of *The Task* (Book VI) to examples of
human cruelty to animals and argument against it:

> The heart is hard in nature, and unfit
> For human fellowship, as being void
> Of sympathy, and therefore dead alike
> To love and friendship both, that is not pleased
> With sight of animals enjoying life...

Some of his lines read as if they were the work of a twentieth-century
ethologist. Cowper also protested against the barbarism of public
schools, the exploitation of colonies, and again and again against
slavery, as unnatural and unchristian, all with a liveliness that makes
him a most readable poet. Other eighteenth-century writers whose
poems increase our awareness of animals are Christopher Smart
(1722–71), Robert Burns (1759–96), and of course William Blake
(1751–1827), whose *Auguries of Innocence* is too well known to need
quotation.

The Romantics and the industrial revolution

The popular image of Burns has unfortunately obscured the poet's
vitality, evident in his few 'nature' poems, but still more so in his
powerful protests against the world of severe moral sanctions he
was brought up in; *Holy Willie's Prayer*, *The Holy Fair* and *The
Ordination* are characteristic examples of the way in which he
responded with warmth and abandon and generosity to people and
events and an unchristian Calvinism. But he had not the occasions
nor the length of life that enabled Blake to set down his vision of
the world and the way it was going. If we find it difficult to grasp
Blake's meaning, we should perhaps recall D. W. Harding's words:

> The miracle is that he produced such work at all. He represents a
> tremendous opportunity in English literature that was largely wasted
> owing to the reading public's restricted capacity for response; and
> the combination of greatness and failure in his work is a reminder
> that a literature consists not of writers only but of their readers too.
> (Ford 5, p. 84)

Blake did stand outside his age, certainly, but even if our under-
standing is of no greater capacity than that of his contemporaries
we can learn what he was driving at, because so many of his
premonitions are now seen to have been well-founded. Moreover
we can see now that, though first, he was not alone in his protests,
after Keats (see *Lamia*, Part II, lines 229ff), Shelley and Wordsworth
had spoken out, as he did, against the prevailing spirit of the age.
The spirit was rational, with Bacon in the background and the
materialist physics of Newton in the foreground; and this ration-
alism and its various manifestations were attacked by Blake on
several fronts – science for example enslaved man and darkened the
imagination. In particular he denounced the industrial revolution
– 'A Machine is not a Man nor a Work of Art; it is destructive of
humanity and art.' He protested against war – 'a warlike State can
never produce art', against slavery (especially in *America, a Pro-
phecy*), against cruelty (*Auguries of Innocence*) and against the
butchery of animals to provide human food (*The First Book of Urizen*,
etc.). He condemned cold, Puritan, negative religion (in *The Ever-
lasting Gospel* and many of the short poems), rigid sexual morality
(*Vision of the Daughters of Albion*) and the starving of child life (*Songs
of Innocence, Songs of Experience*). Blake's view of society is summed
up in *London* – 'perhaps the most vehement and inclusive outcry
that any city or society has had levelled against it' (Coveney, p. 65):

> I wander thro' each charter'd street,
> Near where the charter'd Thames does flow,
> And mark in every face I meet
> Marks of weakness, marks of woe.
>
> In every cry of every Man,
> In every Infant's cry of fear,
> In every voice, in every ban,
> The mind-forg'd manacles I hear.
>
> How the Chimney-sweeper's cry
> Every black'ning Church appals:
> And the hapless Soldier's sigh
> Runs in blood down Palace walls.
>
> But most thro' midnight streets I hear
> How the youthful Harlot's curse
> Blasts the new born Infant's tear,
> And blights with plagues the Marriage hearse.

Blake had little in common with Byron, and Wordsworth did not
resemble Shelley, so that at first glance the term 'Romantic' is a poor
umbrella for such diverse talents. However what they did share was

the assertion of individual protest against 'scientific' thought, the industrialisation it produced, and the impact of the latter on the poor and humble. Their reservations about the doctrine of progress have been justified, and their premonitions verified; for nearly two centuries after their time we can recognise the impulses they shared, and regret that their words went unheeded. Belatedly we can benefit from their insights and take heart from their spirit of resistance. Of the poets labelled 'Romantic', Byron (1788–1824) sorts less readily into the fold than the others. He was enormously popular – a new book of his caused traffic jams, and ten thousand copies of *The Corsair* were sold on publication day. He went down very well with urban radicals in the 1840s; Chartist banners were embroidered with patriotic inscriptions from his poems, and a public-house had scenes from Byron as well as Shakespeare painted on its walls. The Byronic hero influenced generations; for most of the century it supplied Europe with its idea of a literary figure; and it won sympathy for the cause of Greek independence. But unfortunately Byron never escaped from Byronism. The fashion was launched by the publication of the first two cantos of *Childe Harold*, with characteristics carefully adjusted by John Murray the publisher to the needs of the romantic public. Murray urged him to write the same kind of literature, and always arranged not to publish any of Byron's works that would shock his 'Haroldian' public, and consequently left to us a voluminous might-have-been. A sign of change is the fact that Byron's most forceful protests were in prose, his maiden speech to the House of Lords in 1812, for example – in which with cold and angry power he denounced panic action against rioting weavers, unemployed through the introduction of machinery.

Of Shelley (1792–1822) also it seems that his prose protests against the evils of his day were more forceful than his poetry, to judge by the moving *An Address to the People on the Death of Princess Charlotte*, 1817, in which he describes the working of the spy system and its horrible results for men executed on trumped-up political charges. It cannot be dismissed, like his rather routine *Song to the Men of England*, as a product of student activism:

> Men of England, wherefore plough
> For the lords who lay you low?
> Wherefore weave with toil and care
> The rich robes your tyrants wear? etc.

Not that Shelley himself would have thought much of his *Song*. In his Preface to *Prometheus Unbound*, after admitting to 'a passion for reforming the world', he continued it is a mistake to suppose that I dedicate my poetical compositions solely to the direct enforcement of reform, or that I consider them in any degree as containing a reasoned system on the theory of human life. Didactic poetry is my abhorrence; nothing can be equally well expressed in prose that is not tedious and supererogatory in verse.

More clearly than most of his contemporaries he realised the ephemeral nature of political institutions. What (like Blake) he objected to was moralising Christianity, dispensing an oppressive sense of guilt attended by cruelty in action. Positively in *Prometheus Unbound* he upheld the Christian ideal of love, endurance and forgiveness, thus – again like Blake – redeeming from decay 'visitations of the divinity in man' (*A Defence of Poetry*). Shelley's view (Kathleen Raine suggests) was that 'Christian theology, by placing God outside his creation, has deprived "nature" of spiritual life, and prepared the way for that scientific secularization and profanation of the universe from whose deadly results we now suffer.' But here again his prose seems more lucid and specific than his verse, when he writes, in his *Defence*:

> The cultivation of those sciences which have enlarged the limits of the empire of man over the external world, has, for want of the poetical faculty, proportionately circumscribed those of the internal world; and man, having enslaved the elements, remains himself a slave. To what but a cultivation of the mechanical arts in a degree disproportioned to the presence of the creative faculty, which is the basis of all knowledge, is to be attributed the abuse of all invention for abridging and combining labour, to the exasperation of the inequality of mankind? From what other cause has it arisen that the discoveries which should have lightened, have added a weight to the curse imposed on Adam?

The idiom is that of 1817, but the insight remains today. Pope and Blake put their visions into verse; Shelley and most poets after him found it necessary to make a clear distinction between the functions of poetry and those of prose, with prose the medium for a general audience, while poetry was beginning to be reserved for a restricted readership. Shelley himself admitted this: 'My purpose has hitherto been simply to familiarize the highly refined imagination of the more select classes of poetical readers with beautiful idealisms of moral excellence...' (preface to *Prometheus Unbound*).

All the Romantic poets were influenced by the broadside ballads, those composed in their own time as well as the Percy *Reliques* and others still in oral circulation. In the case of Blake 'a number of the *Songs of Innocence and Experience* and some of the miscellaneous poems might be described as street ballads spiritualized and transfigured, and it is highly probable that Blake's beautifully engraved illustrations to these poems are inspired by the example of the crude popular art of the woodcut illustrations to the street ballads'. Pinto and Rodway also point out that Shelley took the metres for his *Arethusa*, *The Cloud* and *The Sensitive Plant* from those found in popular street ballads. Wordsworth (1770–1850) greatly admired both the Border ballads and those that reached the poor orally or in print. He attributed the growth of his own imagination in part to the ballads that he heard as a child:

> the low and wren-like warblings, made
> For cottagers and spinners at the wheel,
> And sun-burnt travellers resting their tired limbs,
> Stretched under wayside hedge-rows, ballad tunes,
> Food for the hungry ears of little ones,
> And of old men who have survived their joys –
> 'Tis just that in behalf of these, the works
> And of the men that framed them, whether known,
> Or sleeping nameless in their scattered graves,
> That here I should assert their rights, attest
> Their honours, and should, once for all, pronounce
> Their benediction; speak of them as Powers
> For ever to be hallowed...
> (*The Prelude*, v, 207–19)

and he went on to compare the education he had received with that offered by the new rationalist instruction, about which he protests at length – an unnatural process which would have dried him up, body and soul, engineered by guides who thought they could control the future, and treated their pupils as machines to run on rails, 'like engines' (lines 223–363 *passim*). In a letter to Francis Wrangham, Wordsworth stated explicitly that he wanted to improve on the printed ballad, and we can see his intention carried out in the themes and stories and metres of the *Lyrical Ballads*, *The Idiot Boy*, for example. In fact a recent writer claims that Wordsworth helped the transmission of the old broadside ballad into the more 'respectable' area of the Victorian ballad (Bratton, p. 14). What Wordsworth was aiming at, in choosing for his poems episodes from the lives of the humble, he explained in a letter of July 1802 to a former prime minister, Charles James Fox, enclosing a copy of *Michael* and *The Brothers*. After describing a disappearing class, the 'statesmen' or small north-country farmers who owned their land, and the way in which their farms served as a kind of rallying point for their domestic feelings, he stated that the two poems were written 'with a view to show that men who do not wear fine cloaths can feel deeply'. His hope was that readers' respect for mankind and their knowledge of human nature would be enlarged by realising that:

> Our best qualities are possessed by men whom we are too apt to consider, not with reference to the points in which they resemble us, but to those in which they manifestly differ from us. I thought, at a time when these feelings are sapped in so many ways, that the two poems might co-operate, however feebly, with the illustrious efforts which you have made to stem this and other evils with which the country is labouring.
>
> (Selincourt 1935, p. 262)

Despite his fear of the mob, Wordsworth, like Coleridge, was deeply moved throughout his life by the sufferings of the poor and afflicted; they supply more than half of the main subjects of the *Lyrical Ballads*. Nearly forty years later, when he was sixty-five, he devoted pages of his Postscript to the poems published in 1835 to an attack on utilitarians, economists, and the cruel, heartless administration of the Poor Law Amendment Act – advocating co-partnership and arguing that

> . . . it is better for the interests of humanity among the people at large, that ten undeserving should partake of the funds provided, than that one morally good man, through want of relief, should either have his principles corrupted, or his energies destroyed; than that such a one should either be driven to do wrong, or be cast to the earth in hopelessness.
>
> (Wordsworth, p. 961)

More penetratingly than the tunnel-visioned economists and complacent utilitarians of the time he saw beyond the immediate distress. In Book VIII of *The Excursion* he described the results of applying science to industry: the destruction of old ways of life, the organic relationship of man to man, the imposition of the inhuman rhythm of the machine in the factory system, the running-up of miserable slums to house near-servile workers, and the plight of the human victims. Industry rolled on relentlessly but Wordsworth had some able converts; John Stuart Mill, for example, records his debt to Wordsworth at some length in chapter 5 of his *Autobiography*. And

> His antithesis of town and country became of increasing importance to a century disfigured by the urban outrage of the Industrial Revolution. His plea for a sensuous relation between Man and Nature became a force among a whole generation of intellectuals at the end of the century dissatisfied with the human sterilities of the vulgarizers of Benthamite utilitarianism.
>
> (Coveney, p. 83)

Towards the end of the twentieth century also the intelligent left, when you have traced it, is found to be firmly based on the implications for today of the insights of Wordsworth, Blake, Shelley and other Romantics. Whatever their politics they saw the far-reaching changes that were going on, and detected trends that have now been recognised and substantiated.

A few more individual poets remain to be mentioned under the heading of poetic protest in the nineteenth century. First is George Crabbe (1754–1832). Though his dates put him in the previous century, he belongs in feeling to romantic disillusion rather than to the age of enlightenment, a point obscured by the current preference for his verse tales to the neglect of his earlier poetry about English life. The latter is a strong, harsh, realistic corrective to the pastoral version of country living and the smug pictures of Miss Mitford. *The Village, The Parish Register* and *The Borough* speak to us today with a clear individual voice. In the first of these, published before he was thirty, he paints 'the real picture of the poor'; after a few lines of neo-classical introduction he settles down to grim descriptions of the lower class, degraded by want and suffering, eking out a miserable existence in rural slums. If there were space the powerfully moving account of the poor-house, early in Book I, would be included, but it is easy to find. Along with it go such pieces as the unwilling marriage and Isaac Ashford from *The Parish Register*. With his large output of poems about birds, animals, plants and rural scenes Clare (1793–1864), belongs mainly to the long and admirable British tradition of protest against cruelty, but he did also record his complaint about the enclosures, in writing of the loss of Swordy Well in *Remembrances*, where children were free to play and moles to make their hills. As he wrote of himself: 'I kept my spirit with the free'.

Late in his life Tom Hood (1799–1845), a journalist and an undistinguished poet, wrote *The Song of the Shirt* (1843), of which the first stanza runs:

> With fingers weary and worn,
>   With eyelids heavy and red,
> A Woman sat, in unwomanly rags,
>   Plying her needle and thread –
>   Stitch! stitch! stitch!
> In poverty, hunger and dirt,
>   And still with a voice of dolorous pitch
> She sang the 'Song of the Shirt!'

It had an enormous vogue; was widely imitated, and was frequently quoted in sermons. His point – that it was not enough for philanthropists to go prison-visiting, but that they should prevent people getting there – was widely taken, and resulted in a certain amount of practical assistance. He followed up the *Song* by such poems as the *Lay of the Labourer, The Workhouse Clock, The Lady's Dream, The Pauper's Christmas Carol* and *The Assistant Drapers' Petition.* He seems to have met precisely the need of the moment by his expressions of concern for the needy, and he did so without recourse to the literary idiom from which the minor 'social' poets never escaped, or the patronising note and religiosity that mark the poems of George R. Sims.

The established poets of the Victorian age did not express dissent; apart from some superficial traits of Romanticism, their common characteristic was a failure to act in any way as the antennae of their time. A partial exception is Matthew Arnold (1822–88). His work, conscientious, brave and intelligent, as an inspector of schools, involved visits to areas which it was almost dangerous for a member of the middle class to enter. His reports go to the heart of the matter, making clear the humanising and civilising function of the schools, and pointing to the ways in which it could be carried out. At the risk of losing his job he condemned the system of payment by results. His major work, *Culture and Anarchy*, complemented his inspecting; he charted the drift of the times, and showed that hope lay in educating the masses of new voters, who would soon exert political control. But none of this affected his poetry, except perhaps *Dover Beach* and the sonnet *West London*. He did not supply the prophetic verse that might have leavened the age, any more than Tennyson (1809–92) or Browning (1812–89). The former achieved great popularity, prosperity, honours and friendship with the powerful, by supplying the middle class with an image, reassurance and some relief from a sense of guilt; its members could easily respond to the only kind of protest Tennyson made, against cruelty to children and animals, as in *In the Children's Hospital*. Browning also raised the right objections to cruelty to animals in *Tray*; and Mrs Browning wrote on the lot of children in factories in her *The Cry of Children*. But apart from Hopkins, unrecognised and unread, the Victorian poets spent their talents on brooding over a set range of themes and emotions – youth, age, time, mortality, love, joy and grief – and Tennyson's *Tithonus* was a typical product.

Throughout the nineteenth century the effective voice of protest was heard in prose, first in the writing of Cobbett, Byron, Shelley and in various pamphlets, and later in *The Times*, T. H. Huxley,

Samuel Plimsoll and General Booth. In addition there was a large output of protest in verse from members of the oppressed working class, but the poetry afforded consolation, relief, a sense of solidarity and some encouragement to go on living, rather than contributing to any change in public opinion. For example when the Tolpuddle Martyrs were sentenced at Dorchester in 1834, one of them in a most moving document recorded:

> As soon as the sentence was passed, I got a pencil and a scrap of paper and wrote the following lines:
>
>> God is our guide! from field, from wave,
>> From plough, from anvil, and from loom;
>> We come, our country's rights to save,
>> And speak a tyrant faction's doom:
>> We raise the watch-word liberty;
>> We will, we will, we will be free!
>>
>> God is our guide! no swords we draw,
>> We kindle not war's battle fires;
>> Be reason, union, justice, law,
>> We claim the birth-right of our sires:
>> We raise the watch-word, liberty,
>> We will, we will, we will be free!!!
>
> While we were being guarded back to prison, our hands locked together, I tossed the above lines to some people that we passed; the guard, however, seizing hold of them, they were instantly carried back to the judge; and by some this was considered a crime of no less magnitude than high treason.
>
> (*Victims of Whiggery*, a pamphlet, 1837)

A page or two of the pamphlet's dignified and forceful prose, close to the rhythms of speech, needs to be read to bring out the contrast with the literary, hymn-like verses.

The literary mode of popular writing died out with Chartism by the middle of the century, though it flickered again in the handful of *Chants for Socialists* by William Morris, published as a penny pamphlet by the Socialist League in 1885. Chartism, founded after a meeting in 1838, seems to have had numbers of poets among its members, including for a short time Ebenezer Elliott (1781–1849), a successful Sheffield business man who attributed the loss of some of his savings to the duty on imported corn. He had been a respectable poet, a follower of Thomson and Crabbe, and was an ardent and courageous radical; so that his anger at the sufferings of the poor unable to afford bread readily flowed into his *Corn Law Rhymes* of 1831. They were quickly popular, his biographer of 1850 claiming that he was 'the pioneer and trumpeter of a great national movement', and apparently effective; the Attorney-General was urged to prosecute him as a promoter of revolution. This Elliott was not. He also seems to have been a Christian, and he followed up the *Rhymes* by *Corn-Law Hymns*, in the hope that they would be sung in churches. No. 8 of the *Hymns* contains these verses:

> Lord, bid our palaced worms their vileness know!
>   Bleach them with famine till they earn their bread,
> And taught by pain to feel a brother's woe,
>   Marvel that honest labour toils unfed.
> They never heard their children's grim despair
>   Cry, 'Give us work, ere want and death prevail,'
> Then seek in crime or in desponding prayer
>   A refuge from the bread-tax-crowded gaol...

Elliott is worth more attention than he has had in recent years; he achieved success within the idiom he inherited, and won the respect of some of the intellectual heavyweights of his period.

But the poems written in a more popular vein have a clearer ring of truth; and here, before we reach the great volume of verse connected with weaving and mining, we must note the complaints centring on the state of agriculture and on the royal family. An early Victorian street ballad deplores the anti-union attitude of farmers; and when in 1837 the government, wishing to bring home the need for economy, proclaimed every Wednesday a fast day, a broadside gave its views on the likelihood of the politicians' obeying their own suggestion. Early in the century a lively ballad, *The Times Have Altered*, attacked the new style of farmer, keeping up a mode of living that cut him off from his men; and in 1841 Dickens wrote an excellent 'new version – to be said or sung at all Conservative dinners' of *The Fine Old English Gentleman*:

> The good old laws were garnished well with gibbets, whips and chains,
> With fine old English penalties, and fine old English pains,
> With rebel heads, and seas of blood once hot in rebel veins;
> For all these things were requisite to guard the rich old gains
>   Of the fine old English Tory times;
>   Soon may they come again!
> (Pinto and Rodway, p. 181)

Another street ballad, *The Bishop's See*, is a bitter ironic attack on ecclesiastical tithes; and others attacked enclosures and spoke up for poachers. 'In the three years alone between 1827 and 1830, more than 8,500 men and youths were convicted as poachers, and a high proportion shipped away in broad-arrowed felt suits...' (Lloyd, p. 246). As a result many songs of protest circulated against the cruelty and injustice of transportation, a fate which removed some of the best country stock, as well as those more readily classed as criminals. Most of the verse mentioned in this paragraph has expressed rural discontent, but with *The Song of the Lower Classes* by the Chartist poet, Ernest Jones, we move to more general complaint, couched in a direct and simple style. After the opening stanza:

> We plough and sow – we're so very, very low,
>   That we delve in the dirty clay,
> Till we bless the plain – with the golden grain,
>   And the vale with the fragrant hay.
> Our place we know – we're so very low,
>   It's down at the landlord's feet:
> We're not too low – the bread to grow,
>   But too low the bread to eat...
> (Pinto and Rodway, p. 187)

Jones goes on to describe the lot of miners, builders, weavers and soldiers, who toil and fight for others without sharing what their efforts have won. The progenitiveness of the royal family and the resulting cost to the country provided another theme for verses of protest. Mayhew, in writing of the patterers, was informed that the inhabitants of lodging houses 'hate the aristocracy. Whenever there is a rumour or an announcement of an addition to the Royal Family, and the news reaches the padding-ken, the kitchen for half-an-hour becomes the scene of uproar – "another expense coming on the b—y country!"' A street ballad, *Old England Forever and Do it no More*, sold by the patterers, begins:

> As the Queen and Prince Albert, so buxom and all pert,
>   Were jovially conversing together one day,
> Old Bull heard them talking as they were awalking,
>   And V. unto A. so boldly did say
> The State seems bewildering about little children,
>   And we are increasing every day, you know we have four,
> We kindly do treat them and seldom to beat them,
>   So Albert, dear Albert, we'll do it no more...
> (W. Henderson, p. 145)

Shuttle and cage

The occupational poems that we now come to are one of the finest single sources for the domestic history of the nineteenth century, for they present, often with a rawness, awkwardness and ugliness that are fully convincing, a picture of what the industrial changes meant for the people who suffered them. When there was employment, the hours were long, the pay poor, the work exhausting and sometimes dangerous, and the conditions physically and spiritually oppressive – there were fines for everything, and even when there was energy for singing, it was liable to be forbidden. When there was unemployment, the effects were less cushioned in the urban than in the rural slums. Strikes, evictions, lock-outs and the constant struggle for better conditions also supplied themes for many songs of complaint. The sufferings of the weavers were among the earliest to be described, perhaps because they had a long tradition of singing at work. In the sixteenth century Deloney in *Jack of Newberrie* had painted an idealised picture (unsupported by contemporary writers) of weaver girls singing at their work in a factory, and in the eighteenth century Burns set down his version of a weavers' song, *My heart ance as blythe and free*. In 1812 Byron published in the *Morning Chronicle* his *Ode to the Framers of the Frame Bill*, of which the second stanza runs:

> The rascals, perhaps, may betake them to robbing,
> The dogs to be sure have got nothing to eat –
> So if we can hang them for breaking a bobbin,
> 'Twill save all the Government's money and meat:
> Men are more easily made than machinery –
> Stockings fetch better prices than lives –
> Gibbets on Sherwood will heighten the scenery,
> Showing how Commerce, how Liberty thrives!

A little later *The Poor Cotton Weaver*, of which there are numerous versions, began to circulate. 'Weavers were working a fifteen-hour day for ten shillings a week if they were fortunate, four shillings if not; they were living on oatmeal and potatoes, onion porridge and blue milk, and hungry women roamed the moors looking for nettles to boil' (Lloyd, p. 325). The song is often printed in a shortened form, but the full one is the better, because it brings out humour as well as courage in the grimmest of conditions. There were many other weavers' songs, some by individual weaver poets like Alex Wilson of Paisley, and Samuel Laycock, who wrote poetry to support his family in the cottom famine of the 60s.

A. L. Lloyd has shown that 'for centuries, English miners have possessed a vigorous song culture relating to their work and their way of life...in poetry and song our coalfield can match the great areas of pit culture in the Carinthian, Saxon-Bohemian and Moravian-Silesian districts'. Certainly an old mining song, *The Colliers' Rant*, had appeared in print before the end of the eighteenth century. In it a miner fights with the devil that inhabits the mine:

> As me and me marrer was going to work,
> We met wi' the devil, it was in the dark;

I up wi' me pick, it was in the neet,
I knocked off his horns, likewise his clubfeet...

Thus when the occasion arose for the venting of grievances, the medium was there, ready. Lloyd has demonstrated in his excellent *Folk Song in England* that the miners' poems of protest against their exploitation by the wealthy were militant from the start, that is from the late 1820s. These early complaints were very much for local consumption; they expressed a feeling of solidarity, urged the justice of their cause, and explained to their fellows the needs for united action. A good example is *The Coal-owner and the Pitman's Wife*, in which the wife explains to a colliery owner that the poor are being turned out of hell in order to make room for the rich; and that therefore the owner should treat his men fairly to avoid being sent below. It is humorous and comparatively mild. The trend however was for the mining poems to become more harshly realistic and more bitter in feeling. *The Durham Lock-out* of 1892 blames the masters for the increasing hunger and starvation in the county, and expressed the wish:

May every Durham colliery owner that is in the fault,
Receive nine lashes with the rod, and then be rubbed with salt,
May his back be thick with boils so that he may never sit,
And never burst until the wheels go round at every pit.

This is not an isolated example. The poetry of mining is extensive, and with its realistic description of conditions and the angry criticism of the owners – no industry more richly deserved nationalising – it supplies a condensed source of social history. One cannot help wondering, in passing, why the history studied in schools neglects such compelling and graphic material, especially for groups of children chosen for their lack of academic ability. The more able too would have their humanity fed and maintained to a degree that is not always attained in specialised courses. The later ballads are more sharply focused – on practical aims for example (the collection of funds for miners' families) and on factual details that were ignored by press reports.

Other occupations had their verses of complaint. The Sheffield grinders had a song tersely describing their work and its dangers. In early Victorian Scotland the young farm workers who were housed in bothies (one-roomed cottages for bachelor labourers) had their own poems; the bothy ballad is a narrative song that deals immediately with he life of these men, their activities at and after work, and the hard conditions they endured. Some of the ballads complained about the inadequacy of their tools, poor food and the meanness and ill-temper of some farmers' wives. David Buchan, who has written so fully and freshly of these and other Scots ballads, notes that 'Instead of escaping from the hard realities of everyday life by singing about another life, the ballad singer relieved his feelings by commenting directly and sardonically on the life he led, day in, day out' (Buchan, p. 268). He points out also the resemblance between these ballads and those evolved by isolated groups of workers elsewhere – in prairies, forests, mines and at sea, with their satirical approach to similar targets. The lumberjack ballads of North America for example flourished particularly when Napoleon's blockade cut off Britain's trade with the Baltic countries, and ended with the disappearance of squared timber camps at the end of the nineteenth century. The early examples have an Irish flavour; some have a European origin; many utter complaints about the hard times. But on the whole they are rather poor stuff, and are degenerate forms of printed ballads.

The sailors' life produced a quantity of songs of complaint, especially in the third quarter of the nineteenth century, when competition was severe; these songs, from *The Banks of Newfoundland* onwards, should not of course be confused with sea shanties, which are purely work songs. The worst of conditions at sea were experienced in whalers, and because of this and its long history, whale-hunting produced a fine crop of complaining songs. *The Greenland Whale*, recorded in several versions, is one of the oldest of these. A whale is sighted, a boat launched, but the whale escapes and a man is drowned:

> Now when the news to our captain came
>   He called up all his crew,
> And for the losing of that man
>   He down his colours drew,
>
> Says he, My men, be not dismayed
>   At the losing of one man,
> For providence will have his will
>   Let man do what he can.
>
> Now the losing of that prentice boy
>   It grieved our captain sore,
> But the losing of that great big whale
>   It grieved him a damn sight more
>   Brave boys,
>   It grieved him a damn sight more.
> (Grigson, p. 217)

Other sea songs described the activities of the crimps, who got men on board by drink, drugs and other means. The monstrous predations of the naval press-gangs were also the occasion of many complaints, of which this little poem is an example:

> Oh cruel was the press-gang
>   That took my love from me.
> Oh cruel was the little ship
>   That took him out to sea.
>
> And cruel was the splinter-board
>   That took away his leg.
> Now he is forced to fiddle-scrape,
>   And I am forced to beg.
> (Grigson, p. 238)

The army also was the source of many songs complaining of vicious methods of recruiting and the horrible cruelty of military punishments. *Arthur McBride* is a splendid example of an anti-recruiting song:

> If we were such fools as to take your advance
> It's right bloody slender would be our poor chance,
> For the Queen wouldn't scruple to send us to France
> And get us all shot in the morning.
> (Lloyd, p. 257)

The barbarous treatment of soldiers led to hundreds of desertions.

> With the deserter such a characteristic figure of the time, the desertion ballads made a deep impression on soldiers and the working country- and towns-folk from whom they came. In general the people were firmly on the side of the deserter, and their sympathy shows in many contemporary reports as well as in several widespread and much-loved songs.
> (Lloyd, p. 259)

America

With an economy originally based on slavery, with social changes taking place at high speed compared with elsewhere, and with capitalism completing its cycle in half the time that it took in Europe, American history is marked by dislocation, exploitation and repression on a large scale; and the cries of those who suffered still echo round the world. First, those of negro slaves, in the form of spirituals, which must go back to the importation of slaves to Virginia in 1631 – four hundred collections of them exist. If none of them are overt protests – for they were sung in front of whites – they are all evidence of discontent, though most of them disguise their sentiments in imagery and symbolism. 'Spirituals are fraught with secret calls for freedom – indeed, the word "freedom" occurs with disturbing regularity in them, as do references to "home", and they evidence an almost pathological concern for the plight of Old Testament Jews held in Egyptian bondage' (Haslam). *Go down Moses* is a well-known example; it begins:

> Go down Moses,
> Way down to Egyptland
> Tell old Pharaoh
> Let my people go.
>
> When Israel was in Egyptland
> Let my people go
> Oppressed so hard they could not stand
> Let my people go...

Most spirituals share the character of the one above; they express a deep discontent; there is a meaning below the surface; they are not entirely without hope. Though it is on record that one slave – Frederick Douglass, who became a leading abolitionist – escaped because the suggestion came to him from the spiritual *Run to Jesus*, the songs did no more than enable the slaves to see that they shared their plight with the Israelites, that Canada was Canaan, the slave-owner Pharaoh.

There are not many negro songs of protest other than the spirituals, and most of them come from prisons and chain-gangs. In a Texas prison the songs were 'devices some of the men developed to keep their heads straight or busy enough to avoid giving in to the vacancy, the emptiness, the terror. They are a weapon against a kind of death' (Jackson, p. xvi). A convict spoke of the younger men who did not know any songs. 'In most cases their world is so modernaire, they're all daydreamin'; they drivin' the Cadillacs and sleepin' on the silk sheets, you know.' It is very interesting to note that day-dreaming, leading a fictitious life, is exactly what modern workers on the assembly line or at a repetitive job indulge in, as a compensation for the rebuffs and failures of life, or just because conversation is impossible. The implications of the contrast between singing and day-dreaming cannot be pursued here, but they are worth considering. Unless the mind is stored with something worth pondering, day-dreaming tends to be about petty matters that deserve no more than a moment's thought; and it is conceivable that this negative state of affairs accounts for much dissatisfaction with work today and perhaps strikes. Certainly (in the words of two very perceptive observers) 'this tendency to endless unprogressive brooding goes far to explain the great force of the *idée fixe*...The notions that have pleased the fancy or have been engendered by emotion are ground into the very substance of the mind by the repeating process of the machine...' (Reaveley and Winnington, p. 79).

In America there exist numerous songs of protest associated with work on river, rail, factory, field and forest, and with the lives of poor whites and hoboes. Two thousand of them survive, going back to 1842–3, when complaints about the control of Rhode Island by hereditary landowners took the form of broadside ballads. Agitation for a shorter working day; against the oppressive paternalism of the Pullman Car Company; and that stirred up by the 1932 depression are other examples. Even in this century the power of song has been recognised and feared. In 1929 Ella May Wiggins, who was highly esteemed as a singer and composer to the National Textile Workers' Union, was murdered in the anarchy that followed a strike at Gastonia; a mob that included Southern fundamentalist farmers attacked union members on their way to a meeting. 'Her fellow workers were convinced that she had been deliberately singled out for death because of her song-making' (Greenway, p. 247). About 1925 'Gospel' music took over from the negro spirituals, as negro workers moved from the agricultural south to the industrial north, and found centres in the churches of the various sects, Pentecostal, Sanctified and others. Gospel music, unlike the spirituals, was provided by individual authors, and in the words of a singer:

> The Gospel was the Black man's weapon; his peace even with all the burdens put upon his shoulders; it was his language, to speak or sing, and was understood by other Blacks but was meaningless to the whites; and it was his sound, a reverberating sound of the oppressed, of God, of his estrangement from the face of human dignity, and the means by which he told his story...
> (Nicholas)

The Gospel music was followed by the blues, rather moaning and groaning stuff, but like the spirituals not without hope. The most recent manifestation of negro dissent is to be found in the songs of the Southern Freedom Movement, which protest against all forms of racial segregation, and are sung in many situations. The words, describing particular episodes, characters or situations in the non-violent struggle, strike one as being much more important than in some songs of complaint; they are often direct, forceful and confident (Carawan).

We cannot do more than mention examples of dissenting poetry of the nineteenth century in tongues other than English. The large

169

conscript armies created self-centred communities, isolated like lumbermen groups, and like them depending for entertainment on their own voices. In Germany especially their ballads expressed the peasants' dislike of conscription, the march to a frontier, the sad or joyful return home. In Czechoslovakia research workers found in the police records a number of songs impounded over years of strikes and demonstrations. And it is arguable that all the poetry of the French symbolists, with the poet in the role of bohemian, was a protest against bourgeois attitudes.

The twentieth century

In this century poetry has played only an insignificant part in the life of western nations. The poets have certainly been protesters: Stephen Crane and Edgar Lee Masters are examples from the United States, and in Europe we have had the poets of the First World War, Ezra Pound, T. S. Eliot, Brecht and others. But the war poets were hardly read at all till more than ten years after the armistice of 1918; and it is not certain that the influence of, say, T. S. Eliot upon ways of thinking and feeling has reached more than a fairly small circle of readers. The need is there and is felt: poetry is thought in a vague way to be appropriate to solemn occasions, such as death, and emotion has found shape in rhyme and jingles. In the First World War British soldiers avoided hysteria by ironic songs about themselves – 'Send out the Army and the Navy...But for Gawd's sake don't send me' – and thus achieved the kind of resignation expressed by John Bates and Michael Williams in *Henry V*. Sometimes the protest was unequivocal, as in the soldiers' satires on their officers and the military system, and in 'Oh my, I don't want to die', sung at Victoria Station in London in the winter of 1915 (see Brophy and Partridge). The Second World War was not the occasion for any considerable poetry, though shortly after it the Campaign for Nuclear Disarmament produced a number of songs for singing on protest marches. However what appears to be the century's most acceptable poetry of dissent comes out of Soviet Russia, and its courage and articulateness appear in the few translated examples available. This is Sergei Chudakov, writing in the underground magazine *Syntax*, whose editor Aleksandr Ginzburg was sent to a labour camp for two years:

> When they call out
>   'Man overboard!'
> The ocean liner, big as a house

Suddenly stops
And the man
   is fished out with ropes.
But when
   a man's soul is overboard
When he is drowning
   in horror and despair
Then even his own house
Does not stop
   but sails on.
(Bosley, p. 27)

The poets in the collection of underground Russian poetry from which this poem is taken give the impression, not always given by volumes of poetry from other parts of the world, of having something to write about. This 'something' in its early stages is described by W. H. Auden in *The Dyer's Hand*:

> In our age, the mere making of a work of art is itself a political act. So long as artists exist, making what they please and think they ought to make, even if it is not terribly good, even if it appeals only to a handful of people, they remind the Management of something managers need to be reminded of, namely, that the managed are people with faces, not anonymous numbers...
>
> If a poet meets an illiterate peasant, they may not be able to say much to each other, but if they both meet a public official, they share the same feeling of suspicion; neither will trust one further than he can throw a grand piano. If they enter a government building, both share the same feeling of apprehension; perhaps they will never get out again. Whatever the cultural differences between them, they both sniff in any official world the smell of an unreality in which persons are treated as statistics. (p. 88)

What has poetry done for the multitudes whose grievances it has voiced over thousands of years? It has spoken for individuals protesting against men, and gods, repression and the clutch of circumstance. It has sought sympathy and support; it has channelled and distanced the flow of feeling; in the case of social protest it has tried to reinforce solidarity and morale, to win converts and perhaps to point to a solution. It is unlikely to have done much to alter the circumstances complained of, but it has countered despair and kept hope alive and helped some sufferers to come to terms with life. The rural singers of folk poems were fortunate in having an environment that offered them symbols by means of which they could master experience; since the songs were the common property of a community it happened that when (say) grief came near to overwhelming one of its members, the emotion was controlled by flowing in courses ready for it. The traditional form of words almost ritualised the feeling generated by the crises of life, and offered some encouragement to go on living. This beautiful folk song from Norfolk provides an example:

Old Thyme

Come all young women and maids
  That are all in your prime,
Mind how you weed your gardens gay,
  Let no one steal your thyme.

Once I had thyme enough,
  To last me night and day,
There came to me a false young man
  Stole all my thyme away.

And now my thyme is done,
  I cannot plant no new,
There lays the bed where my old thyme grew,
  'Tis all over-run with rue.

Rue is a running root,
  Runs all across amain,
If I could pluck that running root
  I'd plant my old thyme again.

However strong the sense of loss, a country-dweller could hardly fail to remember that gardens can be weeded and thyme sows itself.

But prisoners and workers in industry could get no help from traditional song as they endured the desperate grind of toil, ill-treatment or starvation. Yet they shaped their woes into verse, and the fact that they were able to describe their grief, to recount episodes in the struggle, and to unite with others in giving vent to their feelings about masters or overseers, gave them some sort of control over part of their existence. They were seeing things their way, according to their own scheme, and not in a pattern laid down by owner or overseer or gaoler. Emotional or physical starvation did not rob them of the power to make their own response in poems that seem to have little grace or beauty but take a firm grasp of misfortune. (In a South African prison Dennis Brutus found that one of the worst deprivations was lack of music; singing was forbidden. He managed to write poetry by putting his official letters home into verse form.) The day-dreaming that is the only resort of assembly-line workers seems a poor substitute for actual songs or words.

7

The printed poem

The impact of printing

Caxton printed his first book in 1477, but it was more than a century before printing made much difference to writers and readers. At first it was a supplement to the production of books in manuscript, and those who could read continued to do so in the way of readers for hundreds of years, laboriously whispering the words as they traced them with a finger. They read aloud to themselves, just as writers dictated to themselves, and people who could read silently were rarities to be wondered at; according to St Augustine people came to watch St Ambrose indulging in his habit of silent reading. The practice of framing the printed words with the mouth and muttering probably persisted to the end of the sixteenth century; perhaps the dividing line between Shakespeare, who did not regard his plays as literature, and Ben Jonson, who did.

Before the age of reading contact with poetry was a matter of hearing it every day. In church, not only on Sundays but also on the numerous holy days which were the occasion for reading metrical lives of the saints, in the mystery plays, in the folk songs linked with occupations, in proverbs and mnemonics, and on many occasions throughout life, the ordinary man heard verse spoken in the course of daily living. Today, in contrast, we view the poetic and the prosaic as mutually exclusive modes of expression appropriate to different parts of life. 'One does not burst into verse in order to admonish one's children, or dictate a letter, or tell a joke, still less to give orders or draft directives. But [E. A. Havelock insists] in the Greek situation, during the non-literature epoch, you might do just that.' The change from this state of affairs was long and gradual.

When books replaced the living voice as medium, a new relationship developed between poet and audience, and eventually there were new kinds of poet, poetry and readership. Reading poetry became an affair of conscious choice, normally requiring outlay on a book on a scale that has fairly steadily increased since the groundling paid his penny to see a Shakespeare play. Moreover leisure, privacy and reasonable quiet were needed, commodities in short supply at various times. Reading has always been a solitary activity, deliberately undertaken by that part of the population able to read and determined enough to use the ability. From being something which could not be easily escaped, poetry became the profit from a contract between the poet and his reader, and not everyone took steps to reach the point of such considered choice.

Printing made its way because – among other reasons – it was novel and because it was associated with religion. Many writers on ballads and traditional poetry have noted that respect for the printed word caused the living versions of oral poetry to be ousted by stereotyped editions. One such observer was Willa Muir:

> Unlettered people, especially when they are given authoritative scriptures and feel reverence for the printed word of God, extend that reverence to all print that comes their way; they begin to think that the printed version of an orally transmitted song must be correct and that the fluid rendering of an orally transmitted song is somehow full of incorrect deviations. (p. 232)

These 'correct' versions froze the life out of oral poetry, and inferior literary work began to replace it. Face to face contact between poet and audience, and co-operation between them, came to an end; and poetry lost much of its body, the effects of sound and gesture that were part of its meaning. Of course there were gains – poetry of greater range and power which we discuss elsewhere – but the immediate impression is one of loss. The static nature of print precluded the dynamic performance without which oral poetry did not exist – a point again that has been repeatedly made by collectors and sometimes by the singers themselves of folk songs. When Sir Walter Scott printed some of the songs sung by the mother of James Hogg, the Ettrick shepherd, she reproved him: 'There were never ane o' my songs prentit till ye prentit them yoursel', an' ye hae spoilt them awthegither. They were made for singing and not for reading; but ye hae broken the charm now, an' they'll never be sung mair' (Willa Muir, p. 47).

However strenuously the exceptionally capable silent reader tries to recreate for himself the performance demanded by a poem, his 'internal pronunciation' must often fail; probably most readers never achieve much in the way of inner pronunciation, so that communication is only partial. And though the provision of a permanent form for a poem was an enormous gain – so that a reader could re-read and absorb it and later generations enjoy it – the lack of a physical audience seems at first to have been felt by writers; Terence Hawkes finds that 'much of the writing of the Elizabethan–Jacobean period proves to be a pale shadow of notions previously expressed orally with more powerful and ruthless realism in medieval vernacular proverbs and sermons' (T. Hawkes, p. 45).

Literacy moved literature from the world of voice into that of sight, and language lost much of the 'multi-dimensional resonance' it had enjoyed when myth and proverb and wise 'sentences' typified the utterances of oral culture, and every word was 'a poetic world unto itself' (McLuhan, p. 25). The understanding of a poem became an exercise in following a linear sequence rather than a matter of three-dimensional grasp, whereby a poem was heard and felt and experienced by the whole being of a man; so little of a person is called into play by an ordinary silent reading. Time also began to be seen in the way we see it, the present moment being like a train moving at a steady pace on lines unbroken since the creation and stretching illimitably (for practical purposes) ahead. Thus the sense of history we enjoy was developed with print; whereas the pre-literature ballad singer could say that the events described in a particular narrative happened a mile or two away only a generation or two ago, though any historical basis his tale may have had was far away and hundreds of years earlier. The history plays of Shakespeare may have been felt to be much nearer in time to their first audiences than they actually were.

The move from sound to sight found a theorist and an apologist in the work of Pierre la Ramée (1515–72), known by the Latinised form of his name, Petrus Ramus. His *Dialectica* became extremely influential, especially through the esteem it enjoyed at Cambridge. An advocate of order, he methodised everything, using diagrams and other visual methods to present his ideas; language was limited to writing, to marks on a page. 'The Ramist reworking of dialectic and rhetoric furthered the elimination of sound and voice from man's understanding of the intellectual world and helped create within the human spirit itself the silences of a spatialized universe' (Ong 1958, p. 318). Father Ong has elsewhere described the Ramist approach to knowledge as congenial to persons who habitually deal with reality in terms of accounting rather than in terms of meditation or wisdom (Ong 1971, p. 189). Ramism was thus a forerunner of the limited rationalism now pervasive among us. The media have put into circulation half-baked notions of science as a guide and philosophy; they have also given our minds a predilection for the abstract and the cliché, and the cliché is the popular expression of the abstract. 'It tends to make us view life impersonally, as third parties and onlookers, and it inclines to use, even when we are strongly moved, a kind of language which is suited only for general ideas and newspaper reports, or even for headlines' (Edwin Muir 1962, p. 101). The mental consciousness induced by print has no use for the creative, highly-charged language of poetry and imaginative literature, language that has always formed part of being human, and seems essential to our balance and well-being. Thus we suffer from emotional and imaginative malnutrition, and 'the semi-educated cling to the fixity of typographical space as a substitute for the living permanence of truth' (Ong 1971, p. 293). Our technical vocabularies have been grotesquely enlarged, but the vocabulary in which men have expressed their deepest feelings, managed their relations with each other and 'placed' themselves in their world, is no longer fully available. In Pope's words (*Dunciad* IV 162) we have 'hung one jingling padlock on the mind', and the vocabulary of sex, for example, 'is all but neutralized by constant exploitation' (Steiner 1975, p. 174).

Pre-literate poetry tended to be the voice of the people, uttered by an individual skilled in words and moving, in work songs and dance songs, to the rhythms of a basic civilisation. To a certain extent all people were poets and there was a reciprocal relationship between audience and performer. Even when able performers became prominent and the office of poet distinct, he was regarded as an expert who had learned the rules and practised his craft for the benefit of society. Often the purposes of the poems were practical and clearly prescribed. Until the poet was withdrawn from his hearers by the barriers of literacy, poetry could be regarded as the product of a community, and there was less individualising of personal experience. However a reading of pre-literate poems from all over the world does not leave one with the impression that they are group compositions; an individual is always speaking, but the themes are central – birth, courtship, marriage, work, war, illness, death – and the treatment moving and sensitive. One feels the kinship of Polynesian, Indian and African with the European poets who have handled the great commonplaces of experience. Folk song is not really an exception to this lack of individualising; though it developed from 'the communal and hardly differentiated work songs and cult songs of barbarian tribesmen' and was sung by a solo singer, it has been noted all over the world that the singers suppress their individuality, and that personal emotion is externalised and distanced.

Of course there are many exceptions to the character of early poetry as a social product; there have always been people with special gifts as poets and musicians, who composed the original 'folk' song and made the improvements that the body of singers approved and incorporated over the years. From a few survivals we know that there were personal lyrics among the most ancient poetry, but circumstances did not help them in general to survive. Certain tasks too were solitary and afforded the opportunity for more introspective singing. Among religions, Christianity by its nature offered more occasions for personal poetry than other faiths did; some Latin hymns and 'The Dream of the Rood' come to mind as early examples, and in the thirteenth century we have 'Stabat Mater' and 'Dies Irae'. Though it was harder for non-religious verse to escape destruction, the same century saw the emergence of the first individual lyric poet of France, Rutebeuf (c. 1230 – c. 1280), one of the great troubadours; and later Villon (fl. 1460) and Dunbar (? 1465 – ? 1530) strike one as being among the first modern poets, enlargers like the greater Dante and Donne.

In pre-literate cultures there was a strong element of religion and an unrelenting pressure from the need to wrest a living from the environment, and there cannot have been much of the individual life that we enjoy; so much of it was communal and conducted in church and guild rather than in private. One result of this was that in the audience for Shakespeare's plays, for example, 'the power of sharing group-response was highly developed, their threshold of emotional reaction low' (Bradbrook 1955, p. 19). Among primitive peoples the great occasions of life were often accompanied by rites and ceremonies, with the whole of existence affected by magical forces; a consciousness of this kind must have persisted in this country till replaced by the new outlook and the more private life that came in with literacy. 'Much of what we call the literature of medieval England is a symptom of a certain kind of social activity'; (Stevens 1973, p. 228) and the same is true of the mass of devotional verse, which reflects the religious life of a community.

Printing and a sufficient number of readers made it possible for the poet to sit alone in his study and write for readers who would themselves be on their own; he was now an individual setting down his personal feelings, sharing his private life with more or less like-minded people. The older poets of an oral culture could express only material for which there already existed a suitable diction; they could perhaps improve on this, but they could never do without it, never change it entirely. The poet on the other hand of a literate culture employed a different method of composition, seeking at leisure the right words for what he had to say; and as a result in the case of major poets there were new ways of attaining and expressing a fresh consciousness. As writers composed in a more deliberate manner when their work was to be printed, so readers came to accept the poet's offerings more selectively, more critically, and with a more considered but less spontaneous emotional response than that called forth by the ballads and epics of an oral culture. The silent reader cannot applaud the poet, join in a refrain, or throw a present to the singer. He may not be able to demonstrate his approval or disapproval, but he can explore new paths and enjoy an incomparably wider range of experience than was possible before print. The audience could no longer indulge in the collaboration of the old style; the gap between its members and the poet was marked, and the poet could get only a delayed reaction from his readers; but there was greater scope for the poet's exploration and greater rewards for those who could bridge the gap. Poetry became the vehicle for a special kind of experience, so that now the poetic frame of mind seems esoteric and dependent on being artificially kept alive.

There has always been a degree of cultural compartmentalising in civilised Europe. In medieval England the nobles, whose occupations were ruling, hunting and fighting, maintained the social gulf between themselves on the one hand and the peasants and priests on the other. The clergy had a monopoly of literacy, which the nobility did not seek to change, because they had no need of reading and writing – or rather could use priests as administrators. They could get on without it; the first five hundred years of English history 'cannot show more than three kings who were even probably literate' (Galbraith). But the cultural divisions were not watertight; there were great possibilities of education through eyes and ears that crossed the barriers, and at a distance the impression is one of cultural unity rather than of stratification. General illiteracy provided a good deal of common ground between social classes; so that 'a shepherd in an Icelandic homestead...could not avoid spending his evenings in listening to the kind of literature which interested the farmer. The result was a degree of really national culture such as no nation of today has been able to achieve' (Philpotts, p. 162).

By the time of Chaucer there existed a distinctive court poetry. It aspired to an achievement beyond that of the ballads and folk song; it was self-conscious art, and was addressed to a cultivated audience. It was for this audience that Caxton started printing in England in his middle fifties, with books that could not claim to be popular in the sense of 'of the people'; he thus continued the trend of monastic copying, which neglected popular poetry, unless like *Piers Plowman* it was acceptable as a kind of sermon. At this point we can see the opening of a rift that has never been narrowed; ever since Chaucer, English poetry, except in the theatre, has reached only a select audience, and so made permanent a division that could not exist in a pre-literate culture (Goody, p. 59). Something similar occurred in Greek literature without benefit of print, when Antimachus (who flourished at the end of the fifth century B.C.) consciously combined the work of the scholar with that of the artist. Only the educated could have followed such learning, and poetry can be seen withdrawing from the popular audience that it had enjoyed in the hey-day of the Athenian drama. A literary tradition enables the vocabulary dealing with central human concerns to acquire a rich charge of meaning from use in the contexts of major writers, and this accounts for much of the great beauty of English poetry; but such a tradition depends on a high degree of literary cultivation and is not generally accessible.

In the Tudor period most people were illiterate, with reading playing a very small part in the life of the people.

> Songs and stories were handed down by word of mouth from generation to generation, with never a page of print intervening. The life of the imagination and the feelings was still attuned to the ear rather than to the eye. The popular tradition, rich in folk heroes and broad humour and proverbial wisdom and memorable events, a strange and fascinating mixture of local legend and the lore of the Bible and the classics, was part of the very soil, and there was as yet no need for the printed word to supplant it.
> (Altick, p. 29)

But at about Shakespeare's time the printed word began to penetrate the masses, in the shape of printed broadsheets and broadsides – the latter being printed on one side only, so that they could be stuck on walls. They were distributed mainly by peddlers, like Autolycus, who sold them in villages and at hirings and fairs. They consisted of a poem with a woodcut at the top; the poem was often a folk song, but more commonly a set of verses produced by a journalist. The printing of folk songs was fatal to the oral tradition;

the fixed versions eventually killed off the living poetry, since respect for print spread the notion that the settled version was the best. The process has gone so far that nowadays we tend automatically to regard the written word as a paradigm of usage, so that at worst the spoken word tries to imitate the printed one.

At the same time composed ballads began to oust the traditional narratives. They were produced in large numbers; three thousand were registered at Stationers' Hall in the century-and-a-half after 1557, and two hundred ballad writers are known by name from the Elizabethan period. Ballads were still being produced in London in the middle of the last century, but gave way to cheap books and the popular press that was devised to meet the social and psychological needs of an industrialised country. These needs had not arisen by Shakespeare's time; a mass population of emotionally starved slum-dwellers had not come into being, so that the poor quality of the broadsides could not do much harm. Even so, in their variety they anticipated the million-sale daily by hundreds of years. There were sensational accounts of crimes and portents and monstrosities: 'Tydinges of a Huge and Ougly childe borne at Arnheim in Gelderland'. Some sought to win middle-class support by tales of valiant apprentices; and there were ballads of good counsel – 'A ballet against Swerynge', 'The Virgin's ABC', and several on the profitability of godliness:

> They that upon the Poor bestow
> unto the Lord doth lend;
> And God unto such men again
> a thousandfold will send.
> (L. B. Wright, p. 115)

There were ballads against drunkenness, and many provided lessons in diligence and thrift; one of the later and most prolific writers, Martin Parker, was fond of preaching philosophy and industry. Others were tragic, amatory, historical, superstitious, bawdy, humorous; and a large class concentrated on current events, dealt with politics or insinuated patriotic propaganda. So as well as supplying mere amusement and moral exhortation the writers acted as reporters, newspapers, histories and publicists on social, religious and political questions. Commercial interests, raising capital for overseas ventures, found in the ballad a means of influencing the public; other verses were the vehicle of protests; and especially in the middle of the seventeenth century ballads were written to order as political weapons against Parliament. At times the establishment was disturbed by the power of the ballads, especially in the struggle between Catholicism and Protestantism, and an Act was passed against them in 1543. The broadsides helped to form middle-class ideas; they represented a decline in taste, according to seventeenth-century satirists; their emotional threshold was low – 'the intuitive delicacy of traditional verse was unknown to them' – and the kind of appeal they made anticipated many of those found in the first Northcliffe newspapers (Lord Northcliffe being the first English press-baron, who thrived on publishing cheap daily newspapers).

As the broadside gained in popularity, so the professional literary figures denounced them. Richard Puttenham in his *Arte of Poetry* (1589), Thomas Nashe in *Pierce Penniless* (1592) and William Webbe in *A Discourse of English Poetrie* (1586) inveighed against them; the last of the three wrote of 'the uncountable rabble of ringing Ballet makers and compilers of senceless sonets who... stuffe every stall full of grosse devises and unlearned Pamphlets', adding 'I scorne and spue out the rakehelly rout of our ragged Rymers'. The cleavage between Shakespeare, writing for performance and not for print, and Ben Jonson has already been mentioned. The taste of court and city were close till late in the sixteenth century, but in the reign of James I the plays and their audiences were socially differentiated, and with the Restoration the ordinary citizen was driven from the theatre.

The growth of print and the increase in literacy at the end of the sixteenth century were instrumental in effecting several changes; they started the decline of folk song and oral poetry; they developed a new readership with the broadsheets and similar literature; and they made possible the growth of individual poetry of high quality on a large scale. With paper to draft his work on, a poet could revise, take stock, produce deeper, more reflective verse, and fix new images to present his experience. Poetry ceased to be improvisatory, public or prophetic, and occupied itself with catching fleeting sensations and private states of mind. The lyric became the appropriate vehicle for this more complex and more revealing material. The latter too would tend to be more difficult, as it lost the support of the religious framework that supplied the symbols and allegories that were formerly the common property of poet and listener. The truly modern poets of the age of print, from the metaphysicals to (say) Eliot, are individuals exploring on their own; and in their successful wrestling with words in order to develop a new consciousness they achieved great advances. But the lesser poets seem to suffer most from the lack of a reciprocal relationship with their readers and of a more than personal outlook; the great run of contemporary verse seems too much absorbed in the writers' temporary physical life. We are reminded of Lawrence's gibe in *Reflections on the Death of a Porcupine*: 'Man, of course, being measure of the universe, is measured only against man. Has, of course, vital relationship only with his own cheap little species. Hence the cheap little twaddler he has become.'

The age of industry

Industrialisation destroyed the culture that had been the birthright of a majority of the English. Ancient and vigorous, it was part of the agricultural economy, and is evident in songs, dances, proverbs, seasonal festivities and artefacts now treasured by museums. It was wiped out in a generation or two. Long hours of factory work (fifty–sixty hours a week up to the 1890s) left workers with little time or energy for culture, which now had to be sought, whereas before it had normally been geared in with earning a livelihood, however arduous. Meanwhile the lives of those left in the country were impoverished by the agricultural depression of 1870–1900; semi-starvation does not encourage singing. In the factories the employers banned song and so fenced off an area where people could be human; but this is to be noted as an instance of subjecting men to the needs of technology rather than a contribution to the decline of folk song. As the economy changed from agriculture to industry, the machine replaced the seasons as providing the rhythms of life; the new schooling supplied by church and state produced a half-educated proletariat; and Northcliffe and his successors exploited this semi-literacy by selling synthetic entertainment which solidified its consumers into what looked like an undifferentiated mass.

The increase of formal education did little for the working class, because what it offered was vocational. The early backers of the Mechanics' Institutes, for example, were opposed to poetry, fiction and such dangerous fare; they wanted all reading to be utilitarian. Poetry was regarded as a sop: 'Poetry...can enable the man of labour to rise sometimes out of his dull, dry, hard toil, and dreary routine of daily life into forgetfulness of his state, to breathe a higher and serener, and purer atmosphere' F. W. Robertson, 1859 (Altick, p. 196). In schools the poetry supplied was in a form remote from the lives and understanding of the children. Much used was Vicesimus Knox's *Elegant Extracts: or, Useful and Entertaining Pieces of Poetry, Selected for the Improvement of Young People*. A comparable collection, *Original Poems for Infant Minds*, not dated but apparently of the 1860s, contains improving stories – 'The Idle Boy', 'The Industrious Boy', 'Never Play with Fire', 'My Mother', and so on. The shortest complete item is:

The Butterfly

The Butterfly, an idle thing,
Nor honey makes, nor yet can sing,
  As do the bee and bird;
Nor does it, like the prudent ant,
Lay up the grain for times of want,
  A wise and cautious hoard.

My youth is but a summer's day:
Then like the bee and ant I'll lay
  A store of learning by;
And though from flower to flower I rove,
My stock of wisdom I'll improve,
  Nor be a butterfly.

Matthew Arnold complained more than once in his reports about the poor quality of reading matter provided in the elementary schools; and his hopes of humanising-by-literature were blighted by the Revised Code, a system of paying for schools by results that narrowed and deadened the curriculum. The memoirs of those who attended the schools often record that reading was a hated school exercise, performed unwillingly and without understanding.

The new plutocracy aped the ways of the patrician patrons of the arts, and the author had to accept his position as provider of entertainment. Literature in general was turned into a commodity and the poet into the producer of something vendible. Of course good prose and verse continued to be written, and that of middling quality sold in large amounts. But the split in readership became wider; the tight stratification of which we have heard so much in this century began when the half-educated were captured by the press, so that by about 1900 we have a population divided into literate, illiterate and – the majority – semi-literate. Of the latter John Berger has observed:

> There are large sections of the English working and middle class who are inarticulate as the result of wholesale cultural deprivation. They are deprived of the means of translating what they know into thoughts which they can think. They have no examples to follow in which words clarify experience. Their spoken proverbial traditions have long been destroyed; and, although they are literate in the strictly technical sense, they have not had the opportunity of discovering the existence of a written cultural heritage. (p. 98)

Another observer, after noting that nowadays the normality of reading scarcely exists, describes many of the students he saw at a day-release centre as 'famished, starving for something more than the curriculum provides' (Blythe, p. 213).

What we have lost is beautifully and suggestively sketched by Willa Muir in her chapter on children's singing games. These songs, orally transmitted without adult help, were an inheritance from the people who made the ballads; and from her account we can gather some idea of the part played by the ballad culture in the lives of the people. The singing games left the children satisfied and happy; squabbling ceased and there was harmony even among rough-tongued and noisy girls. The songs – the mother-and-daughter games for example – were a part of growing up; the children played out the drama of choosing a mate and being chosen; they were rehearsing for real life. The songs filled a human need, for 'the energies informing the underworld of human feeling search for an objective shape in the light of day, and until they find it are unsatisfied'.

The great loss suffered by everyone except the educated, and close-knit groups like miners and sailors, was language – the language that had been the expression of a way of living. The masses who moved into the factory towns found themselves unable to learn the English supplied to them in schools. There were several results. It looks very much as if the lack of a means of expression can lead to anti-social conduct, so that a purely vocational training that neglects emotional education may turn out to be dangerously defective. The loss of language is likely also to lead to poor thinking, linguistic insensitivity and a weakening hold on reality. The latter especially follows the split between our knowing and our feeling. As Archibald MacLeish has pointed out, we do not seem to feel our knowledge. We have at our disposal a huge amount of information, but we are not thereby seized with more knowledge of these facts; they are there but they do not affect us. MacLeish therefore stressed the need to know with the whole heart.

The displaced language was concrete and expressive, the product of a way of life. It is what R. S. Thomas heard in his parishioners in rural Wales, when he had ceased to misjudge them:

> I have taxed your ignorance of rhyme and sonnet,
> Your want of deference to the painter's skill,
> But I know, as I listen, that your speech has in it
> The source of all poetry, clear as a rill
> Bubbling from your lips; and what brushwork could equal
> The artistry of your dwelling on the bare hill?
> 'A Priest to his People' (R. S. Thomas, p. 29)

It was replaced first by the kind of crude emotional register that the popular press used during the Boer War, followed by the voice of the film and bestseller, the monosyllabic jabs of the headlines, the demotic jargon of television, and the base coinage of the 'ad-man'. 'The mass media first provided the poorly educated with words to express his feelings, and then the feelings themselves to which he was to tailor his own emotional responses' (Vicinus, p. 329).

The working class of the nineteenth century wanted education, and they wanted to read; the accounts in the autobiographies of self-educated men and women of their successful struggles against odds to get learning are most moving. They produced a great deal of poetry themselves. Some of it was literary and rather lifeless, like the Chartist hymns, in a line which petered out with William Morris. There were numbers of individual working-class poets, published in newspapers and books, but none came into the same class as John Clare. Then there were the anonymous poems that came out of factory, mine and mill, which were all the better for having no literary aspirations or trimmings. They speak of the hard and grim lives, and the courage, of the writers and their fellows, but they make rather depressing reading, despite Lloyd's claim for them: 'A new lyric of the industrial towns arose, frail at first but getting stronger, reflecting the life and aspirations of a raw class in the making, thinking new thoughts, standing in novel relationship to each other and to their masters' (p. 317). There is plenty of evidence for working-class achievement, apart from the autobiographies mentioned; Dickens observed in 1853 that 'there are in Birmingham at this moment many working men infinitely better versed in Shakespeare and Milton than the average of fine gentlemen in the days of bought-and-sold dedications and dear books'. They bought books too – not only those by the literary bestsellers like Scott and Tennyson, but also those by John Keble (forty-three editions of *The Christian Year* had been published by mid-century) and Edwin Arnold, whose *The Light of Asia*, a life of Buddha in verse, had large sales. They read Shelley and Wordsworth as well, but the protest of these poets against the subordination of man to machine did not make any impact till this century – and then a limited one. In addition they consumed vast quantities of sensational broadsheets, with half-a-dozen of the murder titles selling over a million each, which were a good deal nastier than those of Elizabeth's time. Other verse read by the working class included such material as temperance songs (see chapter XXXIII of *The Posthumous Papers of the Pickwick Club*) and the lyrics of Adelaide Ann Procter, a regular contributor to Dickens' *Household Words* in the 1850s.

Victorian poetry failed to recognise and respond to the changes that were taking place. Not surprisingly, since it was conceived as an anodyne; in the words of Walter Scott, in a letter:

> A taste for poetry...is apt if too much indulged, to engender a fastidious contempt for the ordinary business of the world, and gradually to unfit us for the exercise of the useful and domestic virtues, which depend greatly on our not exalting our feelings above the temper of a well-ordered and well-educated society...Cultivate, then, Sir, your taste for poetry and the belles lettres, as an elegant and most interesting amusement, but combine it with studies of a more serious and solid cast.
>
> (*Letters*, ed. H. J. C. Grierson, vol. 2, p. 278)

And Mr Weller, whose appearance in *The Pickwick Papers* turned a near failure into a success, spoke for more than himself when he said, 'Poetry's unnat'ral'. Weller was speaking in character, but Dickens voiced his own view when in 1838 in *Sketches of Young Gentlemen* he described 'The Poetical Young Gentleman'. This essay of mixed intentions contains a caricature of a poet that became the standard image for a century – long-haired, tie-less, not over-clean, writing for ladies' albums, ladies' magazines and the Poet's Corner of country newspapers.

The characteristic poetry of the age dealt with a limited range of attitudes. The poets wrote for an urban middle class about topics they could understand, adopting (David Craig suggests in *The Real Foundations*) a lofty Tennysonian style because they had to maintain the equanimity of that class in the face of the bleakness of the age. The lyric was the vehicle for the expression of rather narrow views and selected feelings and moods such as doubt, pessimism or nostalgia. A few titles from the immensely popular Mrs Hemans are indicative: 'The Child's First Grief', 'England's Dead', 'The Better Land', 'Burial in the Desert', 'Bring Flowers', 'The First Grey Hair', 'He Never Smiled Again'. A public lecture on Mrs Hemans was the means whereby an M.P. (in Thackeray's *The Newcomes*) strove to repair his failing popularity. The cult of home, the subject of unlimited sentimentality, was all-pervasive. A review of William Morris's *The Earthly Paradise* in 1870 declared that it was ideal for family reading, being 'adapted for conveying to our wives and daughters a refined, although not altogether diluted version of those wonderful creations of Greek fancy which the rougher sex alone is permitted to imbibe at first hand' (*Saturday Review*, 30 May

1869). But the listeners whom Morris pressed into hearing him read the poem aloud literally fell asleep. The contrast between Morris's vigorous practical activity and his soporific verse illustrates the case of late Victorian poetry. The poets chose subjects deemed to be poetical, without any of the obdurate resistance of theme that is present in so much good poetry, like that of Hopkins. At the end of the century poetry was still fairly popular, because it was uplifting, soothing and deliberately oblivious of the physical and moral ugliness of industry. Thus almost any page of the poets then in circulation is likely to show the influence of Tennyson's idiom, remote from the life of the time and excelling only at conveying a limited range of attitudes. Equally straitened and unrealistic was the popular nationalist and jingo poetry of the music halls, which inspired Kipling to produce his own ballads. These surpassed the music hall fare in arrogance, condescension and crudity of feeling. Kipling seemed to prove that Arthur Symons was right when he told the nineties that 'the poet has no more place in society than a monk in domestic life' (MacLeish 1961, p. 115).

Technology, science and poetry

Of nineteenth-century industrialism it may be said that it produced large quantities of goods and services, but failed miserably to apply them to the relief of poverty and unhappiness. For the present century it may be claimed that it has solved many problems of distribution but has not really much idea of what to do with industry except to let it run on. Industry has not been used to satisfy the true needs of humanity but has continued to serve the well-to-do and has imposed imitations of their affluent ways upon less affluent people. Society has used its energy to produce and consume an ever larger volume of less valued goods. 'The established mechanism of a market society continues to direct human energies into the accustomed economic channels, despite the declining social importance of the activities which fill those channels' (Heilbroner, p. 232). A sort of capitalism has continued to function automatically long after it had achieved the ends proposed for it by its exponents of the previous century. The individuality and non-responsibility which were prominent in that age have been institutionalised, and many qualities of importance to men and society have been suppressed in the market-place because they cannot be quantified. Everything is equated with everything else and rendered exchangeable by being given a price tag, so that even everyday absolute values like health and beauty have to be 'economic'. What has happened is a restriction of freedom (for example by the noise, use of space, consumption of resources associated with transport and other utilities) rather than an enlargement; 'the richer a society, the more impossible it becomes to do worthwhile things without an immediate pay off' (Schumacher, p. 57). The industrial revolution has never been adequately controlled, so that we have been committed to urbanisation, technification and secularisation on a large scale.

This process is accepted equally by all the political parties devoted to what is ironically called 'growth'. That is to say, uncontrolled 'scientific' and technological advance in directions decided by economic interests, nationalism and psychological perversity, and leading to space travel, computerisation, the control of human behaviour, spoliation of the environment and manipulative medico-biology. For all this the ordinary man must pay in the acceptance of the way of life imposed on him, any change being labelled as a rise in the 'standard of living' – the phrase trotted out to stifle any inspection of the truth. Under cover of this mendacity means dictate ends. If a development is technically possible it must be followed up, irrespective of whether it serves human needs. The lie is reiterated in endless variety by the media; the truths that would feed the will and fuel the action required to cope with our problems are obscured, with too little done to alter economic incompetence, environmental pollution and deadening ways of earning a living. 'There is something fundamentally irrational in a society which makes the ways of life of its members conform to the efficiency of technological operations, rather than individual needs and aspirations' (Dubos 1973, p. 286). We have been freed from physical want only to be enslaved as consumers of distractions.

All this amounts to a large-scale distortion of science and its applications. This emerges if we recall that both poetry and science sprang from the same source: the desire of man to understand and meet the situations that confronted him, to recognise patterns and to give shape to his experience, so that the earliest science evolved from poetic cosmologies and gnomic verses. Both science and poetry were originally the outcome of the directiveness and creativeness inherent in life. We can observe this in the young child's questioning use of speech:

> It is his withdrawal from immersion in the environment, his questioning of particular impressions, of the events that come to meet him, that marks the emergence of the child's humanity, the emergence of

the richer intangible world in which he will come to dwell...No
matter how triumphant the forward march of science, no matter how
precise, how far-reaching our formulations, they are founded on a
question mark.
(Grene, p. 175)

And so, in physics for instance, we do not now produce precise
answers, but rather an expression of probabilities; the notions of
pure objectivity and absolute determinism are dominant no more.
We may then adopt Michael Polanyi's definition of science as 'that
which scientists affirm and believe to be true'. Science provides an
emotional satisfaction, but it cannot supplant the modes of aware-
ness that appeal directly to human feelings.

Science exists only with the approval of society. It is no more
autonomous, and no more important than some other human
concerns.

> The social rootedness of science in often associated with the utility
> of applied science; this is an error and a dangerous error. But
> precisely the *detachment* of the theoretical scientist is rooted in the
> institutions of his society and in the evaluative choices which underlie
> those institutions. He can focus his whole attention, bring every
> relevant clue to bear, on a problem wholly without appetitive or
> utilitarian implications...[because] First...he himself has been
> nourished and disciplined by traditions cultivated in his society which
> have produced this kind of devoted attention to impersonal goals.
> And secondly, because the society itself, in its deepest foundations,
> respects those independently self-sustaining traditions of scientist or
> scholar.
> (Grene, p. 180)

Science continues because it accepts the authority of custom and
tradition in society, which for a start supplies it with the language
and writing without which it cannot begin. Moreover scientific
thought, especially modern physics, relies on images; it is a com-
monplace that any significant discovery follows a leap of the
imagination; and day-dreams, like Kekule's vision of snakes (which
gave him the idea of the benzene ring), can be productive. 'It is
probably true that the best ideas regarding our problems come to
us in attitudes that are relatively free from immediate purposive
restrictions. The best thinkers are those who allow themselves a
considerable amount of daydreaming...' (Thurstone, p. 142). A
scientist who limits his thinking to particulars, to concrete reality,
is narrowing and frustrating his science. The 'creative intuition and
perception of the artist and the poets is going to become as necessary
to the future of science as are, and as will remain, the skills of

deductive inference and experimental prowess' (Thorpe, p. 344). As Shelley, arguing the greater value of artists and poets over Locke, Hume, Gibbon and so on, declared: 'The human mind could never, except by the intervention of these excitements, have been awakened to the invention of the grosser sciences, and that application of analytical reasoning to the aberrations of society, which it is now attempted to exalt over the direct expression of the inventive and creative faculty itself' (p. 109). Science cannot thrive without all sorts of 'non-scientific' qualities, including faith, hope and charity. Faith in its methods and the utility of it operations; hope that its activities will produce results, that society will continue to accept science's own valuation of itself and thus go on supporting it; and charity – the good-will of others and the vast contributions of money and resources they are burdened with. (Are the grants for research announced almost daily in *The Times* ever totted up and analysed? How much do they contribute to the quality of life?)

Poetry for a minority?

Since the time of the great Romantics poetry as a whole has failed to meet the experience of change, complexity and technological advance. It has lost the esteem of the intelligent, and the large audience it used to enjoy has faded away, and seems unlikely to return, with leisure now regarded as a time for getting away from anything serious and for conspicuous consumption. Poetry is too exacting to be pleasant. It no longer has any social or prophetic function; it has forfeited the place in the public world that it enjoyed in the nineteenth century. This is not to belittle the achievement of great individual poets like Yeats and Eliot and of lesser figures like Pound and Edwin Muir.

The poet is thus thrown back on himself; he creates a private world for his own satisfaction without concerning himself over-much with his public, if this can be said to exist at all. Even religion does not offer the framework it formerly provided; it is just one more solitary stance, another way of feeling the loneliness that the poet now takes for granted. As Terence Tiller wrote in his poem, 'Substitutes':

> Squeezing the private sadness until words
> pearl round it, and all images become
> the private sadness and the life...

The tendency is for modern collections of verse to consist of such private lyrics, addressed to a very few readers of whose response the poet can never be certain. There is no encouragement to grapple with large issues. The intelligent poet will be aware of complicating factors everywhere, and cannot fail to be influenced for example by psychology and anthropology. Thus much modern poetry appears difficult and lacking in direction. Moreover writers are inhibited from drawing on the poetic; their readers would not understand, might be deterred by echoes from bad 'poetic' verse; and a dry, ironic language is the outcome, even in the best poets. The weaker go in for 'social realism' and a poverty-stricken language. The resources of English literature are not open to them; possibly, like their readers, they have read little of it, now that the poetry of the past seems to exist only as material conserved by academics for use in teaching.

We have reached a position in which poetry, despite the strong case that can be made out for it, is enjoyed only by a small minority of the population, which may or may not keep open communications with the people at large. It is worth bearing in mind that only in small homogeneous groups of 'primitive' people, who manage without leaders or organisation, is there no taking on trust, no explanation of special interests, no decision-making by a few on behalf of others. A country's decisions have as a matter of history been made for it by a small proportion of the population – about one twenty-fifth of it under the Tudors and Stuarts – and in Western Europe at least, thought has been provided by a clerisy of poets, philosophers, priests and artists. At the Renaissance poetry in particular came to be produced for a select society, who admired it because it was the right thing to admire it; and about the same time there began a two-fold attack on poetry, causing it to go more and more on the defensive. On the religious side the early translators of the Bible stigmatised poetry as pernicious; and in the world of affairs the growth of capitalism was inimical. To the mercantile mind of the Jacobean period poetry was worse than useless; it was a waste of time. As the profit motive figured more largely and the need to save one's soul less so in the country's consciousness, a hostility to the arts generally became engrained in the English, among whom nonconformist bankers and factory owners became the dominant class. Thus by the beginning of the present century poetry in the eyes of the man in the street was a frill. The typical capitalist of the nineteenth century regarded the artist as the producer of objects, carrying some inherited prestige, that could be displayed and accumulated; and there was throughout that century a steady decline in accepted artistic standards.

In the present century there is nothing to replace the élite that used to live the political and intellectual life of the nation. On one level, as Michael Polanyi has noted, 'the amplitude of our cultural heritage exceeds ten thousand times the carrying capacity of any human brain, and hence we must have ten thousand specialists to transmit it'. Perhaps a comparable degree of specialisation in things cultural must be tolerated for a time. These specialists may have been what Eliot had in mind when he wrote (in *On Poetry and Poets*) that the development of a culture does not mean bringing everyone to the front, but does mean the maintenance of an élite with the main and more passive body of readers not more than a generation behind. This seems to be an updating of Arnold's belief that poetry could help to purify society by purifying the sensibilities of those men who act as its leaders. The élite postulated by Eliot must be supported by a large and loosely connected liaison group, usefully placed between the active few and the majority who do not wish to be bothered over-much. The liaison group will not be passive handers-on, but will accept the outlook and findings of the specialist group only after it has tested them on general grounds for reasonableness and consistency. There are thousands of such particular interests with their experts handing down their evaluations all the time; and as members of one liaison group or another many of us are helping with this sifting of specialised knowledge and interpretation every day of our lives.

Hostility to poetry and the arts generally still persists. It is active and sometimes virulent, not so much in the entrepreneurs who still find scope in the world of the media, as in those whom they employ to entertain the masses. Many providers of media fare feel insecure and threatened by those who have standards other than their own. In any case they do not wish the consumer to be aware of a different diet, and they make sure that if they do hear of it, it will be only in a distorted, caricatured or emasculated form. The threat is genuine and serious, and one can see the point of F. R. Leavis's case for 'an armed and conscious minority'. But as D. W. Harding wrote:

> Critical analysis of mass culture, with resistance to much of it, is therefore necessary, but a hostile cleavage between mass and minority is not. In the last analysis cultural minorities survive because they enjoy at a high level certain things that the majority also enjoys in a less practised form; and so far there have always been sufficient

numbers of the majority who recognize this, at least dimly, to ensure some support for literature and the arts. A cultural minority, after all, must always be recruited from the majority, spiralling up out of it . . .
(Harding 1969)

Poetry for a minority can never be a satisfactory aim or recipe. It is an activity that depends quite as much as science on the goodwill of society, and it can do for society a great deal that is outside the scope of science.

8

Uses of poetry

To the poet

Many poets have written for pay or advancement. The Homeric epics were composed for recital at festivals, providing a larger audience than that of a court or big house, and made possible by the increased wealth of Greece in the eighth century B.C. In the classical period most poetry was commissioned for pay, to meet a requirement of religion or patriotism or family pride; only Alcaeus and Sappho wrote to please themselves. This is typical of what has happened all over the world; panegyrics and other kinds of official poetry have not usually been composed for love. The bards of Ireland and Scotland became wealthy and powerful landowners; and the professional poets who competed successfully at the verse tournaments of pre-Islamic Arabia were rewarded by gifts of herds and other possessions. In the Middle Ages poetry was a craft acquired by learned men who were in a position to satisfy the wants of patrons – the church and the nobility. By the time of Elizabeth I poetry in the theatre was left to entertainers like Shakespeare; more literary poetry was the accomplishment of gentlemen, who might circulate their work in manuscript but were far above ordinary publication. However, the writers of sonnets could use poetry as a weapon in the competitive life of the court, and in the sixteenth century emblem-writing became 'a gentlemanly accomplishment of the same type as the ability to play the lute or dance the lavolta' (Freeman, p. 3). In the seventeenth century poets wrote for political advancement, or like Herrick, to win fame:

> To Print our Poems, the propulsive cause
> Is Fame (the breath of popular applause).

Dryden and many others sought advancement by dedicating their poems to the rich and powerful; and there was no profession of letters in England till Pope laid the foundations of one by turning to the public, rather than the nobility, as his patron. He was followed in the nineteenth century by bestsellers like Tennyson and Walter Scott – who sold the copyright of *Lord of the Isles* for the then very large sum of £4,200.

Poets have often hoped that their work would bring them immortality or a measure of life after death. Horace (65–8 B.C.) was one of the first, with his ode 'Exegi monumentum aere perennius', and a number of English poets, especially in the sixteenth century, expressed similar sentiments. Shakespeare's

> Not marble, nor the guilded monument,
> Of Princes shall out-live this powrefull rime...

is only one of his statements of the idea, which we find also in sonnets by Michael Drayton and Samuel Daniel. The line continues through Herrick, with a pleasant little poem *His Poetry His Pillar*, and through Waller and many others to our own century, in which the hope is less confident. Siegfried Sassoon wrote, of good poets: 'Who then shall dare to say that they have died?' and C. Day Lewis in *The Poet* was conditional:

> Death's cordon narrows: but vainly,
> If I've slipped the carrier word.

But nowadays the affirmation is rarely heard.

It has been replaced by the theory that the writing of poetry is good for the psychic health of the poet. The notion is perhaps as old as Plato, and it appears in St Augustine's *De Musica*, Book II, which gives the impression already noted: if you can keep your verse in order, your soul will be healthy. There is some support for the theory from the many cases of poets writing under an inner compulsion, of which one of the most astonishing is that of R. M. Rilke. Between 2 and 20 February 1922 he wrote three of his *Duino Elegies* and finished three others; and in the middle of all this produced fifty-five sonnets, which he had never intended to write at all. If one tries to describe the post-Romantic climate in which such a feat can occur, one is reminded of Philip Rieff's observation that 'Religious man was born to be saved; psychological man is born to be pleased' (1966, p. 24). Today we are all psychological men, more or less, so that when a modern poet (in a beautiful poem) wishes to praise John Clare he describes him as 'a voice upon the air That sighed to be delivered of its message' (James Reeves: 'The Savage Moon').

The argument that poetry is good for the poet, and then for his reader, has been eloquently expounded by I. A. Richards in *Principles of Literary Criticism*; in his art the artist attains a balanced poise which the reader or beholder can share. The poet writes to sort himself out, like the child of whom Graham Wallas said in *The Art of Thought*: 'The little girl had the makings of a poet in her who, being told to be sure of her meaning before she spoke, said: "How can I know what I think till I see what I say?"' That is the way in which poets appear to work; of his own writing C. Day Lewis explained:

> I do not sit down at my desk to put into verse something that is already clear in my mind. If it were clear in my mind, I should have no incentive or need to write about it, for I am an explorer, not a journalist, a propagandist, or a statistician . . . The theme of a poem is the meaning of its subject matter for me. When I have discovered the meaning *to me* of the various fragments of experience which are constellating in my mind, I have begun to make sense of such experience and to realise the pattern in it; and often I have gone some way with a poem before I am able to grasp the theme which lies hidden in the material that has accumulated.
>
> (C. Day Lewis 1961)

And again of the poem as a means of self-exploration Michael Hamburger has written:

> One of the great rewards and delights of writing poetry is that poems tell one what one is thinking and feeling, what one is and has been and will be, where one has come from and where one is going. There was a time when I thought that I knew what I believe, and I imposed this knowledge on the poems I wrote. These are the poems which now embarrass me. The ones that don't embarrass me are the ones that surprise me, because they know more than I do – even about myself.
>
> (Dust-jacket of *Travelling*, 1969)

Such expressions come from poets everywhere, including even children at school (Thompson, p. 165).

All this may sound as if a poet is one who carries out spiritual exercises in private, but of course he needs the reassurance of an audience to test the validity of his art and the clarity of his expression, just as a singer minimally needs a room which is not 'dry'. The medieval craftsman-poet, filling a social need, knew his audience well and had to secure and hold its attention. The modern poet feels the need for an audience; T. S. Eliot, for example:

> There is no doubt that a poet wishes to give pleasure, to entertain and divert people; and he should normally be glad to be able to feel that the entertainment or diversion is enjoyed by as large and various a number of people as possible . . . The poet is vitally interested in the *use* of poetry because he naturally desires a state of society in which [his wares] may become popular.
>
> (1933, p. 31)

Theodore Roethke wanted 'to be loved by the people' (Murphy, p. 23) and Walt Whitman demanded full co-operation from his readers:

I myself but write one or two indicative words for the
future,
Expecting the main things from you.

To the reader

The Victorian conception of the poet was summed up in A. W. E.
O'Shaughnessy's *Ode*. He was a 'music-maker' and 'a dreamer of
dreams', whose function it was to celebrate cities and empires:

> With wonderful deathless ditties
> We build up the world's great cities,
>   And out of a fabulous story
>   We fashion an empire's glory:
> One man with a dream, at pleasure,
>   Shall go forth and conquer a crown;
> And three with a new song's measure
>   Can trample an empire down...

But the view of great Victorians like J. S. Mill and Charles Darwin
was rather different. Mill confessed that in his youthful propagan-
dist phase he under-valued poetry, like the Benthamites; but later
he recognised its place in human culture as a means of educating
the feelings (Mill, p. 95). Thinking on similar lines, Darwin described
his plight in a well-known passage:

> My mind seems to have become a kind of machine for grinding
> general laws out of large collections of facts, but why this should have
> caused the atrophy of that part of the brain alone, on which the higher
> tastes depend, I cannot conceive. A man with a mind more highly
> organised or better constituted than mine, would not, I suppose, have
> thus suffered; and if I had to live my life again, I would have made
> a rule to read some poetry and listen to some music at least once every
> week; for perhaps the parts of my brain now atrophied would thus
> have been kept active through use.
> The loss of these tastes is a loss of happiness, and may possibly be
> injurious to the intellect, and more probably to the moral character,
> by enfeebling the emotional part of our nature.
> (Darwin, p. 74)

Thus in the nineteenth century poetry retained a good deal of the
respect with which it had normally been regarded; volumes of verse
sold well and were usually read.

Against this background the position of poetry today stands
sharply contrasted. Its social function is no more, its readers are few
and its study merely an academic concern; and as a result we are
much concerned to make out a case for it. The poet's first aim (in
L. C. Knights's phrase) is 'to activate the reader's mind'. Then it

provides the reader with a means of discovering truths about himself and about human experience: 'poetry puts language to full use as a means of thought, exploration and discovery, and we have so far just about made a beginning...' (Sewell, p. 39). Imaginative literature has often been the best way of learning about the men and women of a particular period, because the creative writer is alive to what is of significance about him; 'what light we possess on our essential, inward condition is still gathered by the poet' (Steiner 1967, p. 25). The poet is in a position to perceive what changes in outlook and feeling are needed and in what direction. His reader, one hopes, becomes more sensitive, and more aware of himself, of other people and of his environment. What poetry offers him is a clarification of life, from which answers can be produced to the two questions posed by W. H. Auden:

> 1. *Who am I?* What is the difference between man and all other creatures? What relations are possible between them? What is man's status in the universe?
>
> 2. *Whom ought I to become?* What are the characteristics of the hero, the authentic man whom everybody should admire and try to become? (Auden, p. 344)

To such questions poetry provides clear replies. A man who recorded how he heard them was Thomas Bewick, who greatly admired the border ballads and at one time engraved headpieces for the copies sold by peddlers. Those who today find the ballads too charged with killing and cruelty may care to observe how he moved on to something more:

> The winter evenings were often spent in listening to the traditionary tales and songs, relating to men who had been eminent for their prowess and bravery in the border wars, and of others who had been esteemed for better and milder qualities, such as their having been good landlords, kind neighbours, and otherwise in every respect bold, independent and honest men. I used to be particularly affected with the warlike music, and with songs relative to the former description of characters; but with the songs regarding the latter a different kind of feeling was drawn forth, and I was greatly distressed, and often gave vent to it in tears.
> (Bewick, p. 10)

Wordsworth too liked the ballads and wished he could emulate them. 'People who did not wear fine clothes but could feel deeply' were the subjects of many poems in which he showed us what he judged as true humanity, a quality found in every station in life. Thus he helped to expand the consciousness of the age, and exemplified the power of art to understand and interpret life. When we see through the eyes of a good poet we can make sense of our experience, understand our world more fully, and see more possibilities for living in it. Of the great poems which had meant much to him D. H. Lawrence remarked: 'all these lovely poems which after all give the ultimate shape to one's life; all these lovely poems woven deep into a man's consciousness' (Lawrence 1930, p. 155). Any good poet sees through surfaces and categories to the lives of individual men and women, and thus keeps us in contact with the essential truths of human existence.

To return for a moment to the ballads. Their poetry provided a picture of life as it appeared to the peasants who transmitted them, and fed their imagination for hundreds of years. They are limited, they are not great poetry, 'they do not contain those universal statements of life which we find in Dante and Shakespeare, but they were once a general possession as Shakespeare has never been' (Edwin Muir 1962, p. 22). Willa Muir described what the ballads did for the illiterate but not insensitive border people:

> The Ballads kept doors open for them into a wider world than everyday experience. As they listened, they translated the themes into familiar terms of local life, but that did not mean that all their interests were narrowly parochial. The Ballads, or, at least, most of the Ballads, were not parochial in theme; moreover, the Ballad stories brought with them, embedded in their material, recognizable vestiges of beliefs and customs from the past of mankind, providing some depth of background for an audience that had no instruction in formal history or geography.   (p. 125)

Every human mind must learn to balance itself, and towards this end it can obtain assistance from poetry and the other arts. The experience of poetry can bring into consciousness what is there but unformed; it can adjust and confirm values; it can help to organise other experiences, the insights gained and the feelings suffered. The experiences of a person nourished by the arts are affected at their inception by his memory of what he has read and seen; the forms they take are shaped by the intentions and attitudes of poets and artists, including bad ones. The crises and testing times of life are lightened by what the sufferer recalls from his reading; his pain or bereavement or disillusion is accompanied by solace and encouragement to go on living, and peace of mind may be achieved. Similarly the intoxication of joy or triumph is sobered and prevented from becoming dangerously obsessive. Thus imaginative literature can become socially valuable

> as having a ritual power. A religious ritual has the effect of stilling

> our anxieties and giving expression to our aspirations. We should not...expect poetry to discharge the functions of religion, but all the same, poetry may have the ritual efficacy of religion in providing formulae which enable man to reconcile himself to his predicaments. This is even true of debased poetry...of the popular song. The music-hall audience or the dance floor clientèle who sing the maudlin words of some popular ballad, may sing with conviction because for them the words express an acceptance of the transience of man, a faith in the enduring power of love, an affirmation of the individual's dignity and worth.
>
> (Nash, p. 94)

Poetry enables people to externalise their emotions, pushing them away to ease the intolerable pressure. Simple examples are the ways in which at times singing has made factory work less oppressive and mollified the harshness of a prison régime. Ruth Finnegan has noted how topical songs have enabled Africans to express what could not otherwise be said, supplied a means of relaxing tensions that would have been retained and repressed, and acted as a vehicle for resigned comment and an attitude of detachment. The gnomic laments of Greece offered consoling words of proverbial wisdom about life and death, 'as though the imposition of order on irrational feelings can effect some control over the disturbing and incomprehensible process of death' (Alexiou, p. 217). In England too, saw and proverb used to articulate the traditional symbolism that coped with the great events of existence. The old collective mourning of Ireland and Scotland was a living illustration of the pristine function of poetry; the part of the mourners had something in common with the response of the audience at a well-acted tragedy. Grief was not only externalised but also institutionalised:

> The cultural value of mourning is that it gives grief its form and rhythm. It transfers actual life to the sphere of drama...Mourning at the court of France or Burgundy [was] a sort of acted elegy. Funeral ceremonial and funeral poetry, which in primitive civilizations are still undistinguished...had not yet been completely separated. Mourning still continued a remnant of its poetical functions. It dramatized the effects of grief.
>
> (Huizinga 1949, p. 52)

The community's duty was to take a share of the bereaved's grief, and death became part of a tragedy, not just a crushing blow to those affected by it.

What poetry can do for its audience is compellingly described by Richards:

> Everybody knows the feeling of freedom, of relief, of increased competence and sanity, that follows any reading in which more than

usual order and coherence has been given to our responses. We seem to feel that our command of life, our insight into it and our discrimination of its possibilities, is enhanced, even for situations having little or nothing to do with the subject of the reading. (Richards 1924, p. 235)

That 'command of life' is exactly what poets wish to secure for their readers. T. S. Eliot made a diffident offer: 'These fragments I have shored against my ruins'; and Ezra Pound in *Commission* was specific at some length about the people whom he wished his poetry to help:

> Go, my songs, to the lonely and unsatisfied,
> Go also to the nerve-wracked, go to the enslaved-by-convention,
> Bear to them my contempt for their oppressors.
> (*Selected Poems*, ed. T. S. Eliot)

The list of unhappy people in Pound's poem is a lengthy one, and points to a sickness in our civilisation. The industrial society, for a start, is cut off from the natural world that provides its physical food and formerly supplied the symbols that human beings need for their health. It seems to be difficult for people nowadays to be at home anywhere. Having made the cities and industrial areas unfit for living, they have moved to the suburbs, themselves now places to be got away from. The work that keeps the industrial machines going does not engage a man's mind or muscles; and too much of what it does produce is expendable or obsolescent. Dissatisfaction with work and mental starvation rather than any material need seem to be among the causes of endemic strikes. The production of consumer goods to be unloaded on purchasers affected by advertising is a poor aim for a society, but no politicians can offer us anything better than 'growth' (i.e. more of the same). We exist as consumers of what technological progress imposes on us, and with so circumscribed a scope we are liable to lose much of our humanity and freedom of mind, exchanging physical want for mental and spiritual poverty. As well as impoverishing ourselves we seem to have lost control, as self-generating research and invention continue their advance without contributing much to the quality of life. 'A life that does not incorporate some degree of ritual, of gesture and attitude, has no mental anchorage. It is prosaic to the point of total indifference, purely casual, devoid of that structure of intellect and feeling which we call "personality"' (Langer 1953, p. 244). What has happened to us in our role as consumers is described by Archibald MacLeish:

> To feel emotion is at least to feel. The crime against life, the worst of all crimes, is *not* to feel. And there was never, perhaps, a civilization

in which that crime, the crime of torpor, of lethargy, of apathy, the snake-like sin of coldness-at-the-heart, was commoner than in our technological civilization in which the emotionless emotions of adolescent boys are mass-produced on television screens to do our feelings for us, and a woman's longing for her life is twisted, by singing commercials, into a longing for a new detergent, family size, which will keep her hands as though she had never lived. It is the modern painless death, this commercialised atrophy of the heart... If poetry can call our numbed emotions to life, its plain human usefulness needs no further demonstration.

The Romantic poets, as we noted in chapter 6, opposed their insights to the dehumanising trend. Shelley perceived that the science which increases our control over the environment also narrows our minds; and one of Wordsworth's aims was 'to reduce the calculating understanding to its proper level among the human faculties'. The poet's function of keeping in touch with the past, as well as finding a direction for the future, is particularly needed, since the consumer society imposes forgetfulness as a duty and makes our spiritual past as out of date as yesterday's technology. But in the last quarter of the century we are much humbler, and this is a most hopeful trend; we are more open to take hints from any source, to learn for instance from non-industrialised peoples. Here poetry can put us in touch with the pre-logical mentality that is thwarted in civilised man, and enable us to recover what Charles Davy has called 'the participating consciousness'. Springs of fresh thought are flowing, in ethology, psychology and anthropology for example as well as in areas less readily labelled, and could quickly grow into a main stream. The present slump might be the opening; it has certainly prompted a revision of attitudes and offered fresh ways of looking to the future. Things will not be the same again.

To society

In the past the poet has often been the spokesman of his society, saying what it wanted said but could not voice for itself. An extreme example is provided by the Sanskrit poets of classical Hindu society; they were well integrated, and in every detail controlled by ancient customs. In Scotland the Gaelic poet was

> an observer, a chronicler, a technician who has learnt the rules and practises his craft for the benefit of society. Even if he puts his verse to therapeutic uses he must not opt out of society. This leads to an externalizing even of personal emotions, and in some of the saddest and most harrowing situations the songster seems to observe her own

predicament rather than become submerged by it...This detachment prevents the songs becoming sentimental.
(D. Thomson, p. 87)

In England up to the time of Elizabeth I, poetry was used to celebrate and comment on nearly every event in life, from birth to death; and this was apart from the court fashion for poetry, which involved the keeping of commonplace books and the exchange of poems in manuscript. Poetry was fashionable, but it was more than that. Nearer our own time the conception of the poet as a useful member of society still held, but only in this idiom: Tennyson was a great teacher because he showed men 'how to live melodious days, bearing their trials and making their sacrifices with purity of feeling and singleness of heart...No man could render more glorious service to his fellows' (Tennyson 1974, p. 353). Walt Whitman tried to revive the notion of bards, who were to be

> native and grand, by them alone can these States
> be fused into the compact organism of a Nation...

and (in *By Blue Ontario's Shore*) he developed it interestingly. However it is unlikely that any western society will enjoy the services that the poet renders to the Acoli people of Northern Uganda, where he 'is the agent of his society. He has the talent, which other members of his social group may not possess, of distilling the thoughts, joy, fears, anger and sorrow, not only of the individual but also of the group, and presenting these in melodic poems' (p'Bitek, p. 9). Of the twentieth-century poets, W. B. Yeats probably came nearest to speaking for his country, in his 'public' poems. In Auden's words, 'Mad Ireland hurt him into poetry': the first poems in which he found his own voice were provoked by events in the life of Ireland, such as the reception given to the first production of *The Playboy of the Western World*. The tone of his poem on this subject, and of others written about the same time, is that of an address to the public; the intention was to exert an influence in public life, and the poems may well have done so. That tone and intention often recur in his poetry, though his subjects changed from those offered by mad Ireland to aspects of a 'botched civilisation'.

Nor are we likely to see again the poet as a judge or man of action. In pre-Christian Ireland poets were *ipso facto* judges, and evolved an obscure language of their own; and according to Julius Caesar the druids of Gaul were judges as well as priests and teachers. In pre-Islamic Arabia, too, poets seem to have acted as judges, and since in the days of multi-functional poetry they were called on to codify laws in a memorable form, they must often have had a say in the formulation and interpretation of legal matters. When Agamemnon went to the siege of Troy he left his wife in charge of a poet; Clytemnestra

> had at hand as her companion
> a minstrel Agamemnon left attending her
> charged with her care, when he took ship for Troy.
> (*Odyssey*, 3, 265–7)

As society became more specialised in its parts, poetry became a side-line of the man of action, as in the sixteenth century, and then something for which the man of action inherited a respect; when Tennyson in *Locksley Hall Sixty Years After* expressed a bitter and depressed view of his age, Gladstone considered it worth his while to reply in *The Nineteenth Century* for January 1887. And when Sir Barnes Newcome (in *The Newcomes*) seeks to shore up his eroded political fortunes he does so by two lectures, on 'The Poetry of Childhood' and 'The Poetry of Womanhood and the Affections'. Thackeray tells us that admission was charged and that the crowded audience was drawn from all classes. The low esteem in which English poetry of the present century is held is fairly suggested by Storm Jameson's comment in reporting without enthusiasm a 1932 Communist meeting in Berlin: 'A woman recited her husband's poems; the police had forbidden him to recite them himself. I tried to remember which of our poets would be dangerous to public order' (*Journey from the North*, p. 277). The poet is no longer a judge or a man of action, but he may still have a social function of the kind to which Richard Eberhart has pointed in *Action and Poetry*:

> The poet against society: stay away from him.
> He sees, but cannot help: passionate disability
> Allows him to do nothing about human error.
> He broods upon the consequence of action,
>
> Wishing some brave intelligence could conquer pain,
> Devise a way amid labyrinthian involvements;
> He feels the brutality and affront of suffering,
> He clings to a remnant of man's nobility.
>
> It is the brutal and primitive power of the poet
> Raises him to his source and height...

The social function of the poet has varied from time to time, as society has changed. The poet passed from having authority to supporting it, still with some of the prestige that attached to the words of verse as a form of magic; and in ancient Egypt, Mesopotamia and China writing was reserved to the ruling bureaucracy. In Wales and Scotland, at a time when the tribe's well-being depended on its chieftain, it was traditionally the poet's job to support authority and an ordered state of affairs. In medieval Europe poetry was generally the handmaid of the church and nobility, with itinerant poets serving as public relations officers, and in the time of Elizabeth verse was regarded by the literary professionals as unfit for common minds. That is very much its isolated position today; the official mind tolerates the academic study of poetry, and universities preserve the poetry of the past in museum cases. Poetry can no longer serve the state, even in a capacity as a barometer of public opinion, as it did in ancient China.

Magician, priest, historian, provider of entertainment at noble courts or religious festivals – these were some of the functions of the primitive poet. In addition he was seer and prophet, maintaining the stability, celebrating the values and speaking out in the best interests of the society he served. These functions have been diluted, and the poet has gained freedom while losing power; but there has remained a constant element: his duty to speak out. Medieval minstrels made themselves unpopular with authority by doing so; Langland and others also spoke out within their church. This obligation was finely put by Marvell in *Tom May's Death*; when justice and religion have been silenced by force,

> Then is the poet's time, 'tis then he draws
> And single fights forsaken virtue's cause.
> He, when the wheel of empire whirleth back,
> And though the world's disjointed axle crack,
> Sings still of ancient rights and better times,
> Seeks wretched good, arraigns successful crimes.

But since his time poetry has not found many occasions to draw its sword. The Romantic poets made a stand, and played a prophetic role, but their example was not followed. The poets of the nineteenth century failed to take cognisance of the changes brought about by technology, even in their own lives. Tennyson wrote about *The Poet*, but vaguely; in the poem the arrows of the poet's mind turn into plants that change the world into a garden, in which Freedom arises. And lesser poets wrote verse of unprecedented badness, like that of Francis Thompson on Queen Victoria and the end of the Boer War. Exceptions like John Davidson were rare; 'The poet [he wrote] is in the street, the hospital. He intends the world to know that it is out of joint.' One is not asking of writers that they should take sides, but if they do it is the quality and nature of their commitment that matter. What is expected of them is that they should 'interpret imaginatively the crisis that is taking place in the mind of man' (P. Henderson 1939). The failure of the conventional wisdom and the present mood of doubt offer large opportunities to the strong-minded poet.

The case for the poet as servant of society is that he is a moralist who dispenses truth. That is how he started, and that is how the Greeks, for example, saw him; they quarried the dramatists for wise sayings about all aspects of life. He was honoured in many cultures, from that of monastic Ireland in the sixth century to the aristocratic households that formed part of the sixteenth-century economy. This was at a time when Philip Sidney placed the poet above the moral philosopher and historian, because he was able more powerfully to move his readers to virtue. Later, Johnson wrote 'The end of poetry is to instruct by pleasing', and in the same century Gray spoke, in 'The Bard', of 'Truth severe by fairy fiction dressed.' Wordsworth saw it as the destiny of his poetry 'to console the afflicted, to add sunshine to daylight by making the happy happier, to teach the young and the gracious of every age, to see, to think and feel, and therefore become more actively and securely virtuous' (Selincourt 1937, p. 126). D. H. Lawrence can speak for this century: 'The essential function of art is moral. Not aesthetic, not decorative, not pastime and recreation. But moral. The essential function of art is moral' (Lawrence 1924, p. 170).

Moral, that is, because it claims to be a road to truth, of which there appear to be several kinds. First there is the scientific kind, with which poetry is not greatly concerned. Beyond the simplest propositions scientific truths are attained by a particular approach and method, often working by exclusion and selection, emotionally influenced to meet certain human needs at particular times. When Yeats wrote, 'The imagination has some way of lighting on the truth that reason has not', he may have been thinking of the scientific kind, and here we can note that in some branches of knowledge poetry can get there more quickly than, say, laboratory psychologists. The insights of Shakespeare, Donne and Blake, for example, have been re-stated but not replaced by twentieth-century research; and 'the exactness, the univocity, of logic is not found in the real world either in physical or in human phenomena; therefore the most accurate descriptions of the world are more akin to poetry than to mathematical logic' (Hesse, p. 160).

Yeats may also have had in mind a different, and to him superior, kind of truth – that which Richards has termed 'acceptability'.

Truths of this kind are not directly verifiable, because they are not part of the empire of science:

> The falsity of happy endings to *Lear* or to *Don Quixote* is their failure to be acceptable to those who have fully responded to the rest of the work. It is in this sense that 'Truth' is equivalent to 'internal necessity' or rightness. That is 'true' or 'internally necessary' which completes or accords with the rest of the experience...
> (Richards 1924, p. 269)

Thus we speak of the 'truths' of mythology and religious experience and credit a particularly fine work of art with the creation of a true image of life: as Keats said in a letter to Benjamin Bailey, 'What the imagination seizes as beauty must be truth.'

The third meaning came in with the Romantics. Before them it had been assumed that the business of poetry was to re-create for each age the traditional wisdom of man, to re-clothe the old themes, to re-tell old tales. To de Quincey, well into the nineteenth century, the great poets were those 'who have made themselves necessary to the human heart; who have first brought into consciousness, and next have clothed in words, those grand catholic feelings that belong to the grand catholic situations of life, through all its stages; who have clothed them in such words that human wit despairs of bettering them!' (de Quincey, p. 143). But to the Romantics poetry was a means of apprehending truths otherwise inaccessible – a superior form of knowledge. 'The poem or the novel may prove of extraordinary use to the community; the proposition it puts forward about life may be authentic and of the deepest validity' (Steiner 1972, p. 127). The truth revealed by literature is metaphorical, but not in the sense that applies to single metaphorical statements, which can be paraphrased, if at some length. For example, when Macbeth mutters about the intended murder of Duncan 'upon this bank and shoal of time' we can translate his phrase into other words, with profit to our next reading of the play; the figure of speech achieves clarity, speed and condensation. Perhaps also, though less certainly, we can put into prosaic words the piece about the creation in the book of Job 38:

> When the morning stars sang together and
> all the sons of God shouted for joy.

The truth of a play or poem is that of an extended metaphor, and it cannot be paraphrased; we must take or leave the whole of *Macbeth* or Job as statements about life.

Such statements are unverifiable; and we test the truth of a poem by our own response: can we accept it all, or part of it? Our second thoughts will be about the reasons: do we find the author sincere, in the sense that there is no 'apparent attempt on the part of the artist to work effects upon the reader which do not work for himself' (Richards 1924, p. 271); is he being faithful to the nature of his medium, is the work consistent within itself? Does it obey 'the laws of poetic truth and poetic beauty' desiderated by Arnold, has it the 'truth of matter and truth of manner' that he found in Burns? Arnold linked matter and manner together, because the truth of poetry is inseparable from its means of expression – rhythm, rhyme, pattern, imagery, arrangement, sound and so on. To weigh the truth of a work of art such as a poem we must rationalise our response, which practice may make more adequate. For those concerned to go deeply into the matter and establish their judgment this will mean a close consideration of the elements of a poem: is the rhythm compelling, how does the rhyme help, what pattern is there, what light is shed by the imagery, what contribution is made by sound and other effects? As Susanne Langer has commented: 'There are no degrees of literal truth, but artistic truth, which is all significance, expressiveness, articulateness, has degrees; therefore works of art may be good or bad, and each must be judged on our experience of its revelations' (Langer 1948, p. 222).

The last claim staked for poetry is the contribution it is said to make to the health and growth of language; in Eliot's formulation, 'the poetry of a people takes its life from the people's speech and in turn gives life to it' (1933, p. 15). This seems to have been the case in the Middle Ages; the poet was a craftsman, specially apt at manipulating the common heritage of words. We can see Langland as one example, and Shakespeare at the very end of the Middle Ages as another. The latter not only drew on the full resources of the language but enriched them; and L. C. Knights makes the point (which he develops) that Shakespeare was a 'poet engaged in the poet's task of retrieving words from the realm of abstraction and bringing them back to human experience in its fullness, whence they draw their life' (Knights 1965, p. 57). But after Shakespeare Eliot's statement has rarely been fully applicable; the poet has never been able just to use the language as it was, and still less has he been able to make a contribution to its vitality, except in a limited way. The language itself changed; with the new prestige of science, 'scientific' precision became the model, so that the poetic potentiality of Elizabethan English came to an end. Poetry became literary, and the significant poets were those who wrested the language back on course, like Donne and Blake and Wordsworth. They did much for language, but it was the language of a public that now read the poetry of a specifically literary tradition from Spenser to the early years of this century.

This line of English verse, which ended with the Georgian poets, had nothing to offer by the time that Pound and Eliot appeared; and they made a fresh start. They faced the difficulties of a language debased and reduced, especially by the press and popular fiction, which have squandered (in Owen Barfield's words) 'a great pile of spiritual capital which has been laid up by centuries of weary effort', but they triumphantly managed to select and organise the resources of everyday language. Thus they enabled other poets and readers to enjoy a new linguistic freedom, and fulfilled the duty of a poet, who 'breaks through the limitation of words used in their everyday prose context and, by using a different discipline, discovers new meanings or discovers lost meanings, providing new symbols to replace those to which we have become too used' (Barnes, p. 94). At present poetry and popular speech do not interact. This is unfortunate if Eliot is right in asserting that it makes a difference 'to the whole people, whether they read and enjoy poetry or not: even, in fact, whether they know the names of their greatest poets or not'. The influence of poetry is difficult to assess, though Eliot believed that if you follow the influence of poetry through those readers who are most affected by it to those who never read at all, you will find it present everywhere (Eliot 1957, p. 22).

Poetry as therapy

Cleanse the stuffed bosom of that perilous stuff
Which weighs upon the heart.
(*Macbeth*, V, iii)

From the earliest times music and poetry have been regarded as healing agents. When Saul, King of Israel, was morbidly depressed his staff advised him to take the music cure, and recommended David as a good musician: 'And it came to pass, when the evil spirit from God was upon Saul, that David took an harp, and played with his hand: so Saul was refreshed, and was well, and the evil spirit departed from him' (1 Samuel 15: 23). The magical influence of music came later to be associated with the singing of psalms; and one of the early church fathers, Diodore of Tarsus, attributed the calming of carnal desires, the banishment of demons and the healing of wounds to the good influence of psalm singing (Scholl and White, p. 23). More seriously, the Psalms were found to provide

something for every mood and need; the authors were close enough
to their hearers for the person wanting help to feel himself under-
stood and explained in them, and in recent years they have come
to provide a helpful adjunct to clinical therapy. Perhaps Psalm 39
supplies an example; it begins:

> I said: I will keep close watch over myself
> that all I say may be free from sin.
> I will keep a muzzle on my mouth,
> so long as wicked men confront me.
> In dumb silence I held my peace.
> So my agony was quickened,
> and my heart burned within me.
> My mind wandered as the fever grew,
> and I began to speak:
> Lord, let me know my end
> and the number of my days...

(Jeremiah 20: 7–9 is also worth looking up, also in the version of
the New English Bible.)

One of the earliest stages in the evolution of clinical psycho-
therapy has been noted in ancient Egypt. It seems that by following
the magic ritual of *The Book of the Dead* Seth, Osiris and all lesser
deities could be compelled by the devout Egyptian to remove his
frustrations. In Greece Hesiod believed in the hypnotic and curative
power of poetry, which was to him 'a forgetting of what is bad and
a respite from anxieties'. Its psychiatric virtue is described at the
end of his *Theogony*; a person may have

> Grief in a spirit newly wounded
> And endure drought in his heart's anguish,

but once he listens to the minstrel 'Straightway he does forget his
dark thoughts, nor are his cares remembered any more.' In Greece
too the three great writers of tragedy explored the basic human
relationships, and 'the Greeks cherished and utilized these dramas
for their deep human empathies and meanings...' (Masserman, p.
184). Similarly the aim of the Indian drama of the second century
B.C. was to produce in the spectator an internal harmony by arousing
various emotions and then blending them. Among American In-
dians the Chippewa aimed at health in life by an initiation at which
each acquired helpful songs, some self-composed, others bought
expensively; while the Navajo are said to have been remarkable
psychiatrists, dealing successfully with both external and internal
fears, and achieving good results by explaining to sufferers the
origin of the evil they were afflicted with (Astrov, p. 24). In their
view it is the spirit of creation that heals: the Navajo medicine man

sinks the sick person in the beauty and perfection of primeval creation with poems about the earth, the stars, the growing corn, and thus the sufferer is placed in the purity of the beginning of all things, when there was no sin and no fear of death. This is the spirit of a short Navajo chant:

> Reared within the Mountains!
> Lord of the Mountains!
> Young Man!
> Chieftain!
> I have made your sacrifice.
> I have prepared a smoke for you.
> My feet restore thou for me.
> My legs restore thou for me.
> My body restore thou for me.
> My mind restore thou for me.
> My voice restore thou for me.
> Restore all for me in beauty.
> Make beautiful all that is before me.
> Make beautiful all that is behind me.
> Make beautiful my words.
> It is done in beauty.
> It is done in beauty.
> It is done in beauty.
> It is done in beauty.
> (Trask 2, p. 250)

Nearer to us in time and space were the speakers of Gaelic, whose songs of celebration or therapy were woven into 'the emotional texture of life...the jilted or bereaved girl assuages her grief in highly wrought song...the Keen, as well as being therapy, was also ritual, and this brings a stylised element into it' (D. Thomson, p. 58). Many of the healing methods involved the use of secret rituals and spells, which had to be repeated accurately.

Early Indian poetry, like that of many countries, includes spells for various diseases; till recently among the folk songs of the Chattisgarh district there were in circulation poems for pregnancy, delivery, sore eyes and headaches. No doubt the poetic form was the best way of ensuring the accurate transmission of important formulas, but there were sometimes other reasons. In Nigeria today poetry plays a central part in the whole process of divination, because 'it is through the imagery of the poetry that the sufferer can recognise his own case' (Finnegan, p. 191). Poetry is also specific for the treatment of the hysteria to which primitive peoples with a less resilient consciousness are liable, the necessary therapeutic magic being administered in the form of a chanted song (G.

Thomson 1945, pp. 19 ff). Many accounts of healing rites mention the importance of actually naming the disease from which a patient is suffering; for instance St Mark's account of the healing of the split-minded lunatic who lived among tombs tells us that Christ addressed the evil spirit: '"What is thy name?" And he answered, saying, "My name is Legion: for we are many."' Here one cannot help recalling the way in which modern doctors relieve the worry of their patients by naming their diseases. The mother who reports that a child is suffering from sickness and diarrhoea is reassured when she is told that 'There is a lot of gastro-enteritis about'; and many of us with persistent headaches feel a little better as soon as the doctor supplies his magic: 'The cephalalgia that's troubling you . . .'

Most of the poetry used for therapy operated in the way summed up by Aristotle's analysis of the effects of tragedy on its audience, whose emotions of pity and fear were purged by the performance. The traditional poetry of Greece and other countries includes laments for a bride leaving her father's house to be married, since popular belief viewed death and marriage as basically similar occasions, as transitions from one stage to another. The expressing of grief lightened the load, and was just as necessary for the mourner as it was for the dead; in such a ritual lament of this century a Maniot woman sang:

> How good are tears, how sweet are dirges;
> > I would rather sing dirges
> > than eat or drink.

Another instance of the safe channelling by words of a dangerous emotion is provided by the verbal contests that replaced actual fighting. Among the pre-Islamic Arabs words in themselves seem to have retained something of their ancient and magical power:

> The man who, by skilful ordering of vivid imagery in taut rightly nuanced phrases, could play upon the emotions of his hearers, was not merely lauded as an artist but venerated as the protector and guarantor of the honour of the tribe and a potent weapon against its enemies. Tribal contests were fought out as much, or more, in the taunts of their respective poets as on the field of battle, and so deeply rooted was the custom that even Muhammad, although in general hostile to the influence of poets, himself conformed to it in his later years at Medina.
> (Gibb, p. 29)

Matches of honour took place between clans, with an official poet for each side. Again the singing duels of the Babar group of islands in the East Indian archipelago that replaced actual violence and murder have their Eskimo counterparts in the contest songs of abuse and ridicule which gave vent to poisonous grudges and supplied an outlet for pent-up aggression. These songs preceded the drumming contest to which an individual would challenge a man against whom he had a grudge. The process actually took the place of judicial decisions.

Much the same pattern has been observed among the Dinka people of the Sudan, where 'songs are one way of modifying grievances by singing about them instead of brooding over them and making them worse' (Deng, p. 79). Thus fighting with songs becomes an institution and goes beyond individual therapy to the pacification of quarrels. In northern Italy too the collective singing of spontaneous poetry – 'ristornelli' – was used as a token duel between groups. In such contests of song, or flytings, in which the competitors hurled versified abuse at each other, the original aim may have been to strengthen deeds by words, but eventually words came to replace deeds.

For the poets themselves their writings have often been cathartic. Among the Anglo-Saxon gnomic verses that have survived there are some lines which tell us that the poet has fewer cares than other men:

> As many men as there are in the world,
> So many thoughts are there; each has his own heart's longing;
> Yet the less for him who knows many songs
> And can play the harp with his hands,
> He has the gift of music which God has given him.
> (Gordon, p. 312)

And there is an apt fifteenth-century tale from Persia about a poet who went to a doctor, complaining of depression and an insideful of knots. The doctor asked if he had composed a new poem, not yet recited (i.e. published), and the poet replied, 'Yes'. The doctor told him to recite it, and again a second and third time; and then said, 'Be gone, you are cured! It was this poem which was tied up in knots inside of you: and the aridity thereof infected the outer part of you; now it has come forth into the open, you have found recovery' (Hillelson, p. 87). It is related of the Icelandic Egill Skallagrimsson that after losing two sons in a short time he shut himself up and refused to take food or drink. His daughter persuaded him to compose an elegy on his sons, and offered to take it down on a rod. It is said that his spirits revived with the effort and he returned to the family circle (Chadwick 1932, I, p. 347). Of the recent more numerous examples a representative one comes from Burns, who wrote in 1787: 'My passions . . . raged like so many devils, till they got vent in rhyme; and then conning over my verses, like a spell, soothed all into quiet.'

A classic case from the nineteenth century is that of John Stuart Mill, who in chapter 5 of his *Autobiography* records a reasoned and impressive account of his rescue from prolonged mental depression and perhaps breakdown by reading the two-volume 1815 edition of Wordsworth's poems. From curiosity and without any expectation of relief he took up the collection, to find that it was precisely what he needed at the time:

> What made Wordsworth's poems a medicine for my state of mind, was that they expressed, not mere outward beauty, but states of feeling, and of thought coloured by feeling, under the excitement of beauty. They seemed to be the very culture of the feelings, which I was in quest of. In them I seemed to draw from a source of inward joy, of sympathetic and imaginative pleasure, which could be shared in by all human beings; which had no connexion with struggle or imperfection, but would be made richer by every improvement in the physical or social condition of mankind. From them I seemed to learn what would be the perennial sources of happiness, when all the greater evils of life shall have been removed. And I felt myself at once better and happier as I came under their influence.

The application of poetry therapy to cases in which patients are disturbed by 'raging devils' is now less common than it used to be; rather more than here appears to have been attempted in the United States, where this form of healing has been practised at the Philadelphia Hospital for nearly two centuries, and is used at 3,500 mental health centres. Patients for example who had avoided and denied their own problems were able to react to a poem: 'That's just how I feel', and to share their fears with the poet and other readers. When patients realised that they were not alone, their sense of strangeness and alienation was alleviated (Leedy, *passim*). An art therapist in England has similarly noted that the reading and discussion of poetry are profitable methods: 'part of the therapy may lie in the catharsis of shared emotion, the poet being a safe fuse which can lead naturally to the individual in the group speaking of his personal experience' (Ball, p. 94). In America J. J. Leedy's 'iso' principle was applied, i.e. the poems were chosen symbolically to represent the feelings that the patients were unable to deal with successfully. A withdrawn, eczematic, alcoholic girl came across Emily Dickinson's poem:

> I'm nobody. Who are you?
> Are you nobody too?
> Then there's a pair of us.
> Don't tell – they'd banish us, you know.

How dreary to be somebody,
How public – like a frog –
To tell your name the livelong June
To an admiring bog.

Once she had accepted kinship with a celebrated writer she improved, and never looked back. 'The lines of communication between her and the outside world needed mending before anything could be done for her at the (skin) hospital.' The actual writing of poetry afforded a means of symbolic externalisation; patients were helped to distance their trouble and understand it without pressure. This example comes from a collection of poems by hospital patients:

First Poem

Waiting, always waiting
For what? Visitors perhaps
But why? What new words can be said?
By whom?
New thoughts die unborn.

Help perhaps. But how?
From inside? Outside?
Maybe to give?
But what is there?
Another stillborn.

Send for the mid-wife to my thoughts!
Let them not die!
Let them live and breathe
Though unimportant.
Give them life!
L. H. (*The Shattered Heart*, p. 7)

The extending of a person's emotional range has been noted in both England and America; in the latter a reading of Robert Frost's 'The Road Not Taken' led a woman to realise that she actually could make a choice, and in an English hospital Arthur Waley's translations from the Chinese were found helpful, in the feeling of kinship with ancient poets who had explored the perennial difficulties of living.

One of the most striking cases recorded is that of a sixteen year-old Puerto Rican, a tough member of a slum gang. Some of the gang's activities reminded the therapist of Homer, so he lent his patient, Francisco, a copy of the *Iliad*. The boy very competently reproduced some of the stories, thus revealing a new literacy; next he gave up his beard and swaggering manner, and developed a true dignity.

It would appear that somewhere in the Homeric skirmishes he had dropped the false values of his gang along with his haunted sense

of fear and anger. He was able to accept his true role, that of Francisco, a young man with a future. Gone was 'Frenchy', cocky but scared; gone also the theatrical routine that led nowhere.
(Leedy, p. 94)

It is interesting to note that this account of an improvement following contact with poetry comes not from a psychiatrist, but from a member of the English department at a New York college – one recalls that to the Greeks Apollo was god of both poetry and medicine. Ever since their day a succession of poets of all kinds has 'ministered to the dependent and the defeated, comforted and lonely and the lovelorn and understood the hostile and the hateful' (Leedy, p. 35).

The view of poetry implied above was clarified by Richards in his *Principles*, in which he expounded a general theory of value and the place of poetry therein. Human happiness lies in reaching a balanced adjustment of all the impulses that make up a man, and anything that helps to attain this balance is of value. His account (from which there is a quotation above in *To the reader*) is not unlike that of a description of what poetry has done for primitive peoples, in enabling them to reach a position where they feel at home, to master and distance their emotions, and to answer for themselves Lear's question 'Who is it that can tell me who I am?' Civilised man in contrast is supplied with rather too many versions of who he is; he is not at home in his environment and too seldom seems to enjoy the 'command of life' that Richards desiderates. In his *A Fortunate Man* (pp. 98, 99) John Berger has described the 'wholesale cultural deprivation' of large sections of the English people in their inarticulacy. They cannot translate what they know into thoughts; though technically literate they are without the words to clarify experience. 'Yet it is more than a question of literature. Any general culture acts as a mirror which enables the individual to recognise himself . . .' Nor is it fanciful to relate this inability to be one's self, to know what to do with one's self, to outbreaks of violence and hooliganism indulged in as an easy way of 'speaking' by those whose language is inadequate. This, or something like it, is the conclusion of those who study young delinquents: being unable to put their frustration into words they act it out in violence. 'A riot', as Martin Luther King observed, 'is the language of the unheard.' The process was analysed by Erich Fromm many years ago:

> It would seem that the amount of destructiveness to be found in individuals is proportionate to the amount to which expansiveness of life is curtailed. By this we do not refer to individual frustrations

of this of that desire but to the thwarting of the whole of life, the blockage of spontaneity of the growth and expression of man's sensuous, emotional, and intellectual capacities. Life has an inner dynamism of its own; it tends to grow, to be expressed, to be lived. It seems that if this tendency is thwarted the energy directed towards life undergoes a process of decomposition and changes into energies directed towards destruction...Destructiveness is the outcome of unlived life.

(*The Fear of Freedom*, 1942)

Some delinquents have been encouraged to try writing poetry, and since few of them had ever met with any acceptance or success the recognition of their achievement caused their feelings of inferiority to diminish, and opened up new directions for them. In William Saroyan's *Time of Your Life* McCarthy expressed this sardonically:

They all wanted to be writers. Every maniac in the world that ever brought about the murder of people through war started out in an attic or a basement writing poetry. It stank. So they got even by becoming important heels. And it's still going on. The thing to do is to have more magazines. Hundreds of them. *Thousands.* Print everything they write, so they'll believe they're immortal. That may keep them from going haywire. (p. 118)

A psychologist remarked once that the most useful part of her training had been reading for a degree in English. This is not surprising. Her profession, the therapeutic branch at least, needs people specially sensitive to their fellows and skilled in understanding them, qualities to which a fine use of language contributes. One who improves his own linguistic power, especially through wrestling with poetry, is not acquiring knowledge or technique, but (one hopes) increasing his understanding and ability to help others. There must be two-way communication. The understanding largely and the help almost entirely are a matter of words. The patient needs to express his thoughts and feelings, through art perhaps as well as language. For example, this poem by a hospital inmate:

The Shattered Heart

Trembling I lay in my bed
Thinking over the words you said
In dreadful pain.

I wanted to die.
In the long night my throat felt dry –
I loved you my darling
I didn't want us to part
But with those words you said
You shattered my heart.

'I love someone else'

That's what you said
And with those words
I wished I was dead.
D.K. (*The Shattered Heart*, p. 8)

Then from the analyst's point of view, 'It seems reasonable to assert that psychoanalysis is best regarded as a method of semantic interpretation rather than a direct treatment for neurotic symptoms' (Storr, p. 84). Another analyst records the help she received from poetry:

> One of the things...that I noticed when I began to write a discursive account of what [the patient] said and did and what I said and did, centring on her drawings, was that certain lines of poetry kept nosing their way into the foreground of my thinking, lines that had been at the back of my mind at different stages of the treatment, but which I had not taken much notice of, since they were my associations not hers...they were nevertheless highly relevant to the progress of the analysis; they were providing essential bridges in my own thinking, bridges from the raw material of what she brought me to the final stage...of my being able to conceptualise it fully.
> (Milner, p. xxi)

Sophisticated as we are, we do to a certain extent share the faith of non-literate peoples in the power of the word. The functional poetry for example that form part of the spells of Yoruba medicine is never recited in public, and those who know the potent words do not readily reveal them. In the medicine of American Indians the words that go with the healing herbs are the essential part; the word is the medicine-man's strongest weapon against disease and death. Shamanism probably contributes to mental health where it affords a means of apparently controlling the destructive powers behind nervous disorders. There are senses in which even among civilised peoples this belief in the magical effects of words is well-founded. The young child acquires a magic language when he finds that his wants are supplied by using the right word; and 'biodynamically the sounds produced by the human voice reach so deeply into the formative layers of experience that at times they appear to have almost magical effects' (Masserman, p. 174). One of the deep roots may reach back to the earliest dances, which gave form and relief to the bodily tensions of fear and desire, and from which lyric poetry was generated and still sometimes maintains a vestigial connection. We can thus begin to understand how some poems may give pleasure and perhaps some relaxation of the strains of living to certain people; and further that poetry generally can often relieve tensions and even prevent them.

Agenda for the arts

Nearly a hundred years ago Matthew Arnold wrote: 'The future of poetry is immense, because in our poetry, where it is worthy of its high destinies, our race, as time goes on, will find an ever surer and surer stay' (p. 1). Not much later the young W. B. Yeats expressed his wish for the future of poetry: 'I would have all the arts draw together; recover their ancient association, the painter painting what the poet has written, the musician setting the poet's words to simple airs, that the horseman and the engine-driver may sing at their work' (Yeats, p. ix). Between the two poets any confidence one could have had in the future of poetry diminished, and by now has completely evaporated. We have large populations whose needs are met, more or less, by mass-production, an excellent process for all sorts of hardware, but not for providing the entertainment the age has become habituated to.

The physical capacities of man have been enormously extended by computers, radio telescopes, space travel, and so on, but his essential humanity has not expanded. There is a contrast between our knowledge of and power over the physical world and our lack of knowledge of and control over ourselves and our social and economic institutions. We have the innate biological equipment for a number of different lives, but despite all the possibilities open to us the changes that actually take place are disappointing. Popular brands of knowledge have caused people to regard themselves as automata, because 'The breed which has probably had the most profound influence on human behaviour is the psychologists and family sociologists who (especially in America) have largely succeeded in foisting upon the public their views on human nature, thus profoundly influencing customary behaviour' (Andreski, p. 25). The behaviour expected of a human being in western civilisation is to consume; the pressures are pervasive, but not consciously felt. In non-literate societies every social situation brings 'the individual into contact with the group's patterns of thought, feelings and action; the choice is between the cultural tradition or solitude' (Goody, p. 59). For modern people the choice is between solitude and the round of spending prescribed by the colour supplements; conformity is promoted as much by pictures as by words: and in the midst of the affluence that so many of us are able to enjoy there is a good deal of poverty of living. There are more narrowed lives and blunted minds than there need be. The current world recession may well be extremely salutary, if it leads us to re-assess this and that activity, to consider what is humanly and not just financially profitable, and generally to take stock.

The misuse of the intellect divorced from intuition and visionary power has imposed an accountants' rationality – 'the slow dying of men's hearts that we call progress' in the words of Yeats, and we seem too little aware of life and its potentialities. An example is that of an academic biologist who remarked, 'All the birds will have to go' – as a result of protecting crops with insecticides. One wonders what sort of an education did so little to prevent this stunting of his humanity and the drying-up of his human awareness. The quantification he exhibits precludes any realisation that there is a problem in destroying a form of life which has always delighted human eyes and ears, providing us with myths and symbols that are part of our humanity. If the birds go, men will be so much less men.

Language is a point at which poverty of living becomes very clear. Our informational vocabulary has reduced the language that expresses life and the emotions. Industrial production has affected the words we use and hence the way we think. 'The operating code of industrial tools encroaches on everyday language and reduces the poetic self-affirmation of man to a barely tolerated and marginal protest' (Illich 1973, p. 90). The currency of press and politics lacks precision and immediacy; hurtful strikes and unemployment lose the impact of truth to those who read about 'industrial action' and 'redundancy'. The vocabulary of poet and novelist is probably diminishing, for

> The ordinary reader has quite lost that sensitivity to language... which a wholly illiterate people is likely to possess. Once again, we are paying the penalty of universal semi-literacy. Semi-literacy destroys the ability to appreciate poetry without giving the ability fully to appreciate prose. It produces a total insensitivity to all aspects of language except the coarse and representational aspects. It produces a taste for uniformity, for the catchword and the cliché, and an impatience with variety.
> (Daiches, p. 144)

As a result of cultural impoverishment many English people seem to be inarticulate in important parts of life; there is a gap between experience and thought; they lack the language to recognise and come to terms with experience. The influences of religion and homely tradition are no more; education has provided the tools but not the skill to use them. The cultural heritage shaped in words no longer filters through to the people who have the right to enjoy it.

The contribution that imaginative literature in general and

especially poetry need to make is to maintain the idea of humanity, to keep human beings human in the face of mountains of information, accumulations of consumer goods, rudderless change and reductionist theories of man. The need has been admirably expressed:

> The artist must be prophetic, not in the sense that he foretells things to come, but in the sense that he tells his audience, at the risk of their displeasure, the secrets of their own hearts. His business as an artist is to speak out...the secrets he must utter are theirs...The poet as prophet suggests no remedy, because he has already given one. The remedy is the poem itself. Art is the community's medicine for the worst disease of the mind, the corruption of consciousness. (Collingwood, p. 336)

The poets themselves agree with the writer on aesthetics. T. S. Eliot tells us that the poet makes his readers more conscious, more aware of what they feel already. As well as teaching them something about themselves, he can make his readers share consciously in new feelings which they have not experienced before. 'Unless we have those few men who combine an exceptional sensibility with an exceptional power over words, our own ability, not merely to express, but even to feel any but the crudest emotions, will degenerate' (Eliot 1957, p. 21). To this statement we may add the words of Yeats: 'Because an emotion does not exist, or does not become perceptible and active among us, till it has found its expression, in colour or in sound or in form, or in all of these...poets and painters and musicians are continually making and unmaking mankind' (Geddes, p. 563).

Poetry must be responsive to the intellectual movements of the day. There are huge fields of knowledge – anthropology, archaeology, ethology, psychology – that can alter the way we think and feel; and it is on these that the imagination should be working and exploring their implications. 'Poetry needs to wake up. It is being neglectful of, irresponsive to, what is happening. In a spring dawn such as never before broke, here is poetry – as though it were old and frail – all huddled up and with, I fear, its head under the bedclothes' (Richards 1968, p. 178).

If the arts are to return to a position in which they have reciprocal contact with people and in turn can offer them nourishment, there will have to be a deliberate effort. A re-thought education will be one approach, and the current sub-literacy will need to be improved on – if it can be, for not enough is known about that. The state of affairs recorded in this note is not limited to East Anglia:

Books? The question brings the inevitable embarrassment. The village people of all ages seem frightened at the mere mention of books. Why isn't this book-fear dispersed at an early time? Why should it exist at all? A seventeen-year old wrought-iron worker, a good craftsman, and an apparently lively youngster, said, 'Yes, I have read books. I read Enid Blyton when I was at school'. The normality of reading scarcely exists. To nearly every person interviewed, it was a strange thing to read a book. The book is a kind of frontier which few seem to have the nerve to pass.

(Blythe, p. 213)

One cannot help recalling in contrast the old sailor, Singleton, in *The Nigger of the Narcissus*, reading Bulwer Lytton in the din of the forecastle, 'lost in an absorption profound enough to resemble a trance'; and there comes to mind also the pathetic longing for reading that Henry Mayhew noted in some of the destitute children he met. (See 'Boy Inmates of the Casual Wards'.) In supplying only a cheap vocational outfit education for all went wrong from the start. It would now be much more practical to provide a general education; mathematics, real crafts, not too much obsolescent science, art and the literature that is the best route to literacy. This would be a solid foundation for the different vocational trainings that the trades and professions themselves would lay on, with state aid.

At present education tends to neglect intuition and the imagination; instead it enthrones 'the absolute rule of the concept in the child's mind' (Read, p. 20). We do not prepare children for the linguistic and symbolic environment in which they will spend their lives. 'They are taught to deal with language in terms of simplistic dichotomies – truth versus falsity, good versus bad, rich versus poor, and so on' (Key, p. 190). But human motives are rarely considered; it is just as important to detect confusion and distortion in one's own or other people's writing as to spell correctly. As for specialist studies of English at universities, an excellent essay (on the central place that ought to be held by poetry) finds it at fault in a way that continues the weakness we note in schools:

Literary education takes place in the university under the sign of fragmentation and reification. By very few teachers is poetry treated as news, however old, about the world. Rather the poem becomes almost an intellectual luxury item in the college curriculum, its structure being examined, not as a revealed structure of the world, but as the ingenious construction of an intellect bent...on proving its own ingenuity as a thing separate from the world. Little emphasis is placed on the student's *undergoing* the experience of the poem; he is encouraged to analyze it, but not to read it aloud, to meditate on it, to learn it by heart.

(Cameron, p. 71)

But in spite of education children still start with a strong impetus to enjoy poetry, and it is a matter of allowing scope for this drive. For children, simple immersion is better than indifferent teaching; and even adults can be reached, because the primitive feeling for poetry still persists. Richards, writing of poetry's need for a good audience, agrees that the present one is small and incompetent, and attributes this to bad techniques in the teaching of reading and in the early stages of language teaching. 'I believe these can be remedied, and that an audience much more capable of reading well enough to explore and enjoy and appraise poetry could be produced pretty quickly if we really tried' (Richards 1968, p. 178). This seems over-optimistic, and takes too little account of what happens outside the classroom – philistinism, indifference and the ideas of parents, for example.

There are two directions in which one hopes for education through the arts: the development of a sense of the past, and the fostering of the imagination. The child of today is deprived, through knowing and feeling almost nothing of the past; nothing was, before the current pop-star was expensively promoted. 'Our students have inherited nothing from their ancestors; they are the true disinherited' (Rieff 1975, p. 96). They are victims of the fashion for obsolescence imposed by the industrial system (against which the feeling for Ye Olde is perhaps a sort of inarticulate protest), which threatens the right to tradition: the recourse to precedent in language, myth, morals and judgment. Our identity is what we stand to lose:

> We are bound...to the past generations by the same bond that unites us with our neighbours, and if only for the sake of preserving the identity of mankind we must cherish that connection. Fortunately, in spite of our machines, the habits of the human heart remain what they have always been, and the imagination deals with them as no other faculty can. It is more urgently needed in our time than ever before.
> (Edwin Muir 1965, p. 226)

At every level retrospection is essential to the functioning of the consciousness that man developed. This knowledge of the past, especially through literature and art, reminds us what we were; a full knowledge is impossible, but we can learn enough to remain human. It tells us the meaning of life. In contrast with men, plants and animals have a genetic constitution by which they develop their own pattern; 'in front of each natural entity there stands "a picture of what it ought to be", a form for whose realization it strives with all its powers' (Sinnott, p. 54). Human beings have much more choice; our picture of what we ought to be is only to a limited extent built in, and largely comes to us from outside.

The imagination also may have evolved as part of the mechanism of survival. A food-gathering family with a father who imagined a winter without food would store nuts and live. Altruism, based on the imaginative capacity to see himself in another's shoes, may have helped a family to continue when a man was prompted to save a nursing mother from a flooded river. The first expression of the imagination in words may have met similar needs:

> The use of language for 'alternity', for mis-construction, for illusion and play, are the greatest of man's tools by far...At first the instrument probably had a banal survival value. Fiction was disguise: from those seeking out the same water-hole, the same sparse quarry, or meagre sexual chance. To misinform, to utter less than the truth was to gain a vital edge of space or subsistence...
>
> In the creative function of language non-truth or less-than-truth is...a primary device. The relevant framework is not one of morality, but of survival. At every level, from brute camouflage to poetic vision, the linguistic capacity to conceal, mis-inform, leave ambiguous, hypothesize, invent, is indispensable to the equilibrium of human consciousness and to the development of man in society.
> (Steiner 1975, pp. 223, 229)

Today we need this power to envisage such possibilities as the ending of our present civilisation through the misuse of atomic power, the destruction of our habitat and the regeneration of mankind. Poetry like the novel needs its heroes; men should see themselves as resourceful and courageous inheritors. For much of its history poetry has had a practical value, and so it should continue. 'Throughout history, and long before it, poetry has been among man's chief sustainers. A big general increase in his understanding of how it works may well be a practical aid towards saner policies' (Richards 1974a, p. 39). Poetry has been a sustainer because it has expressed and made manageable the great problems of existence that are beyond the reach of scientific terms and precise logical analysis. For this mediating we need, as well as great writers, poets of the second order, middlemen with a function comparable to that of Shaw, through whom the peaks will both be higher and more approachable – poets such as Carl Sandburg, Brecht, Edgar Lee Masters, S. V. Benet, W. H. Auden, R. S. Thomas and John Betjeman, who would help their readers to strengthen their imaginative grasp of change. With so small a public for poetry it might be necessary to adopt this idea:

What I would like to see happen is a disappearance of all poets: a return to the anonymity of the Homeric poets or of the ballad composers. A wise and powerful state would establish machinery making it easy to publish poetry but impossible to be identified as its author... Nothing I can imagine would do more for poetry than the evanishment of all poets.
(Richards 1968, p. 153)

Words are very important indeed. They are not just part of an acquired skill, not just a means of communication, communion, or the expression of what could be left unexpressed, but come from the deepest centre of our being. They are the 'meeting points at which regions of experience which can never combine in sensation or intuition, come together'. They are part of our growth and our living and we cannot be human without them. It is a contention of this book that poetry is the finest way of using words, because it can comprehend the whole of experience. If so, there may be truth in the contention that

If one-tenth of the attention which has been given to portraying poets... had been given to making poetry more accessible, the world (I venture to suggest) would be much better off and poetry have a different kind of audience.
(Richards 1968, p. 152)

Bibliography

Abbs, Peter (ed.). *The Black Rainbow*, London, 1973
Abrams, M. H. *The Mirror and the Lamp*, New York, 1953
Achebe, Chinua. *Things Fall Apart*, London, 1958
Alexander, M. *The Earliest English Poems*, Harmondsworth, 1966
Alexiou, Margaret. *The Ritual Lament in Greek Tradition*, Cambridge, 1974
Allingham, William. *A Diary*, London, 1967 edn.
Altick, R. D. *The English Common Reader*, Chicago, 1957
Andreski, S. *Social Sciences as Sorcery*, London, 1972
Andrzejewski, B. W. and Lewis, I. M. *Somali Poetry*, Oxford, 1964
Archer, W. B. *The Hill of Flutes*, London, 1975
Arnold, Magda B. *Emotion and Personality*, Vol. 2, London 1961
Arnold, Matthew. *Essays in Criticism*, 2nd series, London, 1958 edn.
Arvon, Henri. *Marxist Esthetics*, Ithaca, 1973
Ashby, Eric. 'Dons or Crooners', *Communications in the Modern World*, London, 1959
Astrov, Margot (ed.). *The Winged Serpent*, New York, 1946
Auden, W. H. *The Dyer's Hand*, London, 1963
Auerbach, Erich. *Literary Language and its Public in Later Latin Antiquity*, London, 1945
Baldry, H. C. *Ancient Greek Literature in its Living Context*, London, 1968
Ball, Patricia. 'Therapeutic Poetry' in *Social Service Quarterly*, p. 94, London, 1973
Barber, C. L. *Shakespeare's Festive Comedy*, Princeton, 1959
Barnes, Kenneth C. *The Creative Imagination*, London, 1961
Bates, E. S. (ed.). *The Bible Designed to be Read as Literature*, London, n.d.
Bede. *A History of the English Church and People*, Harmondsworth, 1955
Beier, Ulli (ed.). *African Poetry*, Cambridge, 1966
    Yoruba Poetry, Cambridge, 1970
Beljame, Alexandre. *Men of the Letters and the English Public in the Eighteenth Century*, London, 1948 edn.
Berger, John. *A Fortunate Man*, London, 1967
Berndt, R. M. and C. H. *The World of the First Australians*, London, 1964
Berry, Francis. *Poetry and the Physical Voice*, London, 1962
Betsky, Sarah Zweig. *Onions and Cucumbers and Plums*, Detroit, 1958
Bewick, Thomas. *A Memoir*, Oxford, 1974 edn.
Birket-Smith, Kaj. *The Eskimos*, London, 1959
p'Bitek, Okot. *Horn of My Love*, London, 1974
Blackmur, R. P. *Language as Gesture*, London, 1954
Bleek, W. H. I. and Lloyd, L. C. *Specimens of Bushman Folklore*, London, 1911
Blench, J. W. *Preaching in England in the Later Fifteenth and Sixteenth Centuries*, Oxford, 1964

Blythe, Ronald. *Akenfield*, London, 1969
Bodkin, Maud. *Archetypal Patterns in Poetry*, London, 1934
Bosley, Keith (ed.). *Russia's Other Poets*, London, 1968
Bouquet, A. C. *Sacred Books of the World*, Harmondsworth, 1954
Bowra, C. M. *Heroic Poetry*, London, 1961
  Primitive Song, London, 1962
  Poetry and Politics, Cambridge, 1966
Bradbrook, M. C. *The Growth and Structure of Elizabethan Comedy*, London, 1955
Bratton, J. S. *The Victorian Popular Ballad*, London, 1975
Braybrooke, Neville (ed.). *The Wind and the Rain*, London, 1962
Brophy, John and Partridge, Eric. *The Long Trail*, London, 1965
Brown, Peter. *Augustine of Hippo*, London, 1967
Buber, Martin. *Hasidim*, New York, 1948
Buchan, David. *The Ballad and the Folk*, London, 1972
Bücher, Karl. *Arbeit und Rhythmus*, Leipzig, 1896
Byatt, A. S. *Wordsworth and Coleridge*, London, 1970
Cameron, B. 'Language and the Alteration of Social Behaviour', *Agenda*, Vol. 13, No. 1, London, Winter 1975
Carawan, G. and C. *We Shall Overcome*, New York, 1962
Carothers, J. C. *The Mind of Man in Africa*, London, 1972
Chadwick, H. M. and N. K. *The Growth of Literature*, 3 vols., Cambridge, 1932, 1936, 1940
Chadwick, N. K. *Poetry and Prophecy*, Cambridge, 1942
Chambers, E. K. *English Literature at the Close of the Middle Ages*, Oxford, 1945
Chambers, G. B. *Folksong – Plainsong*, London, 1956
Chapman, Raymond. *Linguistics and Literature*, London, 1973
Chaytor, H. J. *The Troubadours and England*, Cambridge, 1923
  From Script to Print, Cambridge, 1945
Colcord, J. C. *Songs of American Sailormen*, London, 1938
Collingwood, R. G. *The Principles of Art*, London, 1938
Cottle, Basil. *The Triumph of English*, London, 1969
Coveney, Peter. *The Image of Childhood*, Harmondsworth, 1967
Crosby, Ruth. 'Oral Delivery in the Middle Ages', *Speculum*, Vol. I, No. 1, Cambridge, Mass., Jan. 1936
Crossley-Holland, K. *The Battle of Maldon and Other Old English Poems*, London, 1965
Daiches, David. *A Study of Literature*, London, 1968
Darwin, Charles. *Autobiography*, 1929 edn.
Davies, R. T. (ed.). *Medieval English Lyrics*, London, 1963
Davy, Charles. *Words in the Mind*, London, 1965
Decarreaux, Jean. *Monks and Civilization*, London, 1964
De la Mare, Walter. 'Poetry in Prose', *Proceedings of the British Academy*, London, 1935
Deloney, T. *Works*, Oxford, 1912 edn.
Deng, Francis Mading. *The Dinka and their Songs*, Oxford, 1973
De Quincey, T. *Recollections of the Lakes and the Lake Poets*, Harmondsworth, 1970 edn.
Dew, W. N. *A Dyshe of Norfolke Dumplings*, London, 1898

Diamond, A. S. *The History and Origin of Language*, London, 1959
Dodds, E. R. *The Greeks and the Irrational*, Berkeley, 1951
Donovan, J. *From Lyre to Muse*, London, 1890
Downey, June E. *Creative Imagination*, London, 1929
Dubos, René. *So Human an Animal*, London, 1970
    A God Within, London, 1973
Dundes, Alan (ed.). *The Study of Folklore*, Englewood Cliffs, 1965
Eberhart, Richard. *Selected Poems*, London, 1965
Eliade, Mircea. *Shamanism*, London, 1964
Eliot, T. S. *Selected Essays, 1917–1932*, London, 1932
    The Use of Poetry and the Use of Criticism, London, 1933
    On Poetry and Poets, London, 1957
Elwin, Verrier. *Folk-Songs of Chattisgarh*, London, 1946
Elwin, Verrier and Hivale, S. *Folk-Songs of the Maikal Hills*, London, 1944
Emeneau, M. B. 'Songs of the Todas', *Proceedings of the American Philo-
    sophical Society*, Vol. 77, Philadelphia
Entwistle, W. J. *European Balladry*, Oxford, 1939
Evans, George Ewart. *The Horse in the Furrow*, London, 1960
Finley, M. I. *The World of Odysseus*, Harmondsworth, 1962
    Early Greece: the Bronze and Archaic Ages, London, 1970
Finnegan, Ruth. *Oral Literature in Africa*, Oxford, 1970
Firth, J. R. *The Tongues of Men and Speech*, Oxford, 1964
Ford, Boris (ed.). *The Pelican Guide to English Literature*, Vol. 5, Har-
    mondsworth, 1957
Fowke, Edith. *Lumbering Songs from the Northern Woods*, Austin, 1970
Fox-Strangways, A. H. *Cecil Sharp*, Oxford, 1933
Freeman, Rosemary. *English Emblem Books*, London, 1948
Freuchen, Peter. *The Book of the Eskimos*, London, 1962
Galbraith, V. H. 'The Literacy of Medieval English Kings', *Proceedings of
    the British Academy*, Vol. XXI, London, 1935
Gammage, R. G. *History of the Chartist Movement*, London, 2nd edn., 1894
Gandz, S. 'The Dawn of Literature', *Osiris*, Vol. 7, Bruges, 1939
Geddes, G. (ed.). *Poetry and Poetics*, Toronto, 1969
Gesell, Arnold. *The First Five Years of Life*, London, 1950
Gibb, H. A. R. *Arabic Literature*, Oxford, 1963
Gibbon, J. M. *Melody and the Lyric*, London, 1930
Goody, Jack (ed.). *Literacy in Traditional Societies*, Cambridge, 1968
Gordon, R. K. (trans.). *Anglo-Saxon Poetry*, London, 1926
Granet, Marcel. *Festivals and Songs of Ancient China*, London, 1932
Greene, R. L. *The Early English Carols*, Oxford, 1935
Gregory, R. L. *The Intelligent Eye*, London, 1970
Greenway, John. *American Folksongs of Protest*, Philadelphia, 1953
Grene, Marjorie. *The Knower and the Known*, London, 1966
Griffiths, M. E. *Early Vaticination in Wales*, Cardiff, 1937
Grigson, Geoffrey (ed.). *The Faber Book of Popular Verse*, London, 1971
Grimble, Arthur. *Return to the Islands*, London, 1957
Gummere, F. B. *The Beginnings of Poetry*, New York, 1901
Hadas, Moses. *Ancilla to Classical Reading*, New York, 1954
Halliday, W. R. *The Pagan Background of Early Christianity*, London, 1953
Hamburger, Michael. *Travelling*, London, 1969

Harding, D. W. *Experience into Words*, London, 1963
   The New York Review, 2 Jan. 1969
   Words into Rhythm, Cambridge, 1976
Hardy, Thomas. *Far from the Madding Crowd*, London, 1957 edn.
   Personal Writings, London, 1967
Harrison, Jane E. *Ancient Art and Ritual*, London, 1913
Haslam, Gerald. 'American Oral Literature', *The English Journal*, Sept. 1971
Havelock, Eric A. *Preface to Plato*, Oxford, 1963
Hawkes, Jacquetta and Woolley, Leonard. *Prehistory and the Beginnings of Civilization*, London, 1963
Hawkes, Terence. *Shakespeare's Talking Animals*, London, 1973
Heilbroner, Robert L. *The Making of Economic Society*, New York, 1962
Henderson, Philip. *The Poet and Society*, London, 1939
   William Morris, London, 1967
Henderson, W. *Victorian Street Ballads*, London, 1937
Hesse, Mary. *Science and the Human Imagination*, London, 1954
Hill, Edmund (ed.). *Nine Sermons of St Augustine on the Psalms*, London, 1958
Hillelson, S. *Week-end Caravan*, Edinburgh, 1937
Hodgart, Matthew (ed.). *The Faber Book of Ballads*, London, 1965
Howes, Frank. *Man, Mind and Music*, London, 1948
Hugill, Stan. *Shanties and Sailors' Songs*, London, 1969
Huizinga, J. *The Waning of the Middle Ages*, London, 1949
   Homo Ludens, London, 1970
Hyde, Douglas. *A Literary History of Ireland*, London, 1967 edn.
Illich, Ivan. *Tools for Conviviality*, London, 1973
   Medical Nemesis, London, 1975
Innis, Harold A. *The Bias of Communication*, Toronto, 1951
Izutzu, T. *Language and Magic*, Keio, Japan, 1956
Jackson, Bruce. *Wake Up Dead Man*, Cambridge, Mass., 1972
Jameson, Storm. *Journey from the North*, London, 1969
Journal of American Folklore, Boston
Jusserand, J. J. *English Wayfaring Life in the Middle Ages*, London, 1889
Ker, W. P. *Form and Style in Poetry*, London, 1966 edn.
   Medieval English Literature, London, 1969 edn.
Key, Wilson Bryan. *Subliminal Seduction*, New York, 1974
Kirby, W. F. (trans.). *Kalevala*, London, 1907
Knights, L. C. *Drama and Society in the Age of Jonson*, London, 1937
   Further Explorations, London, 1965
Kroeber, A. L. *Handbook of the Indians of California*, Washington, D.C., 1925
Lang, Paul Henry. *Music in Western Civilization*, London, 1942
Langer, Susanne. *Philosophy in a New Key*, New York, 1948 edn.
   Feeling and Form, London, 1953
Laslett, Peter. *The World We Have Lost*, London, 1965
Lawrence, D. H. *Studies in Classic American Literature*, London, 1924
   'Hymns in a Man's Life', *Assorted Articles*, London, 1930
Laye, Camara. *The African Child*, London, 1959
Lee, Peter H. *Anthology of Korean Poetry*, New York, 1964
Leedy, J. J. (ed.). *Poetic Therapy*, Philadelphia, 1969
Lenneberg, Eric H. *Biological Foundations of Language*, New York, 1967
   (ed.). *New Directions in the Study of Language*, Cambridge, Mass., 1964

Lesky, A. *A History of Greek Literature*, London, 1966
Lewis, C. Day. 'The Making of a Poem', *Saturday Evening Post*, 21 Jan. 1961
Lewis, I. M. *Ecstatic Religion*, Harmondsworth, 1971
Lewis, M. M. *Language, Thought and Personality*, London, 1963
Lloyd, A. L. *Folk Song in England*, London, 1967
Lord, A. B. *The Singer of Tales*, Cambridge, Mass., 1964
Lucretius. *The Nature of the Universe*, trans. R. Latham, Harmondsworth, 1951
Mabey, Richard. *The Pop Process*, London, 1969
Macaulay, T. B. *Critical and Historical Essays*, London, 1907 edn.
MacColl, Ewan (ed.). *The Shuttle and the Cage*, London, 1954
MacLeish, Archibald. *The Atlantic Monthly*, March, 1959, Boston
   Poetry and Experience, London, 1961
McLuhan, M. *The Gutenberg Galaxy*, London, 1962
Mahood, M. M. *Shakespeare's Wordplay*, London, 1972
Malinowski, B. *Myth in Primitive Psychology*, London, 1926
Mascaró, Juan. *Lamps of Fire*, London, 1961
Masserman, Jules H. *Principles of Dynamic Psychiatry*, Philadelphia, 1961
Mathews, H. F. *Methodism and the Education of the People*, London, 1949
Mayhew, Henry. *London Labour and the London Poor*, 4 vols., London, 1861–2
Mellers, Wilfrid. *Music and Society*, London, 1946
   Twilight of the Gods, London, 1973
Mill, J. S. *Autobiography*, Oxford, 1924 edn.
Milner, Marion. *The Hands of the Living God*, London, 1969
Minifie, F. D. (ed.). *Normal Aspects of Speech, Hearing and Language*. Englewood Cliffs, 1973
Mordell, Albert. *The Literature of Ecstasy*, London, 1922
Morton, A. L. *The World of the Ranters*, London, 1970
Muir, Edwin. *The Estate of Poetry*, London, 1962
   Literature and Society, London, 1965
Muir, Willa. *Living with Ballads*, London, 1965
Murphy, Richard. 'The Poet on the Island', *Penguin Modern Poets*, 7, Harmondsworth, 1965
Nash, Walter. *Our Experience of Language*, London, 1971
Nicholas, A. X. *The Poetry of Soul*, New York, 1971
North British Review. Cited in C. Tennyson, *Alfred Tennyson*, London, 1974
Oakeshott, Michael. *Rationalism in Politics*, London, 1962
O'Malley, R. Review, *The Use of English*, Winter, 1974
Ong, Walter J. *Ramus: Method and the Decay of Dialogue*, Cambridge, Mass., 1958
   Rhetoric, Romance and Technology, Ithaca, 1971
Opie, Amelia and Peter. *The Language and Lore of School Children*, Oxford, 1959
Over to You. BBC pamphlet, London, 1965
Owen, D. D. R. (trans.). *The Song of Roland*, London, 1972
Owst, G. R. *Preaching in Medieval England*, Cambridge, 1926
   Literature and Pulpit in Medieval England, Cambridge, 1933
Oxford Classical Dictionary. 'Juvenal', 'Satura', 'Solon', 'Tyrtaeus', Oxford, 1949

Packard, Vance. *The Hidden Persuaders*, London, 1957
Palmer, Mary (ed.). *Writing and Action*, London, 1938
Paraone, Tiwai. 'A Maori Cosmogony', *Journal of the Polynesian Society*, 16, Wellington, New Zealand, 1907
Park, Mungo. *Travels*, London, 1907 edn.
Parker, K. L. *The Euahlayi Tribe*, London, 1905
Parry, Milman. *The Making of Homeric Verse*, Oxford, 1971
Parry, Thomas (ed.). *The Oxford Book of Welsh Verse*, Oxford, 1962
Peter, John. *Complaint and Satire in Early English Verse*, Oxford, 1956
Philpotts, Bertha. *Edda and Saga*, London, 1931
Pinto, V. de Sola and Rodway, A. E. *The Common Muse*, London, 1957
Plato. *Ion*, trans. B. Jowett
Polanyi, Michael. *Personal Knowledge*, London, 1958
Power, Eileen. *Medieval People*, London, 1924
Quennell, Peter (ed.). *Mayhew's Characters*, London, 1951
Raby, F. J. E. *A History of Christian-Latin Poetry*, Oxford, 1933
Raine, Kathleen. *Defending Ancient Springs*, Cambridge, 1967
Rasmussen, Knud. *The Netsilik Eskimos: Social Life and Spiritual Culture* (trans.) Calvert, W. E. Copenhagen, 1931
Read, Herbert. *The Redemption of the Robot*, London, 1970
Reaveley, Constance and Winnington, John. *Democracy and Industry*, London, 1947
Reed, James. *The Border Ballads*, London, 1973
Reeves, James. *Selected Poems*, London, 1967
Richards, I. A. *Principles of Literary Criticism*, London, 1924
  So Much Nearer, New York, 1968
  Beyond, New York, 1974a
  Poetries: Their Media and Ends, The Hague, 1974b
Rieff, Philip. *The Triumph of the Therapeutic*, London, 1966
  Fellow Teachers, London, 1975
Robbins, R. H. *Secular Lyrics of the XIVth and XVth Centuries*, Oxford, 1952
Rosenberg, B. and White, D. M. (ed.). *The Popular Arts in America*, Glencoe, 1957
Roszak, Theodore. *Where the Waste Land Ends*, London, 1973
Rowlands, Peter. *The Fugitive Mind*, London, 1972
Russell, E. S. *The Directiveness of Organic Activities*, Cambridge, 1945
Sandars, N. K. (trans.). *Poems of Heaven and Hell from Ancient Mesopotamia*, Harmondsworth, 1971
Saroyan, William. *The Time of Your Life and other plays*, London, 1942
Scattergood, V. J. *Politics and Poetry in the Fifteenth Century*, London, 1971
Scholl, Sharon and White, Sylvia. *Music and the Culture of Man*, New York, 1970
Schumacher, E. F. *Small is Beautiful*, London, 1973
Selincourt, E. de (ed.). *The Early Letters of William and Dorothy Wordsworth*, Oxford, 1935
  The Letters of Dorothy and William Wordsworth–The Middle Years I, Oxford, 1937
Sewell, Elizabeth. *The Orphic Voice*, London, 1960
Shakespeare's England. Vols. 1 and 2, Oxford, 1913
Sharp, Cecil. *English Folk Song*, London, 3rd edn., 1954

Shattered Heart, The. An anthology, Harpenden and District Association for Mental Health, 1972

Shelley, P. B. *A Defence of Poetry,* 1915 edn.

Shepard, Leslie. *A History of Street Literature,* Newton Abbot, 1973

Sinnott, Edmund W. *The Biology of the Spirit,* London, 1956

Smalley, Beryl. *English Friars and Antiquity,* Oxford, 1960
  The Study of the Bible in the Middle Ages, Oxford, 1941

Smith, Logan Pearsall. *Words and Idioms,* London, 1925

Smyth, H. W. (ed.). *Greek Melic Poets,* London, 1900

Snyder, E. D. *Hypnotic Poetry,* Philadelphia, 1930

Speirs, John. *Medieval English Poetry,* London, 1957

Spender, Stephen. *The Making of a Poem,* London, 1955

Steiner, George. *After Babel,* London, 1975
  Extra-Territorial, London, 1972
  Language and Silence, London, 1967

Stevens, John. *Medieval Romance,* London, 1973
  Music and Poetry in the Early Tudor Court, London, 1961

Stevenson, W. B. *The Poem of Job,* London, 1947

Stone, B. (ed.). *Medieval English Verse,* Harmondsworth, 1964

Storr, Anthony. 'The Concept of Cure', *Psychoanalysis Observed,* London, 1966

Synge, J. M. *The Aran Islands,* Dublin, 2 vols. 1906
  Collected Works: Prose, London, 1966

Talbot, C. H. *Medicine in Medieval England,* London, 1967

Taylor, Archer. *The Proverb,* Cambridge, Mass., 1931

Tennyson, Charles. *Alfred Tennyson,* London, 1974

Terry, R. R. *The Shanty Book,* Part I, London, 1921

Thomas, R. S. *Song at the Year's Turning,* London, 1963

Thompson, D. *Children as Poets,* London, 1972

Thomson, Derick. *An Introduction to Gaelic Poetry,* London, 1974

Thomson, G. *Aeschylus and Athens,* London, 1938
  Marxism and Poetry, London, 1945

Thorpe, W. H. *Animal Nature and Human Nature,* London, 1974

Thurstone, L. L. *The Nature of Intelligence,* London, 1924

Tongue, Ruth L. *The Chime Child,* London, 1968

Trask, Willard (ed.). *The Unwritten Song,* Vol. 2, New York, 1966

Trevelyan, G. M. *A Shortened History of England,* Harmondsworth, 1959

Underhill, Ruth M. *Papago Indian Religion,* New York, 1946

Vansina, Jan. *Oral Tradition,* London, 1965

Vaughan Williams, R. and Lloyd, A. L. *The Penguin Book of English Folksongs,* London, 1959

Vicinus, M. *The Lowly Harp,* University of Wisconsin dissertation, 1969

Walton, Izaak. *Life of Dr Robert Sanderson,* Oxford, 1927 edn.

Ward, A. W. and Waller, A. R. *The Cambridge History of English Literature,* Cambridge, 1932

Wells, H. G. *The Outline of History,* rev. edn. 1972

Wenger, M. A. and others. *Physiological Psychology,* London, 1956

Wilhelm, Richard. *A Short History of Chinese Civilization,* London, 1929

Williams, Ifor. *The Beginnings of Welsh Poetry,* Cardiff, 1972

Williamson, Henry. *The Village Book,* London, 1930

Winstock, Lewis. *Songs and Marches of Roundheads and Cavaliers*, London, 1971

Wolf, S. and Wolff, H. G. *Human Gastric Function*, London, 1943

Woolley, Leonard and Hawkes, Jacquetta. *History of Mankind: Cultural and Scientific Development*, London, 1965

Wordsworth, William. *Poetical Works*, Oxford, 1914 edn.

Wright, E. M. *Rustic Speech and Folk-lore*, Oxford, 1913

Wright, Louis B. *Middle-Class Culture in Elizabethan England*, Chapel Hill, 1935

Wright, T. *English Political Poems and Songs*, London, 1859

Yates, Frances A. *The Art of Memory*, London, 1966

Yeats, W. B. *Essays and Introductions*, London, 1961

Zimmerman, G.-D. *Songs of Irish rebellion. Political street ballads and rebel songs 1780–1900.* Dublin, 1967

Index